D0818519

ALS

An Orientation

Eliot H. Dunsky, MD

SPRINGDALE PUBLIC LIBRARY
405 S. Pleasant
Springdale, AR 72764

Copyright © 2016 Eliot H. Dunsky, MD
All rights reserved.

ISBN: 1534988661
ISBN 13: 9781534988668
Library of Congress Control Number: 2016911096
CreateSpace Independent Publishing Platform
North Charleston, South Carolina

Note

No liability is assumed with respect to the use of the information contained within this book. Although, the author in the preparation of this book has taken a great deal of care, neither the author nor the publisher assumes responsibility for errors or omissions. Neither is any liability assumed for damages resulting from the use of the information contained in this book. Any information, method, device, opinion, option, recommendations, or treatment described herein are solely for educational purposes and should not be followed or employed except under the direction of a qualified physician.

To my wife, Talia,

Whose love and support have been my rock in good times and bad, and whose smile, humor, and friendship have given me reason to be a happy man.

Contents

Preface

It has been seven years or so since I was diagnosed with ALS. Even though I am a physician, I had never encountered a patient with ALS, and I knew little about the management of this complex disorder.

The diagnosis of ALS both shocked and frightened me. Once I was able to absorb that I really did have ALS after all other diagnoses were ruled out, I suddenly understood that I was facing the greatest challenge of my life. I soon came to the realization that I would have to find a way to deal with what I was feeling and figure out how to respond to what I imagined was coming my way. I also begin to understand that I would need to find an approach to live with ALS while maintaining as good a quality of life as possible while fulfilling my responsibilities for as long as possible.

Over the past several years I have had numerous opportunities to speak with other ALS patients and over time I began to realize that many did not understand their disease well, nor were they knowledgeable about the best options available for managing their symptoms and disability. I began to understand that such a state would seriously interfere with one's ability to cope with ALS. In response to these observations, I decided to put together a book that takes into account my own experience and the experiences of other ALS patients, added my research on ALS management and reviewed ALS as a disease process. I've also combined this information with what I have learned from professionals specializing in ALS. In addition, a collection of more than 750 Internet web site references is provided, which may be the most valuable part of this book.

Instead of learning about ALS in bits and pieces and risk being repeatedly blindsided by new challenges, this book offers a comprehensive view of this multifaceted disease as well as description of options and specific methods one can use to manage the many issues related to ALS that PALS (people with ALS) might encounter.

I hope this book will offer PALS, their families and caregivers insight, context, and much of the information they need to better understand and manage ALS symptoms and disability.

It is my goal is to provide orientation and information that one often needs to make good decisions as well as practical solutions. I also share my approach in dealing with problems that I have encountered and outline how I have been able to enjoy a good quality of life in the face of advancing symptoms and disability. Hopefully this will assist affected individuals to enjoy the best quality of life possible while living with ALS. In this matter, knowledge is power, and that is what this book is about.

Note: I have noticed that some of the Internet web-based references in this book (e.g., PDF files) occasionally might not be accessible through the Safari's Internet browser. In such cases, I have found that the same web address may be opened through other Web browsers including Firefox. A Web address may change; so check site maps when possible. Should a link not work, enter its address into another browser or use a search engine.

https://support.mozilla.org/en-US/kb/how-download-and-install-firefox-mac

About The Cover

The human hand may be the most evolved part of the body's system of voluntary muscle movement, since it is able to carry out hundreds or even thousands, of mundane, essential, and complex tasks every day of our lives.

Hand movements can require extraordinary dexterity, gentleness, and sometimes, great strength. Your hand contains 19 bones and 19 joints, none of which can do much without the more than two-dozen muscles that control its movement. Hand muscles allow for an almost infinite combination of movements needed to perform an incredible variety of daily tasks. The coordination and control of one's hand and wrist muscles originate in the nervous system's motor neurons. Should these motor neurons die, as in the case of ALS, one's ability to perform the simplest of physical tasks can become excruciatingly difficult or impossible. When this occurs, one will quickly come to realize how important muscular control of the hand is in most everything we do.

I chose this pre-ALS photo of my left hand because it represents what is at risk with ALS. Examining this photo carefully, one can clearly see the skin tightly outlining an underlying complex of individual healthy muscles as well as dozens of permanent skin creases that represent the myriad of movements performed by this hand over a period of years or perhaps decades. Aside from the loss of speech, the loss of voluntary control of hand movement is perhaps the greatest blow to one's independence, and this photograph symbolizes the importance of that loss in ALS.

Introduction

Since the ALS ice bucket challenge (2014) and the recent movie about Stephen Hawking, *The Theory of Everything*, I imagine most people have become aware that ALS is a terminal illness characterized by progressive muscular weakness and paralysis, ultimately resulting in severe physical disability and death. Beyond these basic facts, I doubt many truly grasp the complex nature of ALS, its impact on an affected individual, on one's family, or the demanding requirements needed for optimum management of this illness.

The symptoms of weakness and paralysis often progress gradually over a period of years, giving an affected individual the opportunity to adapt and adjust to symptoms and disability and to find ways to enjoy life in spite of living with the challenges posed by ALS. For a minority of individuals, symptoms will advance quickly, which will make things far more difficult. Fortunately, the ongoing development of adaptive and assistive equipment, devices, and advances in technology continues to help ALS patients enjoy mobility and function, supporting their pursuit of a meaningful life. In addition, rapidly advancing discovery in medical research holds the promise that effective treatment for ALS will arrive within the foreseeable future.

When I was diagnosed with ALS in 2009, even though I had studied ALS as a medical student, I understood little about the disease, its management, or how it could affect my life.

I was seriously shaken up by the diagnosis and by the waves of fear and anxiety that I experienced. These feelings made things much worse for me as I suffered not only from the actual symptoms of the disease but also from what I feared would occur. As soon as I was able to comprehend and accept the diagnosis, I began to look for ways to manage living with ALS in a manner that would allow me to enjoy as good as a quality of life possible within the constraints imposed by this illness.

I gradually came to understand that death should not be an imminent concern—the odds favored that I would continue to live for a number of years. What I didn't understand was that the survival time for an individual with ALS is highly variable and in part dependent on the management of one's symptoms. For example, the introduction of ventilation support (e.g., BiPAP) could add years to one's survival time when respiratory muscles begin to fail. Methods to prevent aspiration and malnutrition could also add years to one's life.

From my point of view, the most important issue regarding living with ALS is finding solutions that will allow a person to maintain a quality of life that is both meaningful and one that allows for the presence of happiness in spite of difficulties, symptoms, and physical limitations.

It has been seven years or so since I was diagnosed with ALS, and I can honestly say that while my life has become much more complicated and a quite a struggle at times, I continue to find it to be filled with meaning and happiness for the most part, in spite of advancing symptoms and disability.

I have mobility thanks to a power wheelchair, I no longer suffer from shortness of breath because of the ventilator mounted on the back of my wheelchair, and I have caregivers that help me do whatever I can't do for myself. I feel fortunate in that I have the freedom to choose from among many options. I continue to have the opportunity to spend lots of time with family and friends, pursue my interests and engage in projects that offer me challenge, enjoyment and often provide a sense of fulfillment. This has all been possible because my symptoms and disability have been well managed and are progressing slowly.

As muscular weakness and paralysis advance, I continue to find new methods and adaptive devices that help me maintain function and comfort. I have adjusted to this new normal, and I am OK with it. My approach is to work at focusing on the possible rather than on what is no longer possible, and I have found that this works well.

My symptoms of ALS began one summer afternoon while I was lying on a lounge chair, both exhausted and exhilarated after pushing myself to finish a number of pool laps. Within a few minutes, I began to relax, enjoying the tranquility of the moment. I remember looking up at a blue sky and seeing a passenger jet fly so high above me that passed in complete silence. The combination of the sun's warmth, the smell of suntan lotion, and the quiet of my surroundings allowed my mind to wander in total peace. As I relaxed, I began to notice a subtle but persistent twitching of my right thigh. This signaled the beginning of a process that would dramatically change my life.

Since then, I have learned a lot. I have focused my efforts and energy on studying ALS and the management of its symptoms and progressive disability. Fortunately, I learned early in life to search for solutions when facing difficulties since I have found that other approaches almost always turn out to be poor choices.

About eight years or so have passed since that summer, and at this moment, I am sitting comfortably in a power wheelchair, dictating this chapter while watching a tree heavy with summer leaves move to ever-changing winds, and I feel that it is good to be alive. During these past several years, I have concentrated on learning all I can about ALS as a disease process, finding effective ways to deal with the multiple challenges it poses, and identifying the best management solutions with the goal of maintaining a good quality of life.

Knowing that the time I have left will probably not be that long makes each remaining day, week, and month particularly valuable. I find that I'm now neither willing to waste a single day, nor allow negative thoughts or emotions to disturb my mood for long. Nor will I allow myself to be distracted or deterred from doing my best to enjoy what is still possible. I have learned to regularly set goals and adapt to the reality of my situation.

Long before I was diagnosed with ALS, I began to experience muscular cramps that were severe enough to wake me at night. My internist was unable to provide a diagnosis or offer effective treatment for my symptoms. Years later I developed significant fatigue in addition to muscular twitching. My new internist recommended that I consult with a neurologist. It was my good luck that the neurologist turned out to be a true expert on ALS. That was the start of a long investigation that ultimately led to the diagnosis of ALS.

My training as a physician made it easy for me to research my symptoms and access the medical literature on ALS. I carefully studied the differential diagnosis of my symptoms, desperately searching for a diagnosis other than ALS. Over time, multiple specialists have ruled out all other diagnostic considerations, so I finally had to accept that my diagnosis of ALS was indeed correct.

When I first understood that I really did have ALS, I felt as if I had been hit by a huge wave that suddenly swept me off my feet. Initially, I was disoriented and traumatized; the experience of receiving the diagnosis somehow seemed surreal. I just couldn't believe that this was happening to me.

At the beginning, I struggled with feelings of disbelief, shock, fear, and a deep sense of loss of the life I expected. I had rarely experienced such feelings because I usually had been able to find a way to deal with life's challenges and overcome difficulty. Over time, I have come to realize that neither fear nor acquiescence works well when faced with a catastrophic event and that being determined to find a way to deal with such a challenge is always the best approach. Eventually I accepted the diagnosis.

I understood that from that point forward, I could not be a bystander and passively allow this event to crush me.

When it finally became clear that I had ALS, I suddenly found myself in uncharted waters, and for a while it scared the heck out of me. Nevertheless, I have found that even when a problem is not resolvable, I can still choose how to respond to it and try to find a way to deal with it as well as possible, and I also found this to be the case in dealing with ALS.

Once diagnosed, my anticipated my life course was disrupted. The prospect of dying prematurely was far less frightening to me than the thought of suffering progressive disability and with it, the loss of my independence. Over the past few years, I have learned to deal with these feelings and thoughts, so that they no longer negatively affect my quality of life to a significant degree.

ALS (amyotrophic lateral sclerosis) was first described by Jean Martin Charcot in 1874. Charcot, a French pathologist, linked what he observed in the spinal cord (lateral sclerosis) with progressive neurodegenerative symptoms and findings (muscle weakness, paralysis, and the atrophy) that he observed in his patients. Up until a few decades ago, little progress had been made in understanding ALS. However, in the past 20 years or so, a number of genetic mutations and biochemical defects have been identified in ALS patients, and research into the cause and treatment of ALS is now moving ahead at an ever more rapid pace.

ALS (formally known as Charcot's disease) was hardly known to the general public until it was diagnosed in the famous American baseball player Lou Gehrig. Since then, it has been known as Lou Gehrig disease or ALS in the United States. In Europe, ALS is now referred to as motor neuron disease (MND).

Growing up in the Bronx as a Yankee fan, I knew that Lou Gehrig was one of the great Yankee baseball players and that he had developed ALS. The following has been taken from Lou Gehrig's farewell address to his fans at the Yankee stadium soon after he was diagnosed with ALS: "Fans, for the past two weeks, you have been reading about the bad break I got. Yet today I consider myself the luckiest man on the face of this earth...So in closing I would like to say that I might have been given a bad break, but I've got an awful lot to live for."

I find these sentiments to be inspiring. His remarks offer me a positive perspective even seventy years after they were delivered, probably because they strongly resonate with me. I also believe that even with a diagnosis of ALS, we have an awful lot for which to live, especially when you consider the precious and transient nature of each day. Therefore, it would appear to be wise to find a way to cope and do something meaningful with the time and opportunity that still remain. To do otherwise would be to take a difficult situation and turn it into something much worse.

Each of us can try to push back against encroaching physical limitations by adapting and adjusting in ways that makes sense.

I have come to understand that by studying ALS and its management options, that I could find practical solutions my ALS problems and also prepare for the expected progression of this illness.

By way of example, one could view the life of Stephen Hawking, the English theoretical physicist and cosmologist who was diagnosed with ALS in his youth. In spite of enormous obstacles, he has managed to live with ALS for more than fifty years. Prof. Hawking has a family and has distinguished himself as a leading scientist, pursuing the career he loves even though he is severely disabled. In spite of the fact that he is paralyzed and can only communicate through a computer, he continues to contribute to scientific knowledge, give lectures, travel the world, write best-selling books, and enjoy a social life.

I have found that managing ALS often requires a customized and/or an innovative approach that might not have been apparent at the time a problem emerged. I think it is unrealistic to expect that any single physician or professional will have all the necessary experience, knowledge, and best solutions required for every single ALS problem you encounter. Although a multidisciplinary team at an ALS center will have an expanded capability to manage symptoms and disability, it seems to me that that each of us will also need to do our part in managing problems as well as act as our own advocate, researcher, collaborator, and determined pursuer of solutions.

The good news is that over time, you can become increasingly knowledgeable, skilled, and good at solving ALS problems.

The course of ALS is highly variable; a minority of ALS patients will have a very rapid progression of symptoms and pass away within a year or two while another small group will have a very slow progression and live ten, fifteen, or more years following their diagnosis. In between these two groups reside the great majority of ALS patients, who can expect to live three, four, five, or more years. In addition, new treatments for ALS are likely to emerge in the coming years that will significantly slow down or stop the disease's progression and extend survival rates to well beyond what is common today. Therefore, life will go on following your diagnosis, and if you take a proactive approach and manage your illness well, many of the years ahead can be good ones.

One thing that greatly helped me adjust to my new circumstance was connecting with an ALS center that has provided me with the professional support and guidance I so desperately needed. The clinic staff offered orientation, information, guidance, and helped get me what I needed. Over time, my doctors and the center's staff have gained my trust and respect, and this relationship has relieved me of much anxiety because I know that I'm not alone in this struggle and that they are there to help me.

Once I was able to understand the basics of ALS, I began to intensively research my symptoms and potential difficulties, and this helped me identify options and potential solutions to deal with the problems I encountered as well as for those that I might encounter in the future. I studied the ALS disease process so that I could anticipate and prepare for what I would likely face. This approach has not only reduced my anxiety regarding the future but it has also allowed me to meet each new challenge in a timely manner because I had prepared.

As symptoms slowly progressed from fatigue to weakness, to trouble walking, to the complete loss of the ability to walk and increasing shortness of breath, I have been able to find the information I needed to help me adapt to each of these problems. In this way I have been able to continue to function well enough to spend my time mostly doing what I like, within a world of possibilities.

I have been married for forty-five years, and there is love and complete trust between us. My wife Talia has become a wonderful caregiver and supporter. Family and friends visit regularly, which brings me happiness because these relationships mean so much to me. The highlight of my week occurs when my daughter Yael and my five-year-old grandson, Jake, spend the weekend with us.

I maintain a tight schedule. With the help of caregivers, I begin my morning by doing range-of-motion exercises, showering, and getting dressed, which has now become a two-hour plus process because I can no longer stand or assist. Since I have all the equipment, knowhow, and help I need, it is really not a problem—it's just time consuming. When I finish eating breakfast and reading the newspaper, I usually begin working on a project. The computer makes this task much easier, especially now that I am using voice recognition software. I've published a book for my grandson—*Common Sense Is Not All That Common* (available on Amazon.com)—wherein I try to pass on to him much of what I've learned and what I think is important in life since I know I will not be around to share my thoughts with him when he is older. I have also made a series of DVDs for him where I share my history and ideas. I continue to pursue my hobby of photography even though my mobility and muscular strength continue to decline. With help I can still work the computer, the software, and the printer. At first our social life barely changed, but now, instead of going out to restaurants, we enjoy dinners at home with friends and family.

By adapting and adjusting to each new challenge, I have been able to achieve self-determination within my limitations, which still gives me quite a few good options. Even though I can usually manage things pretty well with help, nevertheless physical limitations still frustrates me at times and this leads to irritability and impatience, which thankfully quickly fade away.

As you can see, I believe that happiness and a good quality of life can be found while living with ALS—if one is determined to make it so.

Living with this illness involves making choices in how to respond to emotional and physical challenges. In this situation, your choices can positively affect the quality of your life and in some cases the duration of your life. I have found that constructive actions have made each year meaningful and worthwhile so far. Furthermore, hope exists that one's quality of your life will be enhanced because of advances being made in medicine and technology. For example, a recent clinical trial for the treatment of ALS using a person's own bone-marrow stem cells (see the web link below) appears to offer significant benefit by slowing down the progression of ALS symptoms (*JAMA Neurology*, January 11, 2016).

www.youtube.com/watch?v=RkTfK6YoYz4

The first section of this book presents an overview of the disease process, including a review of ALS symptoms, the disease's underlying pathology, possible causes, patterns of symptoms, statistics, psychological factors, and other issues related to living with ALS. This should help orient you to how ALS could affect you and bring to light many related issues worth considering when living with ALS. The information provided should offer you perspective, potential resources and solutions that could help support your autonomy, and prepare you to make the most out of a complicated situation.

The second section of this book primarily focuses on the management of symptoms, complications and methods for dealing with everyday challenges. It also reviews equipment, devices, practical solutions, symptom management, approved

ALS treatment, alternative treatments, managing disability and related issues. It is my hope that by raising your level of awareness to current and future ALS challenges, it will help you better prepare to deal with the management of what maybe heading your way. In these matters, knowledge is empowering. I also share my own experience in meeting challenges and navigating the medical system. This book also reviews the financial, legal, and social issues that could strongly impact your life and also touches on important issues related to caregiver assistance and the support you are likely to need as your symptoms advance. Hopefully the information provided will help improve your quality of life, prevent surprises and prepare you to manage future challenges. View the following website for an excellent collection of ALS guidebooks and information.

https://www.mda.org/services/guidebooks-and-pamphlets

Part I

The Basics

One

ALS: A Brief Overview

A LS is not a new disease. It was clearly described about 150 years ago as a degenerative disease caused by the death of motor neurons found in the brain, brain stem, and in the spinal cord.

Motor neurons are specialized nervous-system cells that control all voluntary muscle contraction. As a result, damage to motor neurons can affect the voluntary function of limbs, trunk, neck, tongue, mouth, throat, and diaphragm, since their movement and function depends upon voluntary muscle contraction.

About six thousand new cases of ALS are reported each year in the United States, and there may be about four hundred thousand people living with ALS around the world. Since there are about six thousand new cases of ALS occurring annually among a population of about 320 million in the U.S., the odds of developing ALS in any single year is about one in fifty thousand. However, the risk of an individual developing ALS over a lifetime appears to be less than one in a thousand, and some say it may even as low as one in four hundred.

Symptoms of ALS can vary greatly regarding which muscles are first affected, the pattern of symptoms, the rate of advancement of symptoms, and the severity of disability. One's survival time can also vary greatly. Symptom progression may be so gradual that an individual's diagnosis of ALS could be delayed for more than a year because all the criteria needed for a diagnosis of ALS may not yet have appeared. On the other hand, a minority of individuals will suffer a very rapid progression of symptoms and could succumb to the disease within a year or two. However, most patients with ALS will survive three to five years or more following their diagnosis. Common symptoms include progressive muscle weakness, muscle stiffness, muscle cramps, muscle twitching (fasciculation) as well as difficulty in walking, tripping, clumsiness, paralysis, and eventually muscle atrophy. Less often, presenting symptoms will include difficulty with speech and/or swallowing, which are known as *bulbar symptoms.* In addition, most individuals with ALS will eventually develop difficulty in breathing due to failing respiratory muscles, which is often a cause of respiratory failure and death.

As the disease advances, affected muscles will shrink in size. This is a sign of muscle atrophy, which results from a muscle's loss of its motor-neuron innervation (nerve connection). Weakness and paralysis will continue to advance, as more motor neurons die, and this process will eventually affect most or all voluntary muscles. Rarely, the progression of symptoms will suddenly cease, and the disease will appear to have burned itself out. It has been reported that less than one percent of ALS patients appear to even experience a cessation of the progression of their symptoms at some point, and a few appear to even experience a regression of some of their symptoms. This phenomenon is currently being investigated. Aside from specific neurologic symptoms, many ALS patients also suffer from significant fatigue and weight loss.

In recent years it has been discovered that a number of ALS patients will also experience a diminution in cognitive function over the course of their illness, such as difficulty in making decisions or following complex directions. Some may also suffer language difficulty including difficulty with word retrieval. In addition, some ALS patients have been noted to develop behavioral changes or suffer bouts of inappropriate uncontrollable laughter or crying (e.g., pseudobulbar affect or PBA).

The following is a brief overview of ALS, which will be reviewed in greater detail in subsequent chapters.

The Course of ALS

ALS symptoms can begin at any time between adolescence and old age. However, the majority of patients in the U.S. will have an onset of symptoms somewhere between the ages of thirty-five and seventy-five, with most individuals presenting in their fifties and sixties. Less commonly, ALS can begin during adolescence or in a young adult. It should be noted that the onset at a younger age seems to be associated with a longer survival time. Some populations outside of the U.S. have been reported to have a significantly earlier average onset of ALS.

Progressive muscular weakness, atrophy and paralysis without sensory loss are together the hallmark of ALS. Voluntary muscles grow progressively weaker, begin to atrophy, and becomes paralyzed overtime. Muscle cramps, fasciculations (twitching), and stiffness are common at some point during the progression of symptoms.

Advancing weakness or paralysis of the diaphragm will lead to respiratory symptoms (e.g., symptoms of hypoventilation including shortness of breath, sleep disturbance). It appears that early intervention with respiratory support such as BiPAP (noninvasive ventilation) can significantly increase the survival time of those affected by hypoventilation.

Bulbar symptoms will affect a minority of ALS patients (25 – 30%) at the time of their diagnosis and these symptoms will often contribute to weight loss and malnutrition due to difficulty with swallowing. Bulbar involvement usually affects the muscles the tongue, mouth, pharynx, and larynx leading to difficulty with speech and/or swallowing as well as aspiration.

Most ALS patients will succumb to their disease within 5 or 6 year as a result of respiratory failure, pneumonia or malnutrition. Review the following websites for more information:

https://www.mda.org/disease/amyotrophic-lateral-sclerosis/
signs-and-symptoms/stages-of-als

https://www.mda.org/disease/amyotrophic-lateral-sclerosis/
signs-and-symptoms

http://emedicine.medscape.com/article/1170097-clinical

The Cause of ALS

We know that about 10 - 15 percent of ALS patients have an inherited form of the disease (*familial ALS* or *FALS*) while 85 -90 percent or so of PALS have no affected family members (*sporadic ALS* or *SALS*). Outside of a number of specific genetic mutations found among some ALS patients, no pathologic mechanism or etiology has been identified as the *common or primary cause* of sporadic ALS.

Some but not all patients with the familial form of ALS have specific gene mutations (e.g., SOD 1 {20%}, C9ORF72 {40%}). SOD1 produces an enzymatic protein that converts toxic free radicals (oxidizing forms of oxygen, which are produced as a metabolic by-product of neural cellular metabolism) into non-toxic molecules. Failure to neutralize toxic free radicals could allow them to accumulate in and around motor neurons, causing a motor neuron's injury or death. However, the great majority of nonfamilial or sporadic ALS patients do not have an identified genetic defect or mutation, which supports the possibility that there is probably more than one factor causing of ALS. Furthermore, it appears that abnormal proteins produced by genetic mutation maybe toxic on multiple levels to motor neurons and/or to the neural cells surrounding them. At this point, there may be many possible causes of ALS, and it is more than likely that different mechanisms or more than one pathology play a role in an individual with ALS.

My neurologist, Dr. Heiman-Patterson, tells me tells me that there are more than 30 gene mutations now identified in ALS and that these genes offer clues to etiology and mechanisms involved in ALS. Furthermore, scientists are now identifying modifiers such as well as genes that are not highly penetrant, which may increase the risk of developing ALS when combined with other genetic abnormalities and environmental factors. She further points out that while the majority of ALS patients may not have an identifiable genetic mutation but are likely to have a genetic endowment that predisposes one to develop ALS under the right circumstances (e.g., exposure to toxins).

A large national study directed at evaluating how genes influence the development of ALS is underway with the goal of using future findings to individualized treatment. The project is named the *Genomic Translation for ALS Care (GTAC)* project. Its goal is to perform genetic sequencing of ALS patients upon diagnosis and try to correlate these findings with and individual's clinical presentation and course. More than a thousand ALS patients from many centers and clinics in the U.S. will be studied in order to better understand the role that genes play in the development of ALS.

It is likely that a number of mechanisms, including genetic mutation may contribute to or lead to a final common pathway to cause a motor neuron's death, making it likely that ALS will probably turn out to be a heterogeneous disease regarding its etiology and pathology. Dr. Patterson also notes that in the long-term, the goal for treatment will be to individualize treatment strategies based on the underlying mechanism that is associated with an individual's ALS, and I think she is correct in this matter.

Many theories regarding the cause of ALS have been put forth. For example, some individual's with ALS have a higher-than-normal glutamate level (a neurotransmitter) found in their blood and spinal fluid, and it has been suggested that high levels of glutamate might have a toxic effect on motor neurons. However, treatment with riluzole (Rilutek), which has an inhibitory effect on glutamate release, has only had a very modest effect on extending the lives of ALS patients.

There have also been reports of an increase in the incidence of ALS among individuals who have suffered head trauma and also among those exposed to military service (veterans). However, none of these associations points to a specific common cause of ALS.

Conjecture that motor neurons die as a result of environmental or dietary toxins, nutritional insufficiency, heavy-metal toxicity, or that ALS is commonly caused by an autoimmune disease or a virus has not been proven so far in spite of extensive investigation over a number of years.

However, that being said, it is clear that something is killing motor neurons in ALS. One possibility, not yet excluded, is that a defect has developed in the motor neuron's metabolism or in its neural environment, which is causing the neural cell's death. For example, if a triggered defective cellular process impedes the normal removal of a motor neuron's metabolic toxic waste products or that abnormal proteins are being produced (e.g., genetic mutation) they could accumulate in and around a motor neuron and poison it. Dead motor neurons in ALS have been found to commonly contain abnormal aggregates not found in healthy motor neurons. Many of these aggregates contain abnormal proteins, some of which are a product of mutant genes. Are gene mutations and their production of abnormal proteins a common cause of ALS or is it a combination of factors?

Suggested potential causes for ALS also include: RNA processing defects, programed cell death, cytoskeleton protein defects, mitochondrial dysfunction, defective gene protein production and their clumping within motor neurons, etc.

Although the exact cause of ALS remains unknown, early results of recent clinical trials using neurotrophic stem cells appear to benefit ALS patients who began this treatment early in their disease. One explanation for this observation would be that transplanted stem cells produce neurotrophic factors that somehow repair damaged cells and/or protect undamaged cells by correcting faulty cellular mechanisms. It should be noted that there are a number of other promising potentially effective treatments currently undergoing clinical trials or in development, and this gives one hope for the future.

Review the following websites regarding possible causes of ALS:

http://www.alsa.org/research/focus-areas/disease-mechanisms/

https://www.mda.org/disease/amyotrophic-lateral-sclerosis/causes-inheritance

www.alsa.org/research/about-als-research/sod1.html

https://www.youtube.com/watch?v=lsx9jn3LGxc

http://www.ncbi.nlm.nih.gov/pmc/articles/PMC4404432/

http://www.ncbi.nlm.nih.gov/pmc/articles/PMC3182412/

http://www.ncbi.nlm.nih.gov/pmc/articles/PMC3930370/

http://www.hindawi.com/journals/bmri/2014/925101/

https://www.youtube.com/watch?v=CaD-oF9deNY

https://alsnewstoday.com/2016/08/03/ALS-Culprit-Protein-Chokes-Up-Mitochondria-Killing-Neurons

Diagnosis of ALS

At this time, no specific test for ALS exists; however, diagnostic tests for ALS are being developed (e.g., Iron horse diagnostics). Diagnosis is currently based on observing the development of the typical clinical symptoms and pathologic neurological signs that are associated with the death of both upper and lower motor neurons (more about this in chapter 2). Therefore, at this time

ALS is it clinical diagnosis which accounts for delays in diagnosis as well as occasional misdiagnosis. In addition, other diseases that present with symptoms similar to ALS need to be ruled out since the diagnosis of ALS is based on clinical symptoms and signs. It might take a year or more to finalize a diagnosis of ALS in an individual, especially if symptoms are gradual in their presentation or are atypical.

The most valuable diagnostic information will come from repeated neurological examinations over a period of time that reveal progressive upper and lower motor neuron defects, along with a patient's history of progressive weakness and paralysis.

Clinical observations should include the presence of progressive weakness of voluntary muscles and signs of upper and lower motor neuron damage that are supported by nerve and muscle studies (nerve conduction studies and EMGs) that are consistent with ALS. In addition, blood work, MRI and CT scans, and perhaps analysis of a patient's spinal fluid will be used to rule out other diseases that can mimic ALS symptoms. Getting a second opinion from another ALS neuromuscular specialist is always a good idea, since a correct diagnosis early in the disease's development can be difficult, and making an early diagnosis could help with your management. You may find the following websites useful:

https://www.youtube.com/watch?v=wxr_6DAWZ8U

http://www.alsa.org/als-care/resources/publications-videos/fact sheets/criteria-for-diagnosis.html

http://www.alsa.org/assets/pdfs/fyi/criteria_for_diagnosis.pdf (use Firefox browser to view)

http://www.mayoclinic.org/diseases-conditions/amyotrophic-lateral-sclerosis/basics/tests-diagnosis/con-20024397

http://www.massgeneral.org/als/patienteducation/
DiagnosingALS.aspx

http://ironhorsedx.com/#

Treatment of ALS
Aside from Rilutek (riluzole), there is no other FDA-approved
treatment for ALS at this time. Rilutek appears to extend survival
rates of ALS patient by an average of only three months or so, which
seems to be quite a modest benefit. Current management of ALS is
primarily directed at supportive measures and the use of adaptive,
augmentative, and/or assistive devices. In addition, many patients
with ALS participate in clinical trials, which may offer a potentially
effective treatment. The goal is to help an affected individual maintain function for as long as possible, maintain comfort, and extend
survival (more about treatment can be found in a subsequent
chapter). Check the following websites for more information:

http://www.mayoclinic.org/diseases-conditions/amyotrophic-
lateral-sclerosis/basics/treatment/con-20024397

http://web.alsa.org/site/PageServer?pagename=ALSA_Ask_
Dec2011

http://www.ncbi.nlm.nih.gov/pubmed/22419278

http://www.ninds.nih.gov/disorders/
amyotrophiclateralsclerosis/detail_ALS.htm#4842_6

https://www.youtube.com/watch?v=DCKD3KiCUxc

http://www.news-medical.net/news/20160201/New-study-lays-
foundation-for-future-gene-replacement-therapies-to-treat-ALS-
patients.aspx

Hope for the Future

Experimental stem-cell treatments for ALS have been undergoing clinical trials. Early observations appear to indicate significant benefits for ALS patients enrolled in phase II clinical trials (e.g., Brainstorm, Neuralstem) by slowing down the rate of the progression of symptoms. Furthermore, there are many other promising drugs for the treatment of ALS currently in development. Therefore, there is reason to have hope that effective treatments for ALS will become available in the foreseeable future. To better understand potential therapy, consider reviewing the following websites:

www.youtube.com/watch?v=AuDxBQYeiS4]

www.youtube.com/watch?v=p5OoXkNIvHA

https://www.youtube.com/watch?v=CaD-oF9deNY

www.youtube.com/watch?v=BbKlbwsYcKc

http://www.alsa.org/news/archive/new-copper-therapy.html

http://www.alsa.org/research/about-als-research/therapy-for-als.html

http://www.alstdi.org/als-research/als-clinical-trials/

https://www.youtube.com/watch?v=e50WyILoow4

https://clinicaltrials.gov/ct2/show/NCT02709330

Unfortunately, there are many unproven stem cell treatment and other ineffective or unproven therapies offered to ALS patients in the private clinics around the world (e.g., China, Mexico, etc.) that have not successfully passed rigorously conducted scientific clinical trials with published results in serious refereed journals that supports their safety and efficacy. Therefore, it appears to me that many unproven ALS treatments are being exploited for profit and raising false hopes in PALS. For more on the subject, view the following website:

www.youtube.com/watch?v=ovPZkQYee8Y

It should be noted that there are several new drugs in development for ALS treatment, some of which are already in the pipeline –Edaravone has been approved in Japan and is seeking approval in the US for the treatment of ALS

It also seems that the age of personalized medicine may soon be upon us and this is what it may take to cure ALS. Huge efforts are being made to identify biomarkers of ALS, its progression, and treatment response; trying to identify the mechanism(s) causing ALS in order to stratify clinical trials and ultimately discover an effective treatments.

However, until effective treatment for ALS becomes available, supportive management and adaptive devices can help improve one's ability to function, maintain independence, prevent complications, limit discomfort, and in some cases significantly extend one's longevity. Specifically, the use of noninvasive and invasive ventilation can extend an ALS patient's life by years for those suffering from hypoventilation. Individuals with ALS who have difficulty in swallowing and/or those suffering from malnutrition can receive a feeding tube (a PEG or RIG), which can provide adequate caloric intake and nutrition in such cases. A feeding tube may also prevent aspiration pneumonia in those with swallowing dysfunction. The two main causes of death in ALS are related to hypoventilation (e.g., respiratory failure) and to swallowing dysfunction (e.g., aspiration, pneumonia, and malnutrition). Intervention with respiratory support and/or a feeding tube can often help manage either or both of these problems. Feeding tubes and respiratory support are reviewed in greater detail in subsequent chapters.

As symptoms of weakness and paralysis advance, the use of mobility equipment, adaptive devices, and competent caregivers can help an ALS patient to a live a meaningful and fulfilling life, just as I do.

The rate of advancement in science and neuroscience today is truly breathtaking. The recent development of optogenetic techniques that allows scientists to study individual nerve cells and figure out how they work will have tremendous implications regarding the understanding of many neurological and psychiatric disorders. Further, the recent advances in genetic engineering (e.g., CRISPR) will help researchers to more rapidly identify the role of genes in disorders such as those in ALS and also could potentially be used to correct such defects. This is clearly a big deal since gene mutation seems to play an important role in much of the pathology so far uncovered in ALS.

Currently there are dozens of clinical trials for the treatment of ALS being conducted around the world. In fact, I received an experimental stem cell treatment almost 6 years ago, and it seems to me that it definitely slowed down the progression of my symptoms.

https://www.youtube.com/watch?v=0yOeQa4HgE4

http://www.alsconsortium.org/browse.php

https://clinicaltrials.gov/ct2/results?term=als&pg=1

http://www.alstdi.org/als-research/als-clinical-trials/

Two

Motor Neurons and ALS

A LS is a progressive neurodegenerative disorder that results from dead and dying motor neurons located in the brain, the brain stem and the spinal cord. Motor neurons are specialized nervous system cells that control voluntary muscle contraction. Different types of motor neurons work together to coordinate and control skeletal (voluntary) muscle contraction, and together they are responsible for all voluntary movement. There are two types of motor neurons whose death can lead to the development of ALS. These neural cells are referred to as either *upper motor neurons* or *lower motor neurons.*

- *Upper motor neurons* (UMN) are found in the brain's cortex (outer layer) and in the brain stem.
- *Lower motor neurons* (LMN) are located in the brain stem and the spinal cord.

Each has a very different function; however, they work synergistically together in order to produce desired movement(s). Once you decide to begin a movement, UMNs are activated in order to initiate a desired movement. UMNs relay a signal to stimulate and coordinate specific LMNs to contract muscles under their control in order to initiate and modulate specific muscle contraction and movement. It should be noted that UMNs do not *directly* connect to muscles; instead, they relay signals to LMNs, which in turn initiate muscle contraction. Only LMNs <u>directly</u> innervate voluntary muscles and directly stimulate them to contract.

LMNs, unlike UMNs, do not reside in the brain but are found in the *brain stem* and *spinal cord*. Each LMN sends out its nerve (an axon) to innervate (connect) specific muscle fibers. A LMN, its nerve, and the muscle it controls are together referred to as a *motor-neuron unit* because they all work together as a single unit. Should muscle fibers lose contact with their LMNs, as occurs in ALS when a LMN dies, then voluntary control of that muscle will cease. In such a case the muscle of that lower motor neuron unit will eventually begin to shrink and atrophy. Therefore, the connection of a LMN to its muscle is necessary to maintain a muscle's health and survival.

As the disease progresses, affected ALS patients will eventually reveal the signs and symptoms of both upper and lower motor neuron defects, which are hallmark signs of ALS.

Damage to UMNs will result in an increase of muscle reflexes (*hyperreflexia* or exaggerated deep-tendon reflexes) as well as muscle spasticity (muscle stiffness resulting from an increase in muscle tone). Muscle spasticity occurs when UMNs lose their connection with LMNs, resulting in an increase in muscle tone, muscle stiffness, and increased muscle stretch reflexes. Abnormal neurologic signs that indicate the presence of UMN disease include: the Babinski sign, clonus, clasp-knife reflex, etc. Their presence during the neurological exam will help support the diagnosis of ALS.

Aside from spasticity, symptoms resulting from UMN damage include progressive muscle weakness and clumsiness, imprecise movements, a decline in control over muscle movement, and slowing of voluntary movement(s). However, muscles affected by upper motor neuron damage alone will not atrophy as long as the affected muscle continues to maintain a direct connection with its healthy LMN.

In contrast to UMN defects, the death of a LMN will cause its innervated muscle to lose its nutritive stimulation, which will eventually result in the muscle's atrophy. The death of a LMN will cause an affected muscle to decrease its tone (*hypotonia*), suffer spontaneous muscle twitching (fasciculation), and/or develop sustained intense muscle contractions (cramps). Deep-tendon reflexes will also be reduced (*hyporeflexia*) as a result of the death of a muscle's LMN. Muscle weakness will eventually advance to paralysis as an increasing number of LMNs die. With the loss of LMN innervation, the muscles of the affected lower motor neuron unit will atrophy, and when that process is complete, fasciculation and muscle cramps of the affected muscles will cease because the affected muscle fibers will no longer be functional.

The process of upper and lower motor-neuron interaction permits precise control, coordination, and modulation of complex movements such as walking, running, going up a flight of stairs, lifting heavy objects, throwing a ball accurately, the manual dexterity needed for typing, swallowing function, breathing, and speaking. Patients lacking clear evidence of both upper and lower motor neuron defects will not meet the minimum criteria needed for a diagnosis of ALS.

For additional information about upper- and lower-motor-neuron actions and pathology, review the following websites:

https://www.youtube.com/watch?v=LwA00uqniiU

https://www.youtube.com/watch?v=uO1s9IE5Y3M

http://health.howstuffworks.com/human-body/systems/nervous-system/nerve1.htm

https://www.khanacademy.org/science/health-and-medicine/human-anatomy-and-physiology/nervous-system-introduction/v/motor-unit

www.khanacademy.org/science/health-and-medicine/human-anatomy-and-physiology/nervous-system-introduction/v/upper-motor-neurons

https://www.boundless.com/psychology/textbooks/boundless-psychology-textbook/biological-foundations-of-psychology-3/neurons-33/introducing-the-neuron-141-12676/

http://neuroscience.uth.tmc.edu/s3/chapter01.html

http://www.ninds.nih.gov/disorders/brain_basics/ninds_neuron.htm

Which Muscles Are Affected?

As motor neurons die, the muscles they control will weaken, and in time they will cease to function (paralysis). Dying motor neurons in ALS will affect voluntary (skeletal) muscles under their control. *Nonvoluntary* or *smooth muscles*, such as the smooth muscles of the colon and bladder, are not typically affected in ALS. Smooth muscles are under the control of the *autonomic nervous system,* which are not typicaly influenced by motor neurons. However, incontinence can occur late in advanced ALS should *Onuf's nucleus* be damaged (see reference below) or if dementia is present, which can affect the striated muscles that control sphincter tone.

Smooth muscles control the dilation of your eyes' irises, bladder and colon contraction, and control the muscles involved in erection and ejaculation. Since motor neurons do not affect smooth, incontinence and erectile dysfunction function are usually not consequences of ALS. However, should sphincter control be lost, which is uncommon in ALS, incontinence can occur. Should incontinence occur in ALS it will likely appear in the late stage of the disease. However, it should be noted that incontinence could also occur in PALS due to other causes that are not specifically related to the death of motor neurons.

Clinical symptoms of ALS can include weakness of the extremities (walking, hand function) core body muscles (posture, arising, lifting, etc.), muscles of the diaphragm (breathing), and/or the muscles of swallowing and speech. Initial symptoms may present as fatigue, tripping, falling, hand weakness, slurring of speech or difficulties with swallowing. Many ALS patients first develop muscle weakness, difficulty in walking, tripping and/or going up or down stairs; clumsiness; unexpectedly dropping things; hand weakness; and difficulty getting up from a seated position or getting out of bed. Early symptoms of ALS often consist of twitching of muscles (fasciculation), muscle cramps, and/or muscle stiffness and/or fatigue.

Presenting symptoms of ALS do not frequently include respiratory difficulty although this is in an occasional presenting symptoms. Nevertheless, most PALS will eventually develop difficulty in breathing, which is a sign of muscular weakness of the diaphragm and to a lesser extent, weakness of one's chest wall muscles.

Extra-ocular eye muscles are responsible for eye gaze movement. Although they are voluntary muscles, for some reason they are usually spared from paralysis in ALS. As a result, paralyzed patients in the late stage of the disease are often, but not always, able to use *eye gaze* based technology to communicate.

Less than a third of ALS patients will present with *bulbar symptoms,* which characteristically include difficulties with speech and/or problems related to swallowing. The term *bulbar pattern of ALS* refers to the death of motor neurons located in the brain stem. Patients with bulbar symptoms often suffer slurred speech, difficulty swallowing, along with bouts of coughing and/or choking. Affected patients may also exhibit symptoms of drooling due to swallowing dysfunction. Bulbar symptoms will put affected patients at risk for aspiration of food, drink, or saliva. If aspiration is not quickly prevented, it could lead to pneumonia and lung damage. Aspiration is likely to be life threatening in an ALS patient with a weak cough because it will reduce such a patient's ability to clear aspirated food, drink or saliva from the airway, which could result in lung infection (e.g., pneumonia) and reduce the lungs air exchange ability if the alveoli (air sacs) become filled with aspirated fluids or inflammatory secretions.

The rate of progression of an individual's ALS symptoms tends to remain fairly steady over the long term. That is, if your symptoms are progressing slowly during the early stages of the disease, then symptoms are likely to continue to do so in the future, and the inverse is also true. However, even though the long-term trend of the rate of progression will usually remain steady, there may be periods when one's symptoms temporarily progress more slowly or more rapidly but the rate of progression will usually return to its long-term trend over time.

The process of motor-neuron recruitment will play an important role in ALS symptoms. Motor neurons can innervate a single muscle or a group of muscle fibers, and more than one motor neuron can be involved in controlling a muscle's contraction. When more muscle force is needed for an action, additional motor neurons that innervate the muscle may be recruited to achieve a greater force of contraction. In this way, motor-neuron control over muscles can be modulated. As motor neurons die, the phenomenon of recruitment will become impaired, leading to weaker contractions.

At times, compensatory muscle use will be used to assist weak muscles. For example, if the biceps muscle weakens then the brachoradialis muscle can compensate to some extent. However once the brachoradialis weakens, you may then suddenly find that you can't flex your elbow.

Another form of recruitment can occur when the nerve of a healthy motor neuron take over the function of an adjacent dead motor neuron's innervation of a muscle. This will permit an affected muscle to continue to function and in this way there is remodeling of the motor neuron unit. Unfortunately, as more and more motor neurons die, this compensatory mechanism will also eventually fail as the disease progresses.

It should be noted that the death of motor neurons would have no effect on sensory function; therefore, an ALS patient's sensory functions should remain intact. As a result, ALS patients can suffer from pain just as would anyone else.

Publications about virtually every aspect of ALS are widely available and they can help you better understand your illness and inform you about management options. For example, lots of

ALS information can be found through national organizations such as the Muscular Dystrophy Association (MDA) or from the ALS Association (ALSA). The following websites offer additional information:

https://www.mda.org/disease/amyotrophic-lateral-sclerosis

http://www.alsa.org/als-care/resources/books/

https://en.wikipedia.org/wiki/Motor_unit_recruitment

http://neuroscience.uth.tmc.edu/s3/chapter01.html

https://www.researchgate.net/publication/16041382_The_Onuf's_nucleus_and_the_external_anal_sphincter_muscle_in_ALS_and_Shy-Drager_syndrome

https://www.med.or.jp/english/journal/pdf/2011_01/047_050.pdf

http://www.ncbi.nlm.nih.gov/pmc/articles/PMC4170108/

http://emedicine.medscape.com/article/1170097-overview

https://www.aaet.info/files/documents/Amyotrophic-Lateral-Sclerosis-Paper.pdf (Firefox)

http://www.hindawi.com/journals/bmri/2016/5930621/

http://www.exercisemed.org/research-blog/retaining-muscle-function.html

https://www.ncbi.nlm.nih.gov/pubmed/16155429

http://www.touchneurology.com/system/files/private/articles/10667/pdf/9toshiop46-50.pdf

Three

Life Is Not Over with a Diagnosis of ALS

A diagnosis of ALS does not mean that your death is imminent, nor does it mean that your life is over! However, it does predict that your life will change dramatically as symptoms of weakness and paralysis advance and that you will need to adapt and you adjust to these changes in order to maintain a good quality of life. It will also mean that your survival time on average is likely to be significantly shortened, making time all that more precious.

It seems to me that the biggest challenge of ALS does not concern dying from the disease but rather learning how to live with it in a way that allows for a quality of life that is worthwhile and meaningful, and this has been possible for many.

I have been living with the symptoms of ALS for seven years or so, and in spite of advancing disability, I continue to experience happiness on a daily basis even though I am in the late stage of this disease. What has always been important to me are my relationships, and the most important ones have not really changed—ALS has not stopped me from enjoying them. Further, I continue to have both the opportunity and the freedom to pursue many of my interests in spite of physical limitations. I am able to do much of what I want to do because I have learned to adapt to the constraints of my limitations. A power wheelchair gives me mobility, a wheelchair-accessible taxi will take me to where I wish to go, voice recognition software allows me to write and navigate the computer, and caregivers help me when I lack the necessary strength or dexterity to carry out a task. As a result, I continue to experience freedom, meaning, and happiness.

To illustrate the point that life is not over when diagnosed with ALS, one only needs to examine the life of Steven Hawking, the cosmologist, who has been living with ALS for more than fifty years. Although his longevity may set a record for ALS survival time, it is his attitude that I find inspiring. The following are among his quotes:

"Disability does not really affect my consciousness. I see it as an inconvenience."

"My advice to other disabled people would be, concentrate on things your disability doesn't prevent you doing well, and don't regret the things it interferes with. Don't be disabled in spirit as well as physically."

The odds are that you will have a number of years ahead of you, during which time you can take full advantage of what is possible, and often that is quite a lot.

Considering that some of your current opportunities may be lost as symptoms advance, it would make great sense to concentrate your efforts on doing what is still possible each day. Study ALS, investigate your options of how to best manage symptoms and disability, seek out and accept the support you need, and be determined to find a way to create as good a quality of life by pursuing what is possible.

Finally, in my opinion treatments for ALS in the foreseeable future will likely be able to slow down the disease's progression, improve one's quality of life, and significantly extend ones survival time. I also expect that a cure for ALS will eventually be found based on the ever-increasing rate of progress occurring in science and medicine.

The following websites offer additional information:

http://www.alsa.org/als-care/resources/publications-videos/factsheets/reasons-for-living-with-als.html

https://www.mda.org/disease/amyotrophic-lateral-sclerosis/living-with

http://www.medicaldaily.com/als-diagnosis-age-30-what-its-be-young-lou-gehrigs-disease-patient-how-ice-bucket-348388

http://www.huffingtonpost.com/stephen-finger/als-awareness-month_1_b_5360174.html

http://www.npr.org/2010/03/29/125231223/a-historians-long-view-on-living-with-lou-gehrigs

https://www.youtube.com/watch?v=_d1JLwsvkfo

Four

The Emotional Impact
of ALS

Following the diagnosis of ALS, the first stumbling block I encountered was that of emotional turmoil. At first I felt overwhelmed and frightened. Finding ways to manage the intense and disorienting emotions I experienced helped me to move on with my life following the diagnosis.

Initially I found myself engaged in a struggle trying to avoid being sucked into the darkness of negativism and hopelessness. I knew that I had to accept the reality of my situation and begin to take a constructive approach in dealing with this illness so that I could positively influence how things would work for me. Once I was better able to manage my feelings, I began to study the full spectrum of the disease. In time I was able to begin engaging and optimizing management of my symptoms and advancing disability in a way that allowed me to make the most out of my circumstances. This approach allowed me to begin enjoying that which was meaningful and important to me. This entire process all began with learning how to deal with what I was feeling and by getting help and support when I needed it.

Coping

Each of us is unique in our reaction to stress, and so I doubt there is a single best way that will meet everyone's needs. Nevertheless, there are good answers out there if you look for them. How does one cope with the recurrent waves of intense negative feelings after receiving a diagnosis of ALS? There are no simple answers to this question. When struck with a life-altering illness associated with the prospect of suffering progressive paralysis and an early death, most of us will experience feelings of shock, fear, anxiety, and/or depression.

Although the implications of the diagnosis of ALS are hard to digest, at a certain point one needs to accept reality in order to enjoy what is still possible. To do otherwise would be a waste valuable time and the opportunity that is likely to lead to unnecessary suffering.

Coping has a lot to do with learning how to manage progressive physical symptoms while maintaining a psychological balance. It also has to due with preparing well for expected advancing disability. In order to do this, you will first have to find a way to effectively deal with your feelings so that you can fully engage in managing your physical symptoms and advancing disability.

Taking psychotropic medications (e.g., clonazepam, Lexapro, etc.) can often help take the edge off of feeling anxious and/or diminish feelings of depression. The frequent use of Skype, social media and/or FaceTime can help you to stay in contact with friends and family, which can help prevent isolation and offer you support. Call friends and invite them over to spend some with you. If you can't go out, invite friends and family to your home by reaching out to them. If you belong to a religious organization, speak to your clergyman and asked to be counseled and perhaps they can ask members of their community to offer you support. Contact your local ALS or MDA Association chapter and join their support group for advice and support. If possible, hire a caregiver to assist you or give your family caregiver some time off. Try to be proactive and ask family and friends for the specific help you need or just to spend some time with you. During quiet moments when nothing is going wrong, open a dialogue with your spouse, family and close friends regarding your feelings and their feeling and discuss how important it is to pull together and support each other during this very difficult time. You never know what will work until you try. If your ALS center has a social worker, discuss your situation and asked for help if it is needed. Learn to meditate because it can be a great stress reliever. Consult a psychologist or psychiatrist for professional support. If you're religious or spiritual, your faith can offer you great support. And finally, go online to the ALS and MDA websites; they have a ton of information that can really help you understand what is happening and offer you guidance in the management of ALS symptoms and disability. You can also join an online ALS forum for information, guidance and support.

From the beginning, my way of coping with ALS was to concentrate on to bringing my negative emotions under control, calm down, and begin to focus on what I needed to do. At first I began taking psychotropic medication and used my support system to help me calm down. I did find meditation to be very helpful. Better yet I began to learn as much as I could about ALS as a disease process and in so doing I became less anxious as I learned what to expect and how to handle challenges. Throwing in the towel and giving up were not options for me as long as there were alternatives. I knew that if I remained determined to find a way to manage my symptoms then there could be some good years ahead, and this turned out to be the case. For more information review the following web sites.

http://www.alsa.org/als-care/resources/publications-videos/factsheets/tips-for-newly-diagnosed.html

http://www.alsclinic.pitt.edu/patients/coping.php

http://www.breakthroughals.org/breakthroughblog/entry/mental-health-and-als-staying-mentally-strong-after-an-als-diagnosis

http://alsmaine.org/patients-guide/

https://static1.squarespace.com/static/54e2529ae4b0409b0
6622d23/t/565c6e19e4b0b80773ac40b0/1448898073935/
Holiday_Stress_Flyer.pdf   (Firefox)

http://www.mayoclinic.org/diseases-conditions/amyotrophic-
lateral-sclerosis/basics/coping-support/con-20024397

http://www.alsforums.com

Fear

Fear was probably the first emotion I experienced once I understood that my diagnosis of ALS was definite. I was not looking
forward to dying; however, death has never been a great fear
of mine. What really did scare me was the thought of becoming increasingly disabled, losing my autonomy, being deprived
of the ability to help and protect those I love. I also hated the
thought of giving up my life's work, and being forced to up some
plans and dreams.

At first I was very anxious and needed to take psychotropic
medication (e.g., Clonazepam) in order to calm down enough
to get some sleep. Over time, I came to better understand the
disease process and what was likely to happen to me. As a result,
I began to adapt to each new symptom and prepare for the ones
I could expect. As my understanding and ability to manage challenges improved, my anxiety diminished, and along with it, so
did my feelings of fear. Looking back, I suspect that it was fear of
the unknown that caused much of my distress. As the unknown
became known and methods for managing symptoms became
clear, my level anxiety diminished, and I was no longer afraid.

Under normal circumstances, fear can motivate one to deal
with the very thing that one fears, and that is a good thing.
On the other hand, persistent fear can seriously interfere with
making good decisions if it freezes you into denial, inaction or

indecision. For example, when fear interferes with good decision making or effectively managing symptoms or risks, it can have serious negative consequences.

Fear can also prevent you from enjoying the present if you let it crowd out your ability to enjoy what is still possible. In such a situation, it is fear itself that can cause you greater difficulty and suffering than the discomfort you might endure from your physical symptoms and disability.

When fear interferes with rational decision making, causes you emotional pain, or prevents you from engaging in life, then it has reached a pathological level that requires professional treatment.

As my mom liked to say, "If there is a will, there is a way," and if you have the will to manage ALS symptoms wisely, then there is no reason to be paralyzed by fear since there is quite a bit you can do in spite of symptoms and physical limitations.

Denial
Denial is not an uncommon reaction embraced by some when first diagnosed with ALS. Unfortunately, denial is among the worst responses because it will prevent you from moving forward and making good choices. Ignoring reality when dealing with ALS will likely create a situation in which symptoms or disability related to ALS could suddenly come crashing down upon you because you have not adequately prepared to deal with them.

Not accepting reality and dealing constructively with your symptoms and disability will complicate your life as well as the lives of your loved ones. Refusal to use a walker, rollator, or wheelchair when your lower extremities are very weak will put you at risk for a serious fall as well as limit your mobility and functionality. Falling could result in a broken hip or perhaps a fractured skull, all easily preventable had you accepted reality and taken appropriate measures to manage the situation. Refusing to use respiratory support when needed or accepting a feeding tube when required in a timely manner will cause you both suffering as well as shorten your survival time. When denial gives way to acceptance, the hope of creating an acceptable quality of life as well as extending one's survival time becomes possible. Check out the following web site:

http://alsn.mda.org/article/new-life-als-9

Acceptance

Once I was able to calm down enough to accept the reality of my circumstance, things began to improve.

At first, I felt like a fish caught on a hook, furiously twisting and turning, trying to free myself the reality of my situation. I went to see multiple neurologists at university hospitals for additional opinions. I also went to the Mayo Clinic for a third opinion and even received a fourth opinion at an ALS center outside of the United States. Finally, I began to understand that my diagnosis was without a doubt correct and that I had to accept it.

Acceptance released me from the torture of negative feelings and allowed me to to focus on what I needed to do to in order to prepare to live with ALS. I began to seriously study the disease process and its management so that I could better understand how to best deal with each stage of the disease. Was this approach easy? No, it was not. However, it was doable, and so I did what had to be done. Not accepting the reality of my situation would have been just a waste of valuable time and would have actually made my situation far worse than it needed to be. Review the following web for another person's perspective about acceptance:

http://www.goodtherapy.org/blog/grief-and-chronic-illness-how-to-find-acceptance-0626145

Anxiety and Stress

Anxiety can be defined as fear of the unknown, uneasiness about the future, nervousness, and/or a feeling of dread, and I experienced all of these feelings. Newly diagnosed PALS will undoubtedly be seriously stressed out. Anxiety can lead to sleepless nights, irritability, somatic complaints, panic attacks, and/or a loss of concentration. In any case, uncontrolled anxiety will impede your ability to function at your best, and you are going to need to function well if you want to enjoy as good a quality of life as is possible when dealing with this illness.

It seems to me that emotional distress is often the main hurdle that one must overcome early in the course of ALS in order to enjoy as good a quality of life as possible within the limitations imposed by your illness.

Studying ALS really helped me prepare for each stage of the disease, a disease that is constantly evolving and advancing. Symptoms and disability ALS similar to moving targets that require that you anticipate and prepare for their progression or you may find that you will forever be playing catch-up to nasty events. Knowledge is power in this matter, and it will help you to adapt and manage things wisely. Understanding the disease process should also alleviate a great deal of anxiety, since you will be able to grasp what is happening to you and also help you understand and prepare for what is likely to happen.

Read books and articles about ALS, collect information on the Internet, seek out knowledge and support from your ALS center and national organizations (e.g., MDA and ALSA), and join an ALS support group in order to gain more insight and to help you find what you need. Access the web references throughout this book because they may offer you deeper insight and additional information about a specific ALS issue or problem with which you are unfamiliar and this could help you to optimize management of symptoms or solve problems in a timely manner.

Make a concerted effort to stay engaged with friends and relatives. Such an approach will offer you the emotional support you need, help you remain active in your social network, and avoid self-imposed isolation. Your team of professionals at an ALS center can help allay some of your anxiety once you have established a trusting relationship with them and learn that you can count on their help and expertise when needed. Your physician can also help you deal with feelings of anxiety and/or depression with medication (see below). However, each of us must do our part in dealing with disabling emotions through actively seeking out and participating in treatment.

The diagnosis of ALS shook up me up and the anxiety I suffered was difficult to bear at times. At first I could not eat or sleep. Fortunately, anti-anxiety medication helped moderate these symptoms, and I soon began to calm down and reengage.

Over time, I was able to find the will to push back against feelings of despair, fear, and depression. Slowly I began to move my focus away from negative thoughts and toward constructive ones. Eventually I realized that my life was not over, that I still had years ahead of me, and that they could be good years. This approach helped free me from feelings of hopelessness.

During this period, I learned to accept the reality that I would experience increasing disability as weakness and paralysis advanced and that I had to get over the reluctance or embarrassment of using adaptive equipment (e.g., rollator, wheelchair, nasal mask, BiPAP, etc.). Once I became accustomed to using adaptive equipment, it lost its stigma, and my embarrassment quickly faded.

Over the past few years, I have added all sorts of equipment to my daily life, which has helped me maintain as much independence and comfort as possible. Specifics regarding these issues will be presented in detail throughout the chapters that follow.

Although I have stopped working, I have found ways to participate in projects and activities that interest me and offer me a sense of challenge and fulfillment.

It is true that managing the symptoms of ALS will be very difficult at times, but it is worth the trouble, so hold on tight to what is still possible. I have found that there is a world of possibilities out there out there if you look for them.

Depression

Depression may be the most difficult emotion to manage when living with ALS. Depression will interfere with your decision-making; it will cause you to suffer the pain of despair, which can weaken your will to manage symptoms and reengage in life. Depression may be the result of recognizing that one's life is changing dramatically and that you are facing paralysis, disability, and premature death. Under these circumstances, it is understandable that one could go through a period of grieving for the loss of a life expected. Should depression not be effectively treated, it will make things much worse for you and significantly interfere with your ability to function or enjoy anything.

Symptoms of depression can result in feeling lost, a sense of hopelessness, apathy, bouts of crying, loss of concentration, lack of energy, difficulty sleeping, loss of appetite and weight, and disengagement from friends and family.

Recognize the presence of the symptoms of depression and aggressively treat them before they completely immobilize you. Discuss these symptoms with your doctor so that you can begin treatment as soon as possible.

Those suffering from depression may find significant benefit from antidepressant medications such as:
- Tricyclic antidepressants (e.g., Elavil)
- SSRIs (selective serotonin uptake inhibitors) (e.g., Lexapro, Prozac, etc.)
- SNRIs (serotonin-noradrenaline reuptake inhibitors) (e.g., Effexor, Paxil, etc.)

Push yourself to exit self-imposed social isolation, since isolation itself can promote and reinforce depression. Make a serious effort to reengage with family and friends, and try not to push people away. Social interaction is certainly part of the treatment of depression. Muster your strength to focus on what you *do* have in your life rather than on what you have lost. If you are religious, pursue your faith—it has been very helpful to many suffering from ALS. Take on projects that keep you occupied, focused, and challenged. Participate in an ALS support group if you find it helpful. It is a good thing not to feel alone in your struggle, and you are likely to benefit from the experience of others who may be dealing with the same or similar issues and problems that you are facing.

Make the necessary effort to build a good support system, because you are going to need it.

Seek out professional help from psychologists, psychiatrists, and/or social workers when struggling with depression. Websites worth reviewing:

http://www.massgeneral.org/als/patienteducation/depression anxiety_ALS.aspx

https://drive.google.com/file/d/0B_JwTpNMOI1DeGpaQXpnR ExNY2s/view

http://www.ncbi.nlm.nih.gov/pubmed/17381183 (Firefox)

Meditation

Although *meditation* is not discussed much in the management of ALS, I have found that it can provide significant benefits because it can offer you a respite from constant emotional stress. Although most people, including many physicians, have little or no experience with meditation, it should not be discounted as a potentially valuable aid in stress management including the stress associated with ALS.

In brief, meditation is a discipline or technique involving resting your mind from stressful thoughts and feelings in order to attain a state of peace of mind. Meditation can help you clear and de-stress your mind. In this context, meditation can be a therapeutic tool that a motivated person can learn. There are many types of meditation, and you will need to find one that suits you best. To learn about meditation, go online to research the subject, review books or DVDs on meditation, and/or find a meditation instructor. Check out the following websites for information on meditation:

www.how-to-meditate.org

www.amazon.com/Meditation-Beginners-Depression-Happi ness-Mindfulness-ebook/dp/B00Q1M94XA/ref=sr_1_4?ie=UT F8&qid=1461768322&sr=8-4&keywords=meditation (Firefox)

Book: Full Catastrophe Living (Revised Edition, 2013): Using the Wisdom of Your Body and Mind to Face Stress, Pain, and Illness
    By Jon Kabat-Zin (available on www.amazon.com)

Hypnosis is another method that can be used for stress management. Auto-relaxation is a form of self-hypnosis that is often taught by psychologists. I know that this technique can help diminish anxiety because I've used it. During my allergy fellowship, I studied hypnosis in order to help my asthma patients better deal with stress-induced symptoms, and it works well when practiced. Review the following website for Jacobson's progressive relaxation technique, which is a kind of self-hypnosis:

http://www.healthline.com/health/what-is-jacobson-relaxation-technique#4

Five

Patterns of ALS Symptoms

The initial symptoms of ALS may be subtle in their presentation or slow in their progression. However, as symptoms advance, at a certain point they will become obvious and worrisome. On the other hand, some ALS patients may have a dramatic onset of symptoms, perhaps accompanied by rapid a progression, which is likely to lead to an early diagnosis.

Weakness and progressive loss of control over voluntary muscles may involve your hands, arms, feet, legs, trunk, neck as well as the muscles that control speech and swallowing. Furthermore, damage to or the death of motor neurons that innervate the muscles of your diaphragm and accessory muscles of respiration can lead to the symptoms of hypoventilation (decreased air exchange in the lungs) such as shortness of breath, disturbed sleep and an ineffective cough and eventually cause respiratory failure and death.

Learning to recognize these patterns can help you better understand what is happening to you and help prepare you to manage advancing symptoms.

Limb Pattern
This is the most common presentation of ALS. Such individuals can present with symptoms of muscular weakness of their

upper and/or lower limbs, which progressively worsen over time, resulting in loss of mobility and impairment of function of one's arms, hands, feet, and/or legs. Symptoms may include foot drop, where the front of the foot flops down below its normal alignment with the heel while walking. This will tend to cause you to trip and fall. If weakness begins to affect the upper extremities, things may fall out of your grasp. Hand weakness and loss of function will seriously interfere with you're the ability to function at work and in daily life (e.g., loss of the ability to type, work with tools, grasp and hold utensils, being able to write with a pen, and in the late stage of ALS, the loss of the ability to dress and feed yourself).

Loss of core body-muscle strength can make it difficult to rise from a chair or get out of bed, lift anything heavy, or to maintain normal posture. Those with lower-limb weakness will have difficulty walking, climbing or descending stairs, and in time, even difficulty standing. This will put affected individuals at risk for tripping and falling. Patients presenting with a limb pattern often complain of recurrent muscular cramps involving their calves, quadriceps, back, jaw, hands, feet, and so on. Muscular twitching (fasciculation) is also commonly observed in individuals with limb pattern onset. Muscle spasticity in limb onset can lead to limb stiffness, rigidity or poorly controlled movement. As the disease advances, increasing muscular weakness will lead to progressive muscle fatigue, loss of energy, and eventually to the development of progressive paralysis and muscle atrophy. Muscular weakness and paralysis will frequently advance regionally. For example, if one leg develops symptoms, then ALS symptoms involving the other leg are likely to follow a similar course. In time, all limbs are likely to be affected. However, symptoms can evolve with great variability. Muscular weakness and paralysis may first involve legs and feet and subsequently hands and arms. Less often, upper extremities are the first to be affected. In fact, any combination of symptoms or presentations involving one's limbs is possible. Review the following websites for more information:

http://emedicine.medscape.com/article/1170097-clinical

http://sla-quebec.ca/images/finder/files/als_overview_en.pdf
(Firefox)

http://www.ncbi.nlm.nih.gov/pmc/articles/PMC3182546/
(Firefox)

http://www.nature.com/nrneurol/journal/v10/n11/fig_tab/
nrneurol.2014.184_F1.html

http://jnnp.bmj.com/content/early/2012/04/26/jnnp-2011-
301826.long

http://www.ncbi.nlm.nih.gov/pmc/articles/PMC3154066/
(Firefox)

http://www.mndassociation.org/what-is-mnd/different-types-
of-mnd/

http://alsn.mda.org/article/factors-survival

Respiratory Pattern
Difficulty in breathing will affect most ALS patients at some
point during the course of their illness, although respiratory difficulty is usually not a presenting symptom for most PALS. The
diaphragm is composed of large voluntary muscles that lie just
below the lungs. The diaphragm normally contracts about dozen
or more times a minute and it is the primary muscle responsible
for inspiration (inhaling). With each contraction, the diaphragm
flattens out and moves downward. During inspiration, the diaphragm's downward movement will create a negative pressure
within the chest and lungs by expanding the chest's volume. This
action causes air to be drawn into the lungs (inspiration). When
the diaphragm relaxes, it rises up as the lungs and chest wall

passively contract, forcing air containing the waste gas of respiration (CO_2) to be expired (exhaled) into the atmosphere. The movement of air into and out of the lungs is called *ventilation, respiration* or *air exchange*. Fresh air, rich in oxygen, enters the lungs during inspiration, while the waste gas (carbon dioxide, CO_2) is expelled during expiration.

Each breath begins with a contraction of the diaphragm. The diaphragm's action is under the control of upper motor neurons (located in the brain stem) and lower motor neurons (found in the cervical region of the spinal cord). When these motor neurons are damaged or die, the muscles they innervate (e.g., diaphragm and chest wall intercostal muscles) will weaken and eventually cease to function. All patients with symptoms compatible with the diagnosis of ALS should all undergo breathing tests (pulmonary function testing) early on in their course to determine whether their respiratory muscles are functioning normally or not.

Patients who suffer significant progressive weakness of the diaphragm will sooner or later experience shortness of breath. While one remains in an upright position, gravity pulls the abdominal organs downward, leaving the diaphragm room to easily move downward during inspiration. Respiratory symptoms often begin at night when an ALS patient lies flat in bed and one's abdominal contents, now free of gravity's pull, move upward to press against the diaphragm, which can the resist a diaphragms downward motion. This will make inspiration much harder when one's diaphragm is very weak. In addition, during sleep, the accessory muscles of respiration (e.g., intercostal muscles) relax so completely that breathing becomes totally dependent on the diaphragm's function alone, which is bad news should you have terribly weak diaphragm as may occur as with ALS.

Poor inspiration due to weakness of the diaphragm will result in symptoms of *hypoventilation* (insufficient air exchange within the lungs). Affected individuals may find that they need to sleep on a few pillows in order to elevate their head and chest or sit in a chair in order to diminish shortness of breath. For the above reasons, hypoventilation in ALS is likely to worsen during sleep, disturbing one's sleep. Morning headaches in ALS are usually due to hypoventilation during sleep, which results from a buildup of excessive blood levels of carbon dioxide during the night. As CO_2 increases it can induce dilation of intracranial blood vessels, which in turn can cause morning headaches. Elevated CO_2 levels are also likely to lead to morning drowsiness as well as difficulty with concentration. Initially, headaches due to nocturnal hypoventilation will resolve quickly once a patient awakes and assumes an upright position.

As the diaphragm continues to weaken, affected individuals will begin to experience shortness of breath during the day. Worsening hypoventilation will also cause a decrease in blood oxygen levels and symptoms of shortness of breath. Without intervention, symptoms of hypoventilation will progressively worsen as the diaphragm continues to weaken, and this could eventually lead to respiratory failure and death.

Fortunately, modern technology can compensate for failing respiratory muscles up to a point, with the use of noninvasive ventilation support (e.g., BiPAP) or less commonly with the use of invasive ventilation (e.g., tracheostomy ventilation). Respiratory support devices can assist weakened respiratory muscles to achieve normal ventilation, which will improve one's quality of life as well as extend one's survival time.

I have been using noninvasive ventilation twenty-four seven for several years and I no longer suffer from respiratory symptoms, nor is my sleep disturbed by hypoventilation. Review the following websites for more information related to respiratory issues in ALS:

www.massgeneral.org/als/patienteducation/earlyrespiratoryissues. aspx

http://www.alsa.org/als-care/resources/publications-videos/ factsheets/breathing-difficulties.html

http://amyandpals.com/als-and-breathing-101/

http://www.ncbi.nlm.nih.gov/pubmed/16278079 (Firefox)

http://www.ncbi.nlm.nih.gov/pmc/articles/PMC2843568/
(Firefox)

http://www.ncbi.nlm.nih.gov/pmc/articles/PMC3931301/
(Firefox)

http://www.ncbi.nlm.nih.gov/pmc/articles/PMC2077959/
(Firefox)

Bulbar Pattern

Bulbar symptoms in ALS often present with difficulty in speech
and/or swallowing. About 25 - 30 percent of people with ALS
will have bulbar symptoms at the time of their diagnosis while
others will develop bulbar symptoms later during the course
of their disease. Bulbar symptoms result from damage to or
the death of motor neurons originating in the *brain stem* (e.g.,
medulla oblongata). The percentage of PALS that suffer bulbar
symptoms will increase over their progressive course of ALS.
The term *bulbar* refers to the tulip-bulb-like shape of the brain
stem's neural tissue that extends out from beneath the rear bottom portion of the brain. The brain stem connects the brain to
the spinal cord and gives rise to a number of motor neurons
(e.g., cranial nerves). Some brain stem motor neurons control
the muscles of speech (tongue, mouth, and larynx) and some
control swallowing (tongue, mouth, soft palate, larynx, and
pharynx).

Specific bulbar symptoms can include slurring of speech,
poor articulation of words, hoarseness, and/or the inability to
project one's voice. Symptoms often include drooling, choking, gagging, coughing, and aspirating. Aspiration of food,
drink, and/or saliva into the trachea and lungs can occur if the

epiglottis and glottis at the entrance of the airway fail to close prior to or at the time of swallowing.

Bulbar symptoms will usually prompt an affected individual to quickly seek out a medical evaluation. Difficulty in chewing and swallowing as well as fear of choking can lead to significant weight loss, and in some cases malnutrition. More than a dozen muscles in the mouth, tongue, soft palate and throat need to precisely coordinate for normal speech, chewing, and swallowing.

Normally, chewed food (a bolus) is pushed up against the hard palate and then propelled backward by the tongue. As the bolus moves toward the back of throat (the pharynx), the soft palate moves up to close off the back of the nasal passageway while the tongue continues to propel the bolus of food backward into the pharynx. As the tongue moves backward to initiate swallowing, the epiglottis, which sits just behind the tongue, moves backward to close off the entrance to the larynx. The larynx, which is the beginning of the airway, sits on top of the trachea. As swallowing begins, the epiglottis closes off the airway's entrance. At the same time, the vocal cords shut tight, and the glottis contracts. Together, they normally seal off the airway's entrance during swallowing. This action prevents the aspiration of food or drink into the lungs. As a swallow nears completion, the bolus is propelled back and down toward the esophagus. Aspiration will not occur if the opening of the airway has been closed off during the swallow, ensuring that swallowed food, drink and saliva enter only the esophagus during this complex action.

As bulbar motor neurons die, control and coordination of their innervated muscles (e.g. mouth and throat muscles) will begin to fail to function properly. Should swallowed food or liquid arrive at the entrance of an open airway then the event is likely to lead to coughing or choking, as well as risk aspiration of whatever is being swallowed. Repeated episodes of aspiration will put an affected individual at risk for premature death due to pneumonia and/or respiratory failure.

To prevent aspiration or severe nutritional problems due to swallowing dysfunction, a feeding tube (a PEG or a RIG) can be inserted through the abdominal wall and into directly into the stomach thus eliminating the need to swallow food or drink (feeding tubes are discussed in a subsequent chapter).

Individuals that suffer from difficulty in speaking due to bulbar involvement may be able to improve their communication with the use of assistive or augmentative technology. For example, if you can type, a computer can convert your typing input into audible synthesized speech. One could also write notes or message on a smart phone and other devices as a means of communication. If your voice is barely audible, it can be amplified. Assistive communication technology will be reviewed in a subsequent chapter. In addition, a speech pathologist it Is likely to be able to offer useful strategies to improve your speech. PALS with bulbar symptoms may also develop shortness of breath due to weakness of respiratory muscles and this can also interfere with projection of one's voice making it difficult to be heard.

In addition, it has been observed that a number of ALS patients with bulbar symptoms may also suffer episodes of inappropriate or exaggerated emotional outbursts (e.g., spontaneous laughing or crying without any discernable cause), which is referred to as a *pseudo bulbar affect* (PBA). Others with a bulbar pattern of symptoms may complain of muscle spasm or cramping of the jaw, face, neck, or larynx (laryngospasm) and/or excessive yawning. Facial muscles may also be involved. Review the following websites for related information:

https://www.als.ca/sites/default/files/files/Bulbar%2520ALS.pdf (Firefox)

http://www.nature.com/nrneurol/journal/v4/n7/full/ncpneuro0853.html

http://amyandpals.com/communication-solutions-gallery/

www.youtube.com/watch?v=onbKgDn_maE

http://www.nysslha.org/i4a/pages/index.cfm?pageid=3560

http://www.hindawi.com/journals/bn/2015/183027/ (Firefox)

http://www.ncbi.nlm.nih.gov/pubmed/2921111 (Firefox)

http://www.alscareproject.org/respresearch/RespiratoryCom plications.pdf (Firefox)

http://www.alstexas.org/for-patients/speech-swallowing/

Frontotemporal Dementia Pattern (FTD)
When first diagnosed, most PALS do not appear to have cognitive impairment that interferes with their daily life or ability to function. However, there is growing evidence that supports the observation that a significant number of ALS patients will, over time, develop varying degrees of cognitive impairment similar to that seen in patients diagnosed with *frontotemporal dementia* (FTD). However, the development of dementia itself is not commonly associated with ALS.

FTD is a distinct neurological syndrome that is associated with atrophy of frontal and temporal lobes of the brain.

The brain's frontal lobe is responsible for executive functions (e.g., decision making, cognitive function), emotion, and personality, whereas the temporal lobes are largely responsible for language and working memory. Patients with FTD often have difficulty with performing complex tasks such as exercising the good judgment required to manage finances, taking medications correctly, following directions, solving problems, and so on.

Symptoms of temporal lobe dysfunction in FTD can include language dysfunction (both written and spoken), diminished word comprehension, difficulty with word retrieval, and/or repetitive speech. FTD symptoms can also include changes in emotional responses, behavior, and personality. Some patients with FTD appear to have a flat affect or show little motivation. This should not be confused with depression. Emotional liability, impulsiveness, irritability, inappropriate social or emotional responses, loss of inhibition, emotional blunting, compulsive behavior, and so on have been observed in patients with FTD and in a minority of ALS patients. Difficulty with working memory has also been observed. Working memory is one's short-term memory that is used to hold onto and process new information needed for reasoning, comprehension, and learning.

A *pseudo bulbar affect* (PBA) may also occur in patients diagnosed with FTD, ALS, as well as in other neurological disorders. Symptoms of PBA typically include sudden outbursts of uncontrollable laughter or crying for no apparent reason. These symptoms can start and stop abruptly or can last for several minutes. Affected individual seems to be unable control these outbursts. Treatment with Nudexta appears to help control symptoms of PBA.

The presence of FTD-like symptoms in patients with ALS seems to occur more frequently than had been previously reported. Its presence should be identified early on in ALS to allow for proper management. Identifying faulty decision making due to cognitive decline will help support an affected individual and can prevent harm.

Studies have repeatedly found that between 25 and 50 percent of ALS patients will develop some level of cognitive decline during their course of ALS, although symptoms might be subtle. Perhaps 5% of ALS patients will actually suffer dementia similar to that seen in FTD.

So, what is the connection between FTD and ALS? Some years ago, a mutation was found on chromosome 9 in some ALS patients as well as among patients with FTD. This gene mutation has been termed the C9orf72 mutation. The C9orf72 gene is associated with the production of the TDP-43 protein, which may be found as aggregates in the dead motor neurons in some

ALS patients. Therefore, it appears that the C9orf72 gene mutation may play a role in the causation of FTD and may also have a role in the pathology seen in some PALS. Review the following websites for more information:

http://www.als.ca/sites/default/files/files/ALS%2520and%2520Cognitive%2520Changes.pdf

www.alsa.org/als-care/resources/publications-videos/factsheets/cognitive-changes-family.html

http://www.alsa.org/als-care/resources/publications-videos/factsheets/fyi-cognitive-impairment.html

alsn.mda.org/article/when-thinking-parts-brain-go-awry-als

www.theaftd.org/understandingftd/disorders/ftdal

https://www.hindawi.com/journals/nri/2012/806306/

www.ncbi.nlm.nih.gov/pmc/articles/PMC3801195/ (Firefox)

Six

ALS in 3-D

In order to better understand ALS it might be helpful to think of ALS as a disease with three dimensions. One might view ALS with regard to its:

- Pattern of symptoms
- Rate of advancement of symptoms
- Severity of symptoms and disability, or stage of the disease.

ALS can be classified into early, intermediate, and late stages based on the degree of severity of symptoms and level of disability.

The *first dimension* of ALS relates to which muscle groups are affected (the pattern of symptoms). For example, initial muscle weakness presenting as a limb pattern might primarily involve the lower or the upper extremities, or it could present with respiratory symptoms secondary to diaphragmatic weakness. Most patients will develop two or more patterns over time, while others will also suffer from FTD-like symptoms. ALS symptoms may begin with one group of muscles and subsequently involve an adjacent muscle groups. Progression is highly variable, therefore all known possibilities need to be considered.

A *second dimension of ALS* relates to the rate of progression of symptoms. Symptoms may progress rapidly over a period of months, leading to a person's demise within a year or so. However, symptoms usually progress at a moderate rate over several years in most patients. It should also be noted that a small number of individuals with ALS will exhibit a very slow rate of progression, with symptoms gradually advancing over a decade or even over decades. There are even exceptional instances where symptoms may cease to advance altogether, or even partially regress.

The *third dimension* has to do with the severity and extent of symptoms and disability. Severity will evolve from mild through severe over the disease's course; from weakness to paralysis, from prominent involvement of a few areas to widespread paralysis to most voluntary muscles, from mild hypoventilation to respiratory failure, etc. The stages of ALS are related to this third dimension and are described in a subsequent chapter.

http://bmcneurol.biomedcentral.com/articles/10.1186/s12883-014-0197-9

http://www.livestrong.com/article/18412-progression-als-disease/

https://www.researchgate.net/publication/11273119_Early_symptom_progression_rate_is_related_to_ALS_outcome_A_prospective_population-based_study

https://www.ncbi.nlm.nih.gov/pubmed/27617889 (Firefox)

Seven

ALS Statistics

- About six thousand people are diagnosed with ALS each year in the United States.
- ALS is frequently diagnosed between the ages of thirty five and seventy-five, with preponderance of patients diagnosed in their fifties and sixties.
- About 10 - 15% percent of patients have an inherited form of ALS known as *familial ALS* (FALS).
- The great majority of ALS patients have no family history of ALS symptoms. This group is referred to having the *sporadic form of ALS* (SALS).
- More than half of the patients with the familial form of ALS exhibit gene mutations (e.g., C9orf72, SOD1).
- The majority of ALS patients in the U.S. will live between three and five or six years following their diagnosis; 20 percent will live more than five years, 10 percent will live ten or more years, 5 percent will live more than fifteen years and it has been reported that 1% or less will experience a cessation of the progression of their symptoms and some of these patients made experience some partial regression of their symptoms
- ALS patients that begin assisted ventilation early in the progression of their respiratory symptoms tend to extend their lives beyond what statistics suggest.

- ALS occurs in all races and socioeconomic groups, and it can affect any of the world's populations.
- Men are affected more frequently than women.
- Military veterans appear to have a somewhat higher incidence of ALS than the general population.

http://www.alsa.org/about-als/facts-you-should-know.html

http://www.ncbi.nlm.nih.gov/pmc/articles/PMC3515205/ (Firefox)

https://www26.state.nj.us/doh-shad/indicator/view/ALSInPrSur.Incid.html

http://neuromuscular.wustl.edu/spinal/als.htm

Eight

What Can I Expect?

To better conceptualize what is likely to take place during the coming months and years, it might be helpful to divide the progression of ALS symptoms into three stages; early, middle, and late. In general, the rate of progression of ALS will usually remain fairly steady over the long term. In some cases, a temporary pause in the advancement of symptoms is followed by a continuation of advancement at the previous rate.

Early Stage

Symptoms are usually limited or mild in the early stage, and as a result, your functionality may only be modestly impacted, allowing you to continue much of your normal activity. Although affected individuals will have physical symptoms (muscle weakness, cramps, fatigue, etc.), some of the worst symptoms at this stage of the disease are likely to be psychological in nature. Functional disability at this stage is often mild and may not present significant difficulty, although, this may not true for patients with bulbar symptoms. Affected individuals in this stage may or may not begin to require the use of a walker or rollator. Many will experience cramps, stiffness, and/or weak hands or legs. Foot drop may lead to tripping. The presence of bulbar symptoms will usually cause some degree of difficulty with speech and/or swallowing. Many affected individuals will be able to continue to

SPRINGDALE PUBLIC LIBRARY
405 S. Pleasant
Springdale, AR 72764

work and functioning relatively well during this stage. A minority of individuals at this stage will begin to experience nocturnal shortness of breath and/or sleep disturbance due to hypoventilation and will need to start on BiPAP.

The stage of ALS relates to the severity of symptoms and to the degree of disability but not to the duration of symptoms. A patient can rapidly advance from an early stage to a late stage in less than a year, whereas another PALS may progress from an early stage to a late stage over period of many years. The point is that staging is related to symptom severity and the degree of disability and not to the duration of one's symptoms.

Middle or Intermediate Stage

At this stage of ALS, symptoms of muscle weakness will become prominent and begin to significantly interfere with a patient's ability to function, requiring the adoption of methods to compensate for the loss of motor function. For example, if your legs become unsteady and/or weak, you are you likely need to use a rollator or wheelchair to prevent falling as well as for mobility. Tripping, falling, and/or clumsiness will often worsen at this stage. You may develop foot drop or wrist drop and require a foot-ankle orthotic or wrist brace. You are also likely to suffer diminished stamina and increasing muscle fatigue, which will limit activities. Your appetite may decline to the point that you start to lose weight. You may need to use a shower seat and install grab bars to prevent falling. Many will begin to experience sleep disturbance and /or nocturnal shortness of breath, which will require treatment with BiPAP.

During this stage, some PALS will begin to lose a lot of weight, which could become a serious issue in time. This is particularly true if bulbar symptoms are present. You may need the placement of a feeding tube in order to receive adequate nutrition and/or to prevent coughing, choking, or aspiration. If you have bulbar symptoms, a speech pathologist will begin to work with you to help manage communication and/or swallowing issues.

During the intermediate stage, walking, typing, writing, going up or down stairs, or rising from a chair or a toilet may become increasingly difficult.

Some PALS continue to work at this stage, however accommodations will usually be needed to compensate for increasing disability. You may need to use an adaptive device to open doors or use adaptive clothing to make it easier to dress and undress. The hallmark at this stage is the significant progression of symptoms and increasing disability that interferes with your function, autonomy, safety, and/or comfort.

Late Stage

A marked loss of mobility and worsening disability will become increasingly prominent during this stage. Weakness and/or paralysis are most likely require the daily use of a wheelchair to get around. Almost all patients will opt for a power wheelchair at or before this stage, as it will allow them to independently move about within their home, out-of-doors, around stores as well as to participate in other activities. A wheelchair-accessible van will be needed to get you to where you need to go. The use of non-invasive ventilation (e.g., BiPAP) is often needed to sleep and is often also needed throughout the day. Those with advanced bulbar symptoms and/or significant weight loss will require a feeding tube. As the late stage advances, an ALS patient will become increasingly disabled and will require increasing assistance from a caregiver. Paralysis will continue to advance until the patient is completely dependent on his or her caregiver. Affected individuals will need to be assisted during transfers into and out of bed, into and out of chairs. When one is no longer able to stand, a lift (e.g., a Hoyer lift) will become essential for daily transfers. Bathing and toileting will also require assistance from a caregiver. As paralysis advances, the use of noninvasive respiratory support may prove inadequate, and at a certain point a patient may need to consider invasive respiratory support (tracheostomy ventilation) for continued survival. The late stage of ALS may develop gradually over a number of years, allowing one to adapt and adjust and still maintain a good quality of life in spite of progressive disability.

As paralysis continues to advances, your ability to communicate may require assistive or adaptive technology.

Toward the end of the late stage, one is likely to suffer near total paralysis and may not be able to breathe or speak. Should respiratory support no longer be effective or should a patient reject its use, then hypoventilation will continue to advance, and such a patient will eventually enter respiratory failure and pass away. The effects of malnutrition, infection, or complication (e.g., pneumonia) can also eventually lead to a terminal event during the late stage of ALS.

Several years have passed since my diagnosis. Passing through these stages has given me time to adapt, gain perspective, learn, and find ways to enjoy life while managing symptoms. Your experience will depend on your pattern of symptoms, the speed at which symptoms advance, the level of severity of symptoms and disability, your access to resources and support, your knowledge about ALS management and in particular, how well you are able to adapt and adjust to your situation.

In any case, once you have completed studying and researching ALS you will have a good idea of what is likely to be heading your way, and this will give you the opportunity to prepare for each new challenge. Review the following websites for additional information and to see how others deal with their ALS symptoms:

www.mda.org/disease/amyotrophic-lateral-sclerosis/signs-and-symptoms/stages-of-als

https://www.mda.org/disease/amyotrophic-lateral-sclerosis/medical-management/assistance-in-stages-of-als

https://www.youtube.com/watch?v=ZYM7RKJtxGY

http://www.today.com/id/51147520/ns/today-today_books/t/
until-i-say-good-bye-living-love-face-als/#.WAerK2NpZTc

http://www.alsa.org/als-care/resources/publications-videos/
manuals/

http://www.ncbi.nlm.nih.gov/pubmed/24479577 (Firefox)

http://www.outcomes-umassmed.org/ALS/alsscale.aspx

https://www.rush.edu/health-wellness/discover-health/tools-
living-als (Firefox)

https://www.youtube.com/watch?v=tr6jFySacFQ

Nine

Is My Diagnosis Correct?

At this time, the diagnosis of ALS is primarily a clinical diagnosis, which is based on the presence of symptoms and signs of a progressive, degenerative, neuromuscular disorder that fulfills the specific criteria described below and that all the other causes for your symptoms have been ruled out. The diagnosis of ALS should be supported by an EMG that is compatible with motor neuron disease and ruling out other diseases that could mimic the symptoms of the ALS. Please take note that a laboratory test or biomarker for ALS are likely to become available in the foreseeable future (e.g., Iron horse diagnostics).

The El Escorial World Federation of Neurology criteria for the diagnosis of ALS are a common standard used in making a diagnosis. The diagnosis of ALS is based on the presence of progressive signs and symptoms of both upper- and lower-motor-neuron defects affecting two or three different body segments simultaneously. Your physician's physical examination should reveal signs the upper and lower motor neuron damage without evidence of sensory nerve damage. He or she will check your muscle strength, look for signs of muscle atrophy and fasciculation, and search for abnormal reflexes associated with motor neurons disease. You will be given an *alsfrs-r score,* which will reflect your current functional stage of ALS. Your physician will also look for evidence of sensory loss with a pin and a vibrating tuning fork since finding sensory loss would point to a diagnosis other than ALS or a concomitant condition. In summary, it is expected that if you have ALS your physician will find evidence of muscle weakness, muscle fasciculation, spasticity or atrophy, abnormal reflexes and signs that provide evidence of both upper and lower motor neuron. He or she does not expect to find evidence of sensory loss on physical examination unless it is due to some other medical problem. To review the criteria needed for a diagnosis of ALS check out the following websites:

www.mda.org/disease/amyotrophic-lateral-sclerosis/diagnosis

http://www.alsa.org/als-care/resources/publications-videos/ factsheets/criteria-for-diagnosis.html

http://www.alsa.org/faq/#3 (Firefox)

http:andwww.massgeneral.org/als/patienteducation/Diagno singALS.aspx

www.alsa.org/assets/pdfs/fyi/criteria_for_diagnosis.pdf (Firefox)

www.wfnals.org/downloads/The%20El%20Escorial%20 criteria%20Strengths%20and%20weaknesses.pdf (Firefox)

www.wfnals.org/downloads/A%20revision%20of%20the%20 El%20Escorial%20criteria%202015.pdf (Firefox)

http://www.secondopinion-tv.org/episode/amyotrophic-lateral- sclerosis-als

A diagnosis of ALS may be delayed if your presentation of symptoms are atypical, relatively subtle, or are early in their development and a clear pattern has not yet emerged. Making a diagnosis of ALS may be difficult because presenting symptoms and findings may mimic a number of other disorders or visa versa. As a result, some patients with ALS may initially remain undiagnosed for quite a while or may even be misdiagnosed. It is not a rare for PALS to receive treatment for misdiagnosed with non ALS ailments until they arrive at an ALS center or are evaluated by a neuromuscular specialist experience with ALS.

Without finding clear evidence of both upper and lower motor neuron damage, a diagnosis of ALS should not be made. CT scans, MRIs, laboratory studies, spinal tap, and/or nerve conduction studies (NCS) and electromyograms (EMG) are all used to support the diagnosis of ALS while ruling out other diseases. Genetic studies will be performed if other family members are reported to have ALS or are suspected of having ALS-like symptoms.

A diagnosis of ALS is supported by the absence of evidence of sensory nerve involvement (e.g., as might be found in cervical stenosis) and the presence of abnormal nerve-conduction studies or EMG studies can also support the diagnosis of ALS by revealing activity typical of muscles that have lost their motor-neuron innervation. Together, the clinical symptoms along with the signs of upper and lower motor neuron disease and the studies listed above will help support the diagnosis of ALS. Ruling out other diseases, such as peripheral nerve damage, spinal stenosis with myelopathy, vascular injury, muscle disease (myopathy), or other neurological diseases will support the diagnosis of ALS. Occasionally a muscle biopsy will be needed to rule out muscle disease.

Lab studies will also help rule out heavy metal poisoning, autoimmune disease (e.g., myasthenia gravis), infectious disease (e.g., HIV, polio), and so on. Finally, pulmonary function studies should be performed in order to identify the presence of respiratory muscle weakness typical of ALS. To see an excellent review of the differential diagnosis of ALS, view the following websites:

www.medmerits.com/index.php/article/amyotrophic_lateral_sclerosis/P7

http://pn.bmj.com/content/early/2013/04/23/practneurol-2013-000557.full

http://emedicine.medscape.com/article/1170097-clinical#b3

Ten

Learning What I Need to Know

I f you attend an ALS center, your physician and his or her team of professionals will try to help you understand your diagnosis, symptoms and management options, and more importantly they will try to help you get what you need. However, it is unlikely that everything you need to know will be provided by a single source. It is not that the staff or physician(s) of your ALS center do not wish to provide the exact information needed for an optimal solution for a problem you are having; but rather, the professionals you encounter may not have the best information available for every problem or situation you encounter. Therefore, at times it will fall upon you to find the exact information you need through reading, asking questions, and of course performing your own research. Perhaps you may not be in a state of mind, which is ready to receive the information you need at the time of your diagnosis and you may need time to digest and accept your diagnosis.

Educating yourself to the many issues related to ALS management is key to improving your quality of life as well as to maximizing your longevity. Individuals with ALS might suffer greatly and go through multiple crises, some of which might have been avoided had they just had the knowledge and motivation to optimally manage their symptoms and/or disability. You might ask why do so many ALS patients lack the knowledge they need to make optimal management decisions. The answer to this question may be more complex than might be imagined, particularly when you consider that so much information about ALS is readily available. In part, the reason for a patient's insufficient knowledge often lies with a patient's state of mind (e.g., denial), or by not truly doing their best to deal with the multiple challenges presented by ALS.

When first diagnosed with ALS, some individuals are in such emotional turmoil that they are unable to function very well. As a result, they do not seek out the information they need, or they may just not be receptive to receiving and/or applying the information needed. Some individuals will enter into a state of denial and simply won't participate in trying to improve their situation. Others might be depressed, lack the initiative or energy needed to find and apply solutions. At times, PALS simply fail to ask questions that need answering.

Listen carefully to the advice and information provided by your physician and the ALS clinic staff. Ask questions regarding your symptoms and advancing disability. It would also be a good idea to take another person along with you to clinic visits so that they can help you ask questions, and/or also act as your advocate.

Gather information provided by organizations such as the national ALS Association (www.alsa.org) or the Muscular Dystrophy Association (MDA) (www.mda.org). Read books and articles about ALS that will inform you and orient you toward solving problems.

Research the Internet for information on every aspect of the ALS that you might encounter, and learn about useful devices and equipment. Study adaptive and assistive devices, techniques, methods, and the best practices for the management of ALS symptoms and disabilities. Review the hundreds of Internet websites contained in this book because they can offer you a wealth of relevant information. Armed with enough information and insight, you can become an effective advocate for getting what you need.

Since ALS symptoms are likely to be in constant evolution, you can expect to regularly face new challenges. You need to anticipate where the disease is headed in order to prepare for the future. With enough knowledge, you are more likely to be better prepared to make good decisions when challenged with new problems, which can make a great difference in the quality of your life.

You should familiarize yourself with the many types of eating utensils, mobility equipment, Hoyer lifts/slings, braces, adaptive clothing, bathroom equipment, and so on that have been developed for individuals with disabilities. It is unlikely that a single physician or clinic staff will always be familiar with the exact equipment or method that could ideally meet your need(s). However, by reviewing catalogs of devices for use in disability (e.g., www. pattersonmedical.com, www.spinlife.com, www.rehabmart.com, www.alimed.com/physical-therapy-supplies.aspx, etc.), you will increase the odds of finding exactly what is needed. It is true that optimal ALS management is demanding, stressful, and at times exhausting, but there is no better alternative then to be fully vested in learning everything that one needs to know and doing your best to manage your symptoms of disability to the best of your ability. Review the following excellent educational resources:

Educational Resources

A. <u>The ALS Association</u>

Go to the following site for information:

http://www.alsa.org/als-care/resources/books

Living with ALS manuals: (http://www.alsa.org/als-care/resources/publications-videos/manuals/)
- Manual 1: "What's It All About?"
- Manual 2: "Coping with Change"
- Manual 3: "Managing Your Symptoms and Treatment"

- Manual 4: "Functioning When Your Mobility Is Affected"
- Manual 5: "Adjusting to Swallowing and Speaking Difficulties"
- Manual 6: "Adapting to Breathing Changes"

DVDs:
- *Living with ALS* series
- *Respiratory Decisions in ALS*
- *You Are Not Alone*

B. **Muscular Dystrophy Association (MDA)**
- *Everyday Life with ALS: A Practical Guide*
  www.mda.org/sites/default/files/publications/
  Everyday_Life_with_ALS_P-532.pdf (Firefox)
- *MDA ALS Caregiver's Guide* (this is outstanding resource)
  www.mda.org/sites/default/files/publications/ALS_
  Caregiver's_Guide_P-531.pdf (Firefox)

C. **ALS Foundation of Hope**

www.alshf.org/resources/

D. *Amyotrophic Lateral Sclerosis* (an excellent book by Hiroshi Mitsumoto, MD) A guide for patients and family (Amazon. com).

E. Lots of information about ALS can be also found on the following websites:

http://www.alsfrombothsides.org/index.html

http://webmi.alsa.org/site/PageNavigator/MI_8c_videos. html

Eleven

The ALS Center

A multidisciplinary team led by an experienced and dedicated neurologist specializing in ALS will be best equipped to provide the guidance you will need. Collectively, the group is likely to have more knowledge and resources than any single individual.

For example, respiratory symptoms due to a failing diaphragm are likely to be best managed by a pulmonologist that has experience with ALS. He or she and other team members (e.g., respiratory therapist) will help select the equipment, methods, and settings to best deal with your progressive respiratory symptoms.

When attending an ALS center, your neurologist and his or her team of professionals will follow your progress and bring in various specialists (e.g., physical therapist, occupational therapist, speech pathologist, orthotic specialist, social worker, etc.) to help evaluate, guide, and support you. By the end of your clinic visit, a plan should be developed to address each of your concerns so that little will be overlooked. An ALS clinic/center is likely to be your most important resource in managing your symptoms and disability.

The Director
The director of an ALS center is a board-certified neurologist with subspecialty expertise in neuromuscular disease. He or she

will be experienced in the diagnosis and management of ALS and will have developed a multidisciplinary team to help PALS (people with ALS) deal with their symptoms and related issues. In addition, the director will have secured funding for clinical operations and is often involved in ALS research. He or she will be responsible for the organization and function of this sophisticated health care delivery system that is solely focused on ALS.

Your neurologist is going to be a very important person in your life. If you are lucky, he or she will be compassionate as well as knowledgeable. You are going to need to find someone you trust to guide you and guide you well, someone who can relate to you, someone who will make the effort to get to know you and understand what you need. Such a neurologist will be dedicated to their patients. Therefore, seek out an ALS center headed by a person with the qualities mentioned above because it will make a great difference in your life.

The Physical Therapist

The center's physical therapist (PT) provides evaluation of the mobility and physical therapy needs of each ALS patient. He or she will deliver PT services and education aimed at helping you maintain mobility, muscle strength, joint range of motion and prevent physical complications (e.g., falling, contractures). Physical therapists often focus on lower extremity function and mobility, and will make recommendations regarding musculoskeletal issues (e.g., range-of-motion exercises, etc). Physical therapists can also recommend, mobility equipment (referral for a power wheelchair), and/or adaptive devices to prevent you from falling (rollator, wheelchair, foot-ankle brace, etc.). They can also teach you and your caregiver how to use a lift as well as other methods for transfer and positioning when you are too weak to transfer yourself.

The Occupational Therapist

Occupational therapists (OT) will evaluate your functional ability and needs for daily living. They will often focus on upper-extremities, assessing your daily functional needs, including how you function at work and at home, recommend adaptive and assistive devices to help you to maintain your function (e.g., buttoners and devices for writing and eating). They can teach you to how to use adaptive and/or assistive equipment (e.g., wrist brace, neck braces, and other helpful devices for daily living including eating utensils, buttoners and adaptive clothing). They will advise you on how to remain independent for as long as possible. They can also advise you on how to modify your home regarding access, safety, and function (ramps, hospital beds, transfer techniques, toileting and bathing equipment, etc.).

The Speech Pathologist
A speech pathologist in an ALS clinic is trained to evaluate and help manage difficulties with speech and swallowing, which are expected to occur in those with bulbar dysfunction. A speech pathologist can access swallowing function and can develop strategies to help manage eating and drinking if you are having trouble swallowing. He or she will also be knowledgeable about speech disorders resulting from motor neuron disease. They can assess your ability to speak and suggest which assistive or augmentative technologies and strategies that might be helpful in improving your speech and communication. A speech pathologist can also act as a guide for needed resources in managing bulbar symptoms.

The Dietitian
A dietitian can also help if you are having difficulties with swallowing, suffering from weight loss, or are at risk for malnutrition. A dietitian can perform a nutrition assessment to determine whether or not you are receiving adequate caloric intake and determine whether your diet is providing the nutrition you require. Dietitians can make recommendations regarding the composition of meals in order to help you maintain or gain weight. They may recommend changing the consistency of your food, such as thickening liquids, so that liquids can be swallowed more easily in order to

prevent coughing or choking. They may also make recommendations regarding the need for and the use of a feeding tube and recommend methods and strategies to prevent aspiration.

The Respiratory Therapist

The role of the respiratory therapist is to perform pulmonary function testing during clinic visits in order to determine an ALS patient's respiratory status. They can also explain the correct use of respiratory equipment including the proper use of BiPAP machines, masks, ventilators, etc. They can teach you respiratory exercises including breath stacking and how to use of a cough assist machine. They can also assess whether your equipment is properly functioning and train you regarding the correct use of your respiratory equipment.

The Pulmonologist

A pulmonologist will assess your respiratory status. This will include a review of your pulmonary function tests, chest X-rays, sleep studies, and so on in order to determine whether or not ALS is affecting your ventilation and, if so, to what degree. Pulmonologists can help you decide when to begin respiratory support. They can help determine what type of equipment should be used to treat hypoventilation, and prescribe the correct pulmonary equipment and the appropriate settings. The pulmonologist will monitor your pulmonary function changes as ALS symptoms advance and make recommendations regarding adjustments to equipment and/or settings. Should your pulmonary status deteriorate, your pulmonologist can recommend adjustment of settings, alternative therapies, such as invasive ventilation, a feeding tube, and/or cough-assist equipment. The pulmonologist can also treat pulmonary infections and can treat respiratory failure should that occur.

The Social Worker

A social worker at an ALS center is a specialist who deals with the social, family, financial, and perhaps some of the emotional problems encountered by PALS and his or her family. Social workers have been trained to do psychosocial evaluations. They will provide information, guidance, and support that can help you "work the system" in order to get what you need. They can also provide referrals for community resources. A social worker may offer counseling and emotional support to you and your family. They should also be knowledgeable about health insurance, social security disability benefits, and available community resources and services (e.g., hospice). They can also help advocate for you.

The Nurse Coordinator

A nurse coordinator schedules appointments, coordinates services, and makes sure things get done. He or she will provide information and act as a vehicle of communication between you and the team members. A nurse coordinator can also help evaluate your situation, provide you with guidance, expedite things, and help you get what you need.

The Clinical Research Nurse

The clinical research nurse coordinates clinical trials and qualifies and enrolls patients in ALS studies. He or she will evaluate whether a patient fits the criteria for a particular research protocol or clinical trial. Such individuals will coordinate patients who have entered a clinical trial. The nurse collects lab studies, pulmonary function studies, diaries, questionnaires, and other data on patients in the study. He or she will review the patient's diary and dispense study medications. The clinical research coordinator recruits study patients, provides information about the study, and reviews the informed consent.

The Assistive Technology Professional

An assistive technology professional (ATP) is certified to evaluate the technology needs of a disabled patient. He or she will be able to help an ALS patient acquire and use adaptive and assistive equipment to aid with physical and mobility problems, daily function, and help with communication disability. An ATP can help a patient with mobility devices (e.g., power wheelchair, mobile arm support) and communication devices (eye gaze, voice augmentation, etc.). They are familiar with the methods and equipment needed for accessing computer technology through voice commands, eye gaze, or head movement. An ATP may work for a commercial provider of medical equipment and also have a relationship with the ALS center.

What Else Is Needed?

I recommend that an ALS center have regular access to a physiatrist and/or a highly knowledgeable occupational therapist with deep experience in the management of severely disabled individual, who can help evaluate and make recommendations for such individuals. This specialist should coordinate with the physical therapist and occupational therapist to develop a detailed plan for each patient during the middle and late stages of the disease to be sure that disability needs are being optimally managed. Much of the latter could be assisted through video conferencing in collaboration with rehabilitation specialists who have extensive experience and a broad knowledge of disabilities affecting ALS patients. For example, consulting with a specialist who has lots of experience with neck weakness and head drop could help identify the best options available to meet a PALS's unique needs. The same is true for selecting an optimal mobile arm support for specific patient, etc. Since no one specialist is the master of every aspect disability, it would make sense to develop a broad network of disability expert consultants that could be accessed via telecommunication.

Regular home visits by an occupational therapist or/or an experience ALS social worker can help identify problems, demonstrate disability equipment, and make equipment and management recommendations. It would also be a great help if the ALS center's OT had an up to date list of all equipment available for loan in order to expedite the delivery of disability equipment in a timely manner.

It would also be a good idea for the clinic/center to assign an experienced liaison volunteer to each PAL and/or a caregiver so that they would have someone to call in real time when they have a problem, questions or need direction.

A comprehensive ALS course for PALS and their caregivers should be developed in video format, updated yearly, and disseminated to each ALS patient and caregiver. It should at least cover all the material found in this book. This should also be a collaborative project among a number of ALS centers and funded by the ALS and MDA associations.

It would also be incredibly helpful for the clinic/center to develop a community outreach program to recruit and train part-time volunteer caregivers to offer support for those ALS patients who have no other means for receiving such support or to give caregivers a break.

Dozens of well organized and qualified ALS centers should band together to form a clinical research consortium that would involve dozens and dozens of centers, which would allow patients from across the country better access to participate in clinical trials that would be coordinated within a common protocol in order to more rapidly enroll patients that meet the necessary criteria and speed the completion of a trial.

If your ALS center is not meeting your needs, speak up and if that doesn't work, find a better a better center. Finally, work on developing greater self-sufficiency regarding getting what you need because it is in your best interest.

See the following web sites for more info:

http://www.alsa.org/community/centers-clinics/

https://www.mda.org/sites/default/files/ALS_Centers_and_Clinics-05_2014.pdf
(Firefox)

https://www.youtube.com/watch?v=qlfEFIFZdD0

Twelve

Preparing for Your Clinic Visit

If you wish to get the best possible treatment, you will need to partner with your physician and staff at your ALS center. Supply your physician and team with up-to-date information on the status of your symptoms as well as any other relevant medical information. To carry out this task, provide a written list of all your medications and any change in symptoms, noting what equipment you are currently using and how it is working for you. You should mention all new relevant events, other medical problems, and in particular any unmet needs, discomfort, new symptoms and/ or disabilities and how they are being addressed. This is exactly what I have been doing with each of my clinic visits. It would be a good idea to prepare a written list of questions and concerns in order to be sure all issues are addressed before the end of your visit. Do you need refills or referrals? Record all recommendations for review following your visit so that nothing will be forgotten. Finally, carry out the recommendations made, keep follow-up visits, and communicate with your team when you have questions or run into a problem.

During the clinic visit, you will be asked about your clinical symptoms. You will undergo a neurologic examination to determine the rate at which your illness is advancing with the help of an ALSFRS-R scoring system. You'll probably undergo pulmonary function testing. You'll be evaluated by a number of team members, including the neurologist, PT, OT, and so on. Tests may be ordered, medications prescribed or refilled, equipment ordered, referrals made, and your next appointment scheduled. You may be invited to participate in a clinical study for an experimental ALS medications or other types of ALS studies. Finally, remember that your clinic visit is the best time to directly ask your doctor questions from the list you have prepared. For example, if there were something you don't understand, something that worries you, or something you just heard or read about that you think might help you; the best time to discuss such matters would be face to face during your clinic visit. For more information about a clinic visit view the following website:

http://alsn.mda.org/article/lowdown-following

Thirteen

Advocate for Your Needs

ALS is or will be a demanding disease to manage because eventually you will have multiple needs, which will continue to increase as your symptoms advance. Some ALS symptoms or problems may be minor while others will put you at significant risk. Symptoms should be addressed early in their development, before they have had a chance to cause you harm or significant discomfort. For example, aspirating food or drink could induce violent choking episodes, pneumonia and/or respiratory failure, if not effectively addressed in a timely fashion.

Speak to your physician if you begin to have difficulty swallowing, talking, walking, breathing, sleeping, coughing, suffer pain, discomfort, or develop worsening disability. Identify developing disabilities, pressure discomfort, or have difficulty with daily living. As for adaptive and supportive equipment before they are needed so that you will be prepared (rollator, wheelchair, Hoyer lift, etc.). If solutions aren't forthcoming in timely manner, point that out and ask for a referral to a professional who is capable of managing your specific problem. This approach should stimulate your physician and his or her staff to focus on your problem and prompt him or her to help find a solution. The point is that in these matters, timeliness and information are essential.

Therefore, you will need to be part of the solution through self-advocacy and seeking out professionals who will assist you. Since recommendations aren't always optimal, you may need to pursue alternatives approaches by consulting widely, perform your own research, and re-addressing unresolved problems with determination and persistence.

If you do not have the ability to be a strong self-advocate, then ask someone close to you to fill this role.

https://www.medicalhomeportal.org/living-with-child/navigating-transitions-with-your-child/transition-to-adulthood/self-advocacy

http://www.canceradvocacy.org/resources/advocating-for-yourself/becoming-a-self-advocate-2/

http://www.med.umich.edu/1libr/Neurology/ALS/Living_with_ALS_Guide.pdf (Firefox)

https://books.google.com/books?id=zFo7SBPKZSoC&pg=PA34&lpg=PA34&dq=self+advocacy+in+als&source=bl&ots=pw3-fFdxF-&sig=ELw25OypROKbfd4akxOvdttBM44&hl=en&sa=X&ved=0ahUKEwjilbO1p57OAhWKGB4KHRiLAjU4FBDoAQghMAE#v=onepage&q=self%20advocacy%20in%20als&f=false

Fourteen

Develop a Management Plan

Once you have been diagnosed with ALS, it would be wise to seriously study everything about the disease in order to put together a comprehensive plan to manage symptoms and disability, organize needed services and equipment, and to figure out how to live the best quality of life possible in spite of advancing disability. Can your home be adapted to meet your needs throughout all the stages of your illness? Will you need to move to a new home that will be wheelchair accessible? What equipment will you need, and when should you get it? For example, I purchased a Hoyer lift while I was still walking, and we began training with it well before it was needed. About a year later, I fell and could not get up. My wife was able to use the lift, and within a few minutes, I was lifted up from the floor and transferred to a transporter wheelchair, and the crisis quickly ended.

How are you going to manage your financial needs when medical expenses begin to rise? What kind of psychological support do you need, and where and when will you get it? When and how will you hire a caregiver? How do you plan to manage a medical emergency or an ALS-related crisis, should one occur? Finally, what is your end-of-life plan? You might not have answers to all of these questions right now. Nevertheless, it's never too early to start researching these matters and come up with thoughtful answers so that when the time comes, you will be prepared. By focusing on managing your life as well as possible while living with ALS you will improve your quality of life and allow room for a sense of well-being much of the time while preventing unnecessary discomfort, mental anguish, accidents and complications.

http://www.alsa.org/als-care/resources/fyi/planning-for-the-future.html

http://web.alsa.org/site/PageNavigator/emergency_preparedness.html

http://www.alsa.org/als-care/resources/als-insight/articles/feb2014-financial-planning.html

https://www.youtube.com/watch?v=68r6kYqhcA0

http://www.als.ca/sites/default/files/files/Physicians%20CD/A%20Guide%20to%20ALS%20Patient%20Care%20For%20Primary%20Care%20Physicians%20English.pdf (Firefox)

http://www.bioethics.jp/licht_advals.html

http://www.ncbi.nlm.nih.gov/pmc/articles/PMC3182548/\ (Firefox)

http://www.alscareproject.org/organizations/AMA-Home CarePhysicians.pdf (Firefox)

Fifteen

Quality of Life and ALS

One's quality of life (QOL) is likely to be perceived quite differently by any number of individuals living with ALS even though they may have the exactly the same or similar symptoms and problems. In part, one's QOL while living with ALS will depend upon one's insight and knowledge of managing symptoms, the rate of symptom progression, a PALS perspective and ability to cope, access to resources and support, and social circumstances, etc. Although there are many tools used in medicine to measure quality of life in illness; I doubt that any of them are able to truly accurately ascertain the QOL experienced by a single individual since each of us is unique in our perspective and tolerances. Furthermore, one's perception is also likely to change over time as we learn from our experiences and increase our knowledge. In other words, what might have been unacceptable at one point in time might be entirely acceptable at another point.

Your ALS center can play a key role in helping you maintain a good quality of life as symptoms and disability advance by providing information, guidance, and support.

Finally, your determination and ability to play a constructive role in getting what you need, will certainly have a major impact on your quality of your life when living with this illness.

QOL in ALS will also be affected by your ability to cope and adjust to the reality of your situation, deal with diminished physical ability, manage discomfort, and remain engaged in a life that is still possible and desirable.

Your QOL will also depend largely upon your state of mind, your support system, and access to resources. This includes your relationships, support from family and friends, availability of a competent caregiver(s), meeting your own expectations, feeling secure and valued, and—most of all—finding meaning in the life you are living.

Individuals with ALS who understand their illness and learn to manage their symptoms and disability as well as possible will increase their chances of achieving a good quality of life in spite of considerable difficulty and limitation. Although my life has changed dramatically as a result of ALS, nevertheless, it continues to be a good life from my standpoint and it is one that I appreciate. I am sure that there are others in similar or even far more difficult situations that feel the same way.

Your QOL will be positively affected by your ability to remain engaged in life, feeling loved and connected, and in many cases it may also be greatly influenced by strong spiritual beliefs.

I believe that having meaningful relationships and a sense of fulfillment plays a key role in enjoying a good quality of life while living with ALS.

QOL will also depend on one's ability to manage worries, including the anxiety and fear associated with the prospect of a premature death, increasing dependency or concerns about having unmet needs. Finding a way to cope with such feelings will be an essential element in maintaining a good quality of life.

Learning how to use adaptive equipment (e.g., a Hoyer lift, wheelchair, BiPAP, etc.) and finding ways to optimally manage symptoms will definitely improve your QOL.

Isolation and a lack of ALS knowledge are the enemies of a good QOL. Spending time with family and friends as well as actively pursuing your interests will greatly improve your QOL, so work at staying engaged.

An ALS support group could offer you valuable guidance as well as emotional support, since some members will have already dealt with the same problems and issues that you are facing.

Adequate nutrition could help you to maintain a good energy level. Maintaining comfort will allow you to focus on what is meaningful in your life, so learn to do what is necessary to accomplish this goal.

If you like your work, then continue to for work as long as possible—it should positively contribute to your well-being.

Even though I am in wheelchair because I cannot walk or even stand, have very significant physical limitations, and also require 24/7 respiratory support, I still view my quality of life to be quite good. Each morning, my caregivers help me out of bed and into a shower wheelchair. After showering, I am helped with dressing, and a Hoyer lift is used to transfer me into a power wheelchair. From that point on, I have control over my mobility, and I am free to go wherever I like with my power wheelchair and to do whatever is within my capability.

After breakfast, I usually read the newspaper via the computer and then begin working on a project. Today I'm writing the book that you are reading using voice recognition software. At other times, I might be working on my photography, reading, doing research, making plans, managing finances, learning, or consulting. On most days, friends, family, neighbors, former coworkers, or acquaintances stop by for a visit. Each Saturday, my daughter and grandson visit for the weekend and we have a great time.

I speak regularly with friends and relatives on the phone or, better yet, on Skype or FaceTime. When the weather is pleasant, I go outdoors on my power wheelchair. By the time dinner rolls around, I've had a full day. After dinner and conversation, I often watch a movie, read, or go over some paperwork. Sometimes friends join us for dinner, or I will talk to a family member or a friend. I almost always have a good night's sleep because I'm sleeping on a comfortable adjustable bed and receive respiratory support (e.g., BiPAP) that prevents nocturnal hypoventilation.

Each morning, I wake up rested and in a good mood, and look forward to the day's experience that is likely to contain some enjoyment or challenge. When I think about the issues of quality of life and ALS, I remember that the scientist Stephen Hawking, who is completely paralyzed and has lost his power of direct speech, has managed to enjoy a full and exceptional life while living with ALS for more than fifty years.

So cut yourself a break, grieve for what you have lost, and let go of negativity. Get support and treatment for any feelings that are causing you pain, and move forward with your life in order to enjoy what is still possible. Maintain a positive and proactive outlook, and plan a daily schedule of activity in order to remain engaged while opportunities are still available. And should you have the opportunity, help someone else with ALS so that they can benefit from what you have learned.

As it turns out, research has shown that a large number of ALS patients are satisfied with their quality of life, which surprisingly appears to have more to do with the general or global issues affecting their lives (e.g., family support, relationships) rather than their stage of their disease, level of disability, or specific ALS symptoms.

Taking charge of your life to the fullest extent will allow you to achieve self-determination within the realm of what is possible. All of this requires focus, commitment, planning, and the ability to adapt to the reality of your situation. In so doing, you should be able to find a way to enjoy a life that is possible, and much may be possible.

http://www.alsphiladelphia.org/NetCommunity/Document. Doc?id=155 (Firefox)

http://link.springer.com/article/10.1007%2Fs13311-014-0322-x

http://onlinelibrary.wiley.com/doi/10.1002/mus.24659/abstract

https://www.sciencedaily.com/releases/2008/06/080620120002.htm

http://bjo.sagepub.com/content/67/12/551.abstract

https://www.youtube.com/watch?v=51hcwFAhRlI

http://bmcneurol.biomedcentral.com/articles/10.1186/s12883-015-0340-2

http://www.cnsuwo.ca/ebn/downloads/cats/2010/CNS-EBN_cat-document_2010-07-JUL-15_in-people-with-amyotrophic-lateral-sclerosis-overall-quality-of-life-was-related-to-psychological_DD23C.pdf (Firefox)

http://www.alsa.org/als-care/resources/publications-videos/factsheets/reasons-for-living-with-als.html

https://uu.diva-portal.org/smash/get/diva2:919994/FULLTEXT01.pdf (Firefox)

http://www.alsmndalliance.org/wp-content/uploads/2010/12/005-Yoga-and-ALS-R-Rhodes.pdf (Firefox)

http://www.ncbi.nlm.nih.gov/pmc/articles/PMC3994974/ (Firefox)

http://alsworldwide.org/care-and-support/article/benefits-of-meditation

http://alsandwellness.blogspot.com/2015/01/your-attention-please.html

Sixteen

Prevent Accidents and Prepare for Emergencies

I f your legs grow weak or you develop foot drop, you will then be an accident waiting to happen unless you take preventive measures. For example, not using a rollator, walker, or wheelchair when your legs grow weak or you are unsteady, or if you have had a previous fall any of these indicates that you are at significant risk for a fall. In addition, failing to use a wheelchair when you sense that you are too weak to walk unassisted will cause you to experience unnecessary fatigue and possibly exhaustion. Not wearing a safety belt while sitting in a wheelchair, especially a power wheelchair, can end badly should you slip out of the wheelchair.

Remove obstacles from your home that could impede your access or put you at risk for a fall. Have handrails and grips installed in your bathroom and in other locations where a risk of falling exists.

Prepare for emergencies—because they will happen! Do you have backup power for all the electrical equipment you need? Do you have a backup for your caregiver? How will you manage without one? Do you have backup equipment for those devices upon which you are completely dependent?

What will happen if you start to choke on a piece of food or develop laryngospasm that could leave you unable to breathe or speak? Do you have a plan to manage these situations? Is your caregiver trained to perform a Heimlich maneuver should you begin to choke on a piece of food?

What will happen if you fall and can't get up? What if no one is with you and you get into trouble—how will you call for help? Backup plans will be discussed in a subsequent chapter. The following websites offer additional information:

http://alsn.mda.org/article/take-falls-seriously-prevent-further-injuries

http://alsn.mda.org/article/what-will-you-do-if-power-goes-out

http://www.alsa.org/als-care/living-with-als/emergency-preparedness.html

http://www.mndassociation.org/wp-content/uploads/px017-mnd-in-acute-urgent-and-emergency-care.pdf (Firefox)

Seventeen

Caregivers and Health Care Aides

When first diagnosed, you are likely to need psychological support, guidance, and ALS education. However, it is unlikely that you will need much physical assistance at first. However, as time passes, muscular weakness and disability will increase, necessitating physical assistance with daily tasks. Initially, you might find that your gait (way of walking) has become unsteady, that you suffer muscular weakness of your extremities or that you are having coordination problems. During the late stage of ALS, you are likely to lose your ability to walk, stand, get out of bed, use the toilet or shower unassisted, or perhaps may not be able to feed yourself. Therefore, you will eventually become heavily dependent on a caregiver for assistance.

Progressive weakness and signs of increasing disability indicate that you should begin searching for a caregiver who can help you with those daily activities that you can no longer perform on your own or those that put at risk.

A caregiver's presence may imply dependence, but actually, the presence of a competent caregiver offers you independence since he or she will help you express your will and assist you to pursue your interests and fulfill your needs. In such a case, your caregiver's hands will do your bidding and assist you with the tasks you wish to undertake when disability prevents you from acting yourself.

A caregiver can be anybody who is competent with regard to meeting your needs, who is willing and able to learn, and is reliable and responsible.

At first, your need for a caregiver's assistance is likely to be modest. A family member or a friend might be able to provide the support you need. However, as your symptoms progress and your need for assistance increases, the demands made on your caregivers availability, skill, strength, and commitment are also likely to increase. For example, moving a 150 or 200 pound disabled person who is partially or fully paralyzed from his or her bed to the bathroom and then assisting with showering and dressing will require skill, knowledge, strength, and the use of specialized equipment. An ideal caregiver will strong but gentle as well as patient, knowledgeable, understanding, and sensitive to your needs and comfort.

A spouse might be willing and able to carry out these tasks; however, even the most loving partner will need relief on a regular basis so as not to suffer "burn out."

A caregiver may be a family member, a close friend, or a paid homecare aide. A professional homecare aide is trained and licensed to provide daily care to a disabled person. He or she can be hired through an agency or may be found through a network of friends or acquaintances. Initially you may only need a caregiver for a few hours a day. However, over time, your disability will increase, and you will eventually need the assistance of a full-time caregiver or a team of caregivers.

Caregiving for an ALS patient whose disability is progressive is a demanding job. It requires both physical and mental strength as well as the ability to develop the necessary skills to meet an ALS patient's ever increasing needs. Your caregiver will need to know how to operate a lift and be able to transfer you safely, manage your respiratory equipment, help you perform range-of-motion exercises, position you correctly, and/or manage a feeding tube if you have one. Your caregiver will need to be patient and sensitive to your needs and attentive to your risks and comfort in order to help support as good a quality possible for all. He or she will need to be strong enough to lift or reposition you in a safe manner when you are no longer able to assist or move. Caregiver such as a spouse that is taking care of you 24/7 may suffer burnout, which could lead to depression, anger, and/or resentment. Therefore, arrange to give your caregiver, such as a spouse, scheduled breaks that will allow him or her time to recuperate.

For example, a spouse can alternate shifts with a paid healthcare aide, family member, friend, or others who are willing to help. It is important for a 24/7 caregiver's mental health that they get out of the house from time to time and maintains an outside social life. A paid caregiver can also work with a spouse to lighten the load or to provide a respite.

The presence of a homecare aide will allow your spouse to go to work, carry out childcare chores, manage the household, and/or have enough free time to socialize so that burnout does not occur. Sharing the work among family and friends will also help reduce the costs of engaging a paid caregiver.

One paid eight-hour homecare aide working 5 days a week could cost $35,000 to $40,000 or more per year (2016). If you are severely disabled and without caregiver help from family or friends you might need three eight-hour or two twelve-hour daily shifts of paid caregivers to provide around-the-clock care if you are fully disabled. The cost for such services could easily exceed $120,000 per year. If an individual with ALS were to require tracheostomy ventilation, caregiver costs are likely to be far higher.

Health care workers hired through an agency will be significantly more expensive than directly hiring an individual.

The costs for long-term home healthcare aides are not usually covered by medical insurance. Long-term personal care policies may cover some of these costs, but many do not have such policies. Medicaid may offer to pay for a very limited amount of home healthcare aide time. Both Medicare and Medicaid currently cover hospice care but this will not replace the need for a fulltime daily homecare caregiver in the late stage of ALS.

Choose a homecare aide that has experience. He or she needs to be compatible with your personality, physically strong enough to meet your needs, alert, attentive, and willing to meet growing needs as your disability progresses. References and background checks should be carefully reviewed, but you will only understand the quality and the capability of a caregiver once he or she begins working with you.

Over the years, I have observed that some homecare aides are truly outstanding while others leave much to be desired regarding their work habits, knowledge, skills, initiative, attentiveness, capability, and/or reliability. Some are truly outstanding, others not so much. The interesting thing is that the costs for someone who is excellent may be the same as for someone who is below average in their job performance. You can't assume that the person you hire will meet your needs or will be good at his or her work without a trial run, training, and observation. Hiring caregivers through an agency is not a guarantee of their quality, contrary to the claims of some agencies.

I have found that it's best to hire a person who has been recommended by someone you know well, has good judgment and has had considerable experience with the person they recommend. Regardless, you should clearly state your expectations from the outset, including your specific needs, and the fact that your needs will increase over time as ALS symptoms progress. To avoid misunderstandings or disappointments, try to describe the caregiver's job as precisely as possible. If early on, a caregiver fails to meet your needs, does not respond to your guidance, or is not willing or able to learn to fulfill your needs, it will be best to quickly find a replacement. The role of your caregiver should not be entrusted to a person who is not on top of his or her business, responsible, and competent. When you find a good caregiver, treat him or her well—they are valuable, and they deserve it.

For the past five years, I've been fortunate to have Veronica, a healthcare aide who shares caregiving responsibilities with my wife. Veronica is experienced, competent, and kind, and she has adapted to fulfilling my increasing needs. She has a good sense of humor and is fun to be around, and clearly cares about my welfare. She is highly reliable and responsible. Talia works with Veronica in the morning. In the evening Talia manages things alone. On Saturdays and Sunday mornings, other part-time health care aides complete the team, so I am never without a caregiver.

If your significant other or a family member plays a role as a caregiver, they could benefit from joining an ALS caregiver support group, where they can receive advice, guidance, and literature, including an ALS caregiver manual. Try viewing the following websites for more information and excellent caregiver guidance on the management of ALS:

http://www.alsa.org/als-care/resources/fyi/how-to-know-when-to-hire.html

www.mda.org/sites/default/files/publications/Everyday_Life_with_ALS_P-532.pdf (Firefox)

https://www.mda.org/sites/default/files/publications/ALS_Caregiver's_Guide_P-531.pdf

www.alsa.org/als-care/caregivers/caregiving-tips-and-hints.html

www.alsa.org/als-care/caregivers/for-caregivers.html

http://www.alsa.org/als-care/resources/fyi/hiring-in-home-help.html

http://www.huffingtonpost.com/margaret-m-kruse/the-social-security-con-h_b_9369742.html

http://quest.mda.org/news/mda-study-reveals-cost-illness-als-dmd-mmd

http://www.alsa.org/als-care/caregivers/from-one-caregiver-to-another.html

Eighteen

ALS Support Groups

You should be able to find an ALS support group in most major metropolitan areas in the United States. The easiest way to find one is by contacting the ALS Association, the muscular dystrophy association (MDA), or through your ALS center. They will refer you to a local support group.

Support groups are made up of ALS patients, their families, friends, caregivers, volunteers, and professionals. Members come together to learn from each other, teach each other, share their knowledge and feelings, express their concerns, and ask questions. Members offer and receive support and advice from members who can relate to what you, your family, and caregiver are going through.

Over time, group members may get to know each other better, grow closer, and may offer you support in your time of need. When you enter a crisis, you may be able to call upon other members for advice, because you know that they will do their best to help you. Some may even have experienced a situation similar to yours and will be able to provide you with the information or direction you need.

A support group may invite speakers that can provide you with new information, insight, and perhaps direct you to previously unknown resources or methods. You will learn how others cope with their symptoms and problems, and you will also come to understand that you are not alone in your situation.

In addition, online support groups and/or forums can also provide valuable support, information about clinical drug trials, new technology, as well as advice about the management of a specific ALS problems and issues. The following websites might prove helpful:

www.alsa.org/community/

http://www.mayoclinic.org/healthy-lifestyle/stress-management/in-depth/support-groups/art-20044655

http://www.alsa.org/community/support-groups/

http://alsn.mda.org/article/mda-als-support-groups

http://www.alsforums.com

http://www.alstdi.org/forum/

http://www.alsa.org/als-care/resources/informative-web-links/

https://www.patientslikeme.com/conditions/9-als-amyotrophic-lateral-sclerosis

Nineteen

Family Issues

I think it is best to have a frank discussion with your immediate family members as soon as you are able to understand and absorb the significance of your diagnosis and you are in an emotional state that allows you to logically and calmly explain what you have learned. Family members should be made aware of your diagnosis and its implications so that they will have an opportunity to share in your struggle and help when and if they are able. As your symptoms become obvious, even children will eventually figure out that something is going on. The news should be broken in an appropriate and sensitive manner and in a way so that each individual will be able to understand what is happening.

I struggled for some time regarding how to deliver the news of my diagnosis to my adult children. The psychologist I consulted helped me understand that I was not protecting my children by withholding this information; rather, I was depriving them of the opportunity to make their own decisions in how to deal with what was happening.

If you need help from family members, ask for it. If offered, accept what makes sense. At the same time, discuss how you expect your condition might affect you and the lives of other family members on a need to know basis.

Also, discuss how it would be best to use the time that remains in a meaningful way so that each family member can make the best use of that time.

Consider how your progressive disability is likely to affect your spouse and children, and discuss how things might be best managed. Together with your spouse and family members, work out a plan that will allow your needs to be met without burning out a family caregiver or unnecessarily worrying family members.

Finally, consider the financial impact of your illness and how it might affect your family. Specifically, you don't want your medical bills and related expenses to bankrupt your spouse or impoverish your family. Regarding this matter, you may have enough time early in the course of your illness to put your assets into a trust or shift their ownership in a legal way to protect your spouse and your family's financial state after you have passed away. If you do have assets that you think might be at risk (e.g., your home), you might want to consult with an estate attorney. On the other hand, if you have few assets, you should ask a social worker to help you to develop a plan to conserve what you do have by applying for social security disability, and if you qualify, for Medicaid, and/or for hospice care at the appropriate time. Find ways to access what other resources might be available in your community. In addition, some nonprofit organizations may be able to offer services and equipment that could benefit you and thus relieve some of the financial pressure. Check the following websites for more info:

http://www.alsphiladelphia.org/telling-your-children-or-grand children

http://www.alsphiladelphia.org/document.doc?id=1685 (Firefox)

http://www.breakthroughals.org/breakthroughblog/entry/
how-to-talk-to-children-about-an-als-diagnosis

http://www.columbian.com/projects/2015/11/30/family-
adjusts-to-the-new-normal-with-als/

http://www.usatoday.com/story/news/nation/2014/08/29/
for-als-families-coping-is-real-challenge/14829723/

http://alsn.mda.org/article/social-workers-offer-wealth-re
sources

Twenty

Social Life

It has been to my observation that without meaningful relationships, one can definitely exist—but I would hardly call that living. Without social connection, friendship, or loved ones in your life, you remain isolated from what is most worthwhile. It is my view that happiness is mostly derived from one's relationships. It is not unusual for individuals diagnosed with ALS to become anxious and in some cases, depressed. Under such a circumstance, an affected individual might isolate himself by pushing friends and family away. Although this might be a natural response to the shock of the diagnosis and the emotional turmoil it causes, it is an unhealthy response, and could undermine the one thing you need the most—supportive relationships.

Make a determined effort to connect with friends and family, drawing support and enjoyment from these relationships.

Work at maintaining your social network, and pursue social activities that you enjoy while is still possible, and when going out with friends becomes too difficult, invite them to your home.

http://als-ny.blogspot.com/2009/05/what-do-i-do-what-do-i-say.html

Twenty-One

Financial Issues and ALS

A LS is an expensive disease to manage, and it will become more expensive as your disability worsens and your need for resources increases.

At some point, particularly during the disease's late stage, medical expenses will be largely related to the costs of a home healthcare worker(s), modification of your home, and the purchase of medical equipment and treatment not covered by your medical insurance. If you qualify for Medicaid, many of your medical expenses may be covered but not most of the costs of a home healthcare aide, however this can vary from state to state. In the future, new treatments for ALS will become available, perhaps before they are covered by health insurance, and such treatment could prove to be very expensive. For example, when I was diagnosed with ALS, I was able to receive a legitimate experimental stem-cell treatment for ALS outside of the United States at a top notch University Hospital. The costs for this treatment were approximately $40,000. None of this expense was covered by my medical insurance. Therefore, I had to pay for it out of my own pocket.

An ALS patient's greatest medical expense will most likely be the ongoing expense for a home healthcare worker. As a caregiver's hours increase, so will expenses, especially if you don't have family members or friends who can and will act as caregivers. Even those with long-term homecare insurance policies may be limited to a term of two or three years; therefore, you could easily outlive your policy.

Considering these issues, you will need to come up with a plan to deal with current ongoing and future potential expenses. For example, family members, friends, and other potential support could be mobilized to provide as much caregiver help as possible in order to help conserve on the use of a paid homecare aide. Organize your homecare aide's schedule so that their time is managed efficiently.

Although medical insurance in many cases will cover expensive equipment such as a power wheelchair, this is not always the case. For example, a power wheelchair that fits you correctly and meets all your needs might cost $30,000 or more. Insurance coverage can be tricky. For example, if you use your insurance to buy a power scooter early in your course of ALS, your medical insurance might reject paying for a power wheelchair later on because its rules may state that only one power wheelchair, or scooter will be covered per patient once every five years. Mastering the nuances of medical insurance regarding these issues is essential; therefore, consult with knowledgeable people (e.g., a social worker, an occupational therapist, better yet a wheelchair specialist or supplier) regarding insurance rules before making major purchase. Your alternatives for getting the equipment you need include finding inexpensive used equipment for sale, or if you are lucky enough to have access to an ALS center or MDA "loan closet," you may be able to borrow the equipment you need. A number of charitable organizations might be able to help in this matter.

If you are a veteran you will find that many ALS expenses we'll be covered by the veterans administration including a power wheelchair and possibly the wheelchair accessible minivan and home renovations needed for your disability.

Renovate your home so that it is wheelchair accessible and that you will have good access to your bedroom and bathroom with a wheelchair. This can be expensive. An alternative would be to move into a rented wheelchair-accessible apartment.

Finally, you will need to consider the state of your family finances after you have passed away in order to develop a plan that will not leave your family with the burden of a large debt or without the necessary means of support. A social worker, an accountant, or perhaps an estate lawyer may be able to help you deal with these issues. Check out the following websites for more information:

http://quest.mda.org/news/mda-study-reveals-cost-illness-als-dmd-mmd

http://www.jakesan.com/page1/page18/page31/page31.html

http://alsn.mda.org/article/social-workers-offer-wealth-resources

https://www.fifthseasonfinancial.com/blog/financial-help-als-patients-families/ (Firefox)

http://www.ncbi.nlm.nih.gov/pubmed/25245119 (Firefox)

http://money.usnews.com/money/blogs/the-best-life/2013/06/05/living-with-als-money-issues-need-care-as-well

https://www.simplesanutrition.com/blog/finding-financial-assistance-for-als-patients/

http://www.alsa.org/als-care/living-with-als/navigating-your-tax-burden.html

http://www.schomerlawgroup.com/elder-law-report/living-als-legal-financial-resource-guide/

http://www.alsa.org/als-care/veterans/service-connected-benefits.html

Twenty-Two

ALS and Driving

At the time of my diagnosis, I had no difficulty with driving. Although I had muscle weakness, it was moderate. However, one day I noticed that I began to have difficulty in turning on the ignition key because of hand weakness. Over a period of months, turning the key became so difficult that I needed to start using a small screwdriver, which I would insert through a slot at the top of the key in order to give me enough leverage to turn the key.

As I became weaker, I also developed foot drop, and so I decided it would be better to stop driving before I was actually forced to stop driving. I was concerned that should I need to execute an emergency maneuver, I would not have the strength to do what was needed to avoid an accident. Once I made that decision, I found others to drive me to where I needed to go.

If you are unable to decide whether or not it is safe to continue driving, you can undergo an evaluation by an occupational therapist or similar specialist to assess your driving competency.

Once you've decided to stop driving, you can usually find family and friends who are willing to help drive you to where you need to go. Organize your appointments and set a schedule so that you are efficient in your arrangements for errands and appointments. When no one is available for a necessary trip, consider using a taxi (a wheelchair-accessible one, if needed), Uber, or public transportation.

http://www.alsa.org/als-care/living-with-als/driving-challenges-with-als-1.html

Twenty-Three

Work and ALS

I was diagnosed with ALS in 2009. At the time, I was working full-time as a physician in a very busy practice. The demands of my work were great; however, I loved my work, so it rarely seemed stressful. In 2010, I was evaluated at the Mayo Clinic and was told that based on the rate of progression of my symptoms, I shouldn't plan to continue working for much longer. Nevertheless, I continued to work for about a year or so. Around that time, I started to experience marked fatigue by the end of the workday. One day, I found I was barely able to make it up a flight of stairs at the entrance to one of my offices. I finally realized that I would have to stop working—I simply could no longer physically manage the demands of my work.

Since ALS is a highly variable disease, it may be possible for you to continue to work for some time following your diagnosis. Of course, your decision will depend upon your degree of disability, the demands of your work and the accommodations I am made.

I think it is a very good idea to continue to work for as long as possible, for both psychological and financial reasons. If you enjoy your work, I see no reason to stop working until you can no longer function properly even with accommodations. On the other hand, if you receive little fulfillment from your work, and your financial situation will permit you to "go out" on disability, then the disability route might be a good choice.

Fortunately, some years ago social security disability allowed automatic qualification for disability payments to ALS patients because ALS carries with it a presumptive qualification for disability.

If you decide to continue to work, and you are able to carry out your work with accommodations, then it would be a good idea to speak with your employer about receiving those accommodations at the appropriate time.

For example, you can ask for a flexible work schedule that would work for both you and your employer. You can request modification of your workplace regarding wheelchair access, rest breaks, and ergonomic modifications of your desk, keyboard, and so on, so that you could continue to function. You may also require special accommodation for your wheelchair. However, it might not be a good idea to discuss your diagnosis with your coworkers or employer much before the time you require accommodation because responses can be unpredictable. See the following websites for additional information:

https://askjan.org/soar/other/als.html

www.alsphiladelphia.org/document.doc?id=846 (Firefox)

http://digitalcommons.ilr.cornell.edu/cgi/viewcontent.cgi?article=1319&context=edicollect (Firefox)

http://www.adainfo.org/sites/default/files/Best-Practices-in-Developing-RA-in-the-Workplace.pdf (Firefox)

Twenty-Four

ALS, Sex, and Conception

The neuropathology of ALS will not affect erectile function, ejaculation, or orgasm since these functions are all under the control of the autonomic nervous system, which is not influenced by the death of motor neurons with rare exception. Further, sensory function will remain unaffected in ALS. However, as muscle weakness and paralysis advance, the loss of voluntary muscle function can interfere with the physical act of sexual intercourse. Nevertheless, intimacy can continue to be possible, even in the presence of significant physical disability. Finally, ALS does not affect a man's or a woman's fertility. However, conception in ALS might require the assistance of a fertility specialist in some cases as symptoms advance. The effect of ALS on pregnancy will depend on an individual's respiratory status and muscular functions and this should be discussed with your physician if conception is desired. These matters are explored on the websites below:

www.massgeneral.org/als/patienteducation/ALS_sexuality intimacy.aspx

http://alsworldwide.org/whats-new/article/sexual-intimacy

http://www.ncbi.nlm.nih.gov/pubmed/15083290 (Firefox)

https://www.als.ca/sites/default/files/files/Sexuality,%2520Int
imacy%2520And%2520Chronic%2520Illness.pdf   (Firefox)

http://alsn.mda.org/article/having-children-after-als-diagnosis

http://www.ncbi.nlm.nih.gov/pubmed/8378011 (Firefox)

http://www.tandfonline.com/doi/abs/10.3109/174829608025
78365?journalCode=iafd19

Twenty-Five

Legal Issues

There are three things an individual with ALS can anticipate. First, at some point in the future, you will become severely disabled and may have difficulty with competently managing your own affairs. Second, your life span will be significantly shortened; therefore, you would be wise to get your legal and financial affairs in order sooner rather than later. Third, you should expect that your future medical expenses are likely to increase significantly, which could lead to financial hardship.

A severely disabled individual with ALS might develop communication difficulty, lose his or her physical competency, or suffer some level of cognitive decline. In the latter case, such an individual would likely benefit from appointing someone to safeguard his or her interests and carry out wishes.

If you think that your assets will be at risk at some future point, you can protect those assets against financial claims by putting them into a trust as soon as you suspect you have ALS and you perceive a risk exists. A trust's assets will be protected from financial claims arising from your debts or liabilities. In addition, you can create legal documents than will ensure your future wishes will be carried out in the event that you lose your competency, can't communicate, or die.

Advanced Directives or a Living Will

Advanced directives or a living will is a written set of legal instructions regarding how you wish your future healthcare to be managed in the event that you are unable to competently direct your own medical care. For example, if you are unable to express your wishes due to the inability to communicate, loss of consciousness, confusion, or loss of mental competency, then your advanced directives will guide decisions made by your family and/or medical personal regarding your healthcare management. Such a document should relieve some of the stress of decision making and can help ensure that your desires are carried out according to your wishes.

Do Not Resuscitate Document (DNR)

A DNR order is a written document instructing medical personnel to not resuscitate you in the event that you require CPR (cardio pulmonary resuscitation) in order to sustain your life. In other words, you will have instructed the medical staff to allow you to expire naturally without intervening with aggressive medical measures. If this is your desire, you should sign such a document, and a copy should also be given to your doctor. The original should be kept with you. This should ensure that medical decisions regarding this issue will be managed according to your wishes.

Medical Power of Attorney (POA) or Health Care Power of Attorney (HCPOA)

A HCPOA is similar to an advanced directive except that it appoints a specific person to act as your agent, someone who will be empowered to manage your healthcare and follow your instructions and wishes should you're unable to do so yourself. A HCPOA is more secure than a health care directive.

Durable Power of Attorney

This is a legal document in which you appoint a person to act as your legal agent regarding financial matters, health matters, and even legal matters. Your agent can be a spouse, a relative, a trusted friend, a lawyer, or even a trust company. Your durable power of attorney will continue to remain in effect until you either revoke it or you die.

There are many types of power of attorney, some with quite broad powers and few limitations whereas others are very limited in scope, perhaps covering a single specific activity or action. In general, a power of attorney is either a medical power of attorney (HCPOA) or a legal and financial power of attorney; however, a POA can include any or all of these functions.

A *durable power of attorney* can be written to either take effect immediately (on the day that it is signed), or it can take effect under a specified set of circumstances or on a specific date. For example, your medical POA might only begin when you are no longer able to competently make decisions, as would be the case should you become incapacitated and/or unable to communicate. Without such a document, your loved ones may not be able to make decisions for you, which is a good reason to prepare POA well in advance of need. The POA is considered *durable* because it will remain in force until you revoke it or when it expires automatically upon your death. It is very important that someone you trust be given POA when you are diagnosed with ALS, otherwise a great deal of time and expense might be required for a court to appoint a guardian to manage your affairs should you lose the ability to communicate or are deemed to be no longer competent.

A financial or legal POA appoints an agent to act as your proxy regarding matters involving finances and legal issues. This will allow your agent to manage your bank account, pay your bills from your account, manage your assets and investments, and so on. Your POA agent can also act in your stead in legal matters.

Should you become incapacitated without a power of attorney, your family may not have access to your bank account or have the legal right to use your money to pay your bills or make legal decisions for you. Lacking power of attorney, your family will need to apply to a court requesting that a representative (e.g., family member) be appointed as your legal guardian in order to make decisions (financial, and legal) for you. This usually takes time and can incur significant legal fees. Finally, in order to be sure that your bank will recognize the POA, it would be a good idea to sit down with your bank manager and review the POA document to be sure that the bank will accept it.

Estate Planning:
- **Your Will**

Your last Will and last testament is a legal document that you create in which you give instructions on how your estate and personal property are to be distributed or managed following your death. In order for your Will to be legal and enforceable, you simply need to be of legal age and mentally competent at the time of its creation. The Will needs to be signed by you, and it would also be a good idea to have the document witnessed and notarized. You will need to name an executor of the Will, someone who will be empowered to administer your estate according to the Will's instructions. The Will should name your beneficiaries and contain details of how your assets are to be distributed. Destroy all prior Wills and their copies in order to avoid confusion and to prevent your current will from being successfully challenged. If you are concerned that your Will might be challenged, get a letter from your physician stating that you are mentally competent at the time of the Will's creation, and be sure to date the will at the time of its signing.

Should you die without a Will or if your Will is declared invalid, then the distribution of your assets and property will be determined by a probate court based on the laws of your state. Under such a circumstance, the court will appoint an attorney to manage and distribute your assets according to state law, and your estate will pay significant legal fees for this service.

- **Trusts**

A trust is a legal entity, usually created by a lawyer, used to hold assets (money, real estate, securities, etc) that are given to the trust by the owner of the assets (the grantor, which could be you). Once assets are given to a trust, the assets no longer belong to the grantor (which would be you) but will then belong to the trust. A trust is one of the best ways to protect your assets from liabilities or claims arising from the grantor's personal debts or liabilities (e.g., medical bills), thus preserving your estate (e.g., your home) for your beneficiaries. The trust contains the Grantor's specific instructions for distribution of its assets to designated beneficiaries.

There are a number of distinct types of trusts. One is a *revocable trust* (a temporary one), and the other is an *irrevocable trust* (a permanent one). Each has its benefits and limitations, which should be reviewed with an estate attorney. In general, trusts are used to protect assets for an intended purpose. For example, a trust avoids probate court and, if properly written, can protect assets from being wasted by a beneficiary. Married couples can created a trust within their wills so that upon the death of a spouse, the deceased's assets are held in a trust and will pass directly to the surviving spouse are used to support a spouse, avoiding death taxes or probate of the assets. Review the following websites for additional information:

http://www.alsmndalliance.org/about-us/policies/advanced-directives/

http://www.alsclinic.pitt.edu/patients/living_will.php

http://www.schomerlawgroup.com/elder-law-report/living-als-legal-financial-resource-guide/

http://alsn.mda.org/article/stay-control-making-advance-directives

Twenty-Six

Understand Your Options

When you encounter a life-altering event such as ALS, you should take into consideration the beginning, middle, and end stages of the illness in order to make good decisions. Of course, you can passively let nature take its course through inaction and avoid the stress of making difficult decisions, but first ask yourself if this is in your best interest and if it is what you truly desire.

Understanding that ALS is a terminal illness and also knowing that you are likely to continue to live for a number of years during which you will become increasingly disabled, should give you good reason to come up with a well-thought-out plan on how to best handle all your options throughout all phases of the illness.

During the early stage of ALS your challenges may be mostly psychological in nature. The middle stage of ALS will demand a greater degree of adapting and adjustment to symptoms and physical disability as they advance. However, the "heavy lifting" will really begin during the late stage of the disease when weakness and paralysis reach a point that you require considerable daily physical assistance, need more adaptive and mobility devices, and require frequent physical assistance in order to maintain an acceptable quality of life.

Study your options regarding every day aides for living with disability, management of ALS symptoms, the use of lifts, various types of wheelchairs, cough assist machine, respiratory support equipment, medications, orthotics etc., so that you can find what you need in a timely manner. Review the references in this book, which will present you with hundreds of options.

For example, as ALS advances, difficulty in breathing is likely to occur at some point when respiratory muscles weaken. Should symptoms suddenly worsen, a crisis could occur if noninvasive ventilation becomes ineffective and should you enter into a state of respiratory failure. If this happens, what do you plan to do? If noninvasive ventilation is no longer effective will you choose to begin tracheostomy ventilation in order to prolong your life, or will you choose to begin hospice care and pass away peacefully? Nobody wants to think about these issues but the sooner you research them the better.

Hopefully, you will carefully weighed your options and put a plan in place. Barring complications, tracheostomy ventilation can often restore effective ventilation when an ALS patient enters respiratory failure due respiratory muscle weakness or paralysis. Intervention with respiratory support may allow you to breath comfortably for years. However, only 5 percent or so of ALS patients in the United States will choose to begin tracheostomy ventilation when it is required for survival. The decision regarding this matter will depend upon one's state of mind, outlook for the future, family issues, culture, medical guidance, resources, spiritual beliefs, fears, and wishes.

Decisions regarding end-of-life care should be discussed with your physician and family earlier rather than later in order to avoid being forced into making a decision during a crisis. Such decisions need to be written and fully delineated in a living will and/or in a health care power of attorney's instructions. A copy of your living will should be given to your physician and presented whenever you are hospitalized or enter an emergency room. Otherwise, an ER physician is likely to institute resuscitation, intubate you, and put you on a ventilator should you enter respiratory failure. It would also be a good idea to keep a copy of these documents at home should respiratory failure suddenly occur and an arriving rescue team wants to begin resuscitation. Review the following websites regarding decision-making in ALS:

http://www.alsa.org/als-care/resources/publications-videos/factsheets/fyi-advance-directives.html

www.ncbi.nlm.nih.gov/pmc/articles/PMC3182548/ (Firefox)

http://www.alstexas.org/for-patients/just-diagnosed/what-next/

http://als.ca/sites/default/files/files/ventilation.pdf (Firefox)

http://emedicine.medscape.com/article/1170097-treatment

http://abcnews.go.com/blogs/health/2013/05/27/deciding-to-live-with-als-not-die-from-it/

http://www.pennstatehershey.org/c/document_library/get_file?folderId=375615&name=DLFE-8920.pdf (Firefox)

http://alsworldwide.org/care-and-support/article/feeding-tube-decisions

http://www.alsphiladelphia.org/doent.doc?id=828

Twenty-Seven

Planning Ahead

When first diagnosed with ALS, it is unlikely that you will truly comprehend what lies ahead or what will be required of you to manage advancing symptoms and disability. Initially each of us will need to find a way to effectively deal with the emotional stress that is universally experienced following the diagnosis of ALS. In order to make good decisions, you will need to gather a great deal of information—ALS management is complex, and each of us is likely to have our own unique problems. To make the best of the situation, you will need to thoroughly understand the disease process. Further, the management of ALS will require significant resources, so you will need to come up with a strong plan that will take everything (potential needs, resources, desires, etc.) into consideration. Focusing on each stage of the disease, the rate of the disease's progression, and taking into account the preparations needed for the probable as well as the possible will help you create a better designed plan.

Project how symptoms and needs might affect your life and the lives of those you love. In order to grasp future needs, begin reading the ALS literature until you fully understand the disease process and have researched the specific topics that concern you. Seek out guidance and information from your ALS center and from your support group. Review the websites offered as references in this book, since they contain a wealth of information.

Once armed with enough information and insight, you will be ready to develop a comprehensive plan.

Since ALS is a progressive disorder, you should expect your symptoms to worsen over time and to be repeatedly challenged with new problems. Knowing this, you would be wise to prepare to manage predictable symptoms rather than try to play catch-up as each new problem unfolds.

For example, you know that you will become increasingly disabled over time and will need physical assistance at some point to manage your daily activities. This should give you a strong impetus to identify, hire, and train a caregiver that can meet your needs earlier rather than later. Even if caregivers are family members or friends, it will take time for them to learn how to operate the equipment you need (e.g., a Hoyer lift, BiPAP equipment, etc.). Your caregiver(s) should also be trained to know what to do in the event of an emergency. Finding such a person(s) could take a while, so allow yourself the time necessary to find and train a good caregiver—The right person will make a great deal of difference in the quality of your life.

Since you know that you will eventually need a wheelchair, you should plan in advance to modify your home so that it is wheelchair accessible and safe. Other modifications may be needed to allow you to carry out daily activities (e.g., toileting and showering). Medical equipment, such as a lift or power wheelchair, should also be ordered well in advance of need so that you don't risk long delays in its acquisition (e.g., insurance approval). Research what equipment and methods are available to deal with each stage of your illness in order to increase your safety, comfort, and longevity.

Develop a contingency plan for each potential need or emergency that you can reasonably anticipate. Review your medical insurance policy coverage before you need to use it. Review your financial situation and create a budget to manage all anticipated costs. Consult a lawyer, an accountant, and an ALS social worker to help you develop plans that will meet your future needs as well as those of your family.

Finally, you will need to create an end-of-life plan, because you are going to need it. This is something that will need to be reviewed from time to time and discussed with your physician and family. Check the following websites and review chapter 78.

http://www.alsa.org/als-care/resources/fyi/planning-for-the-future.html

http://alsn.mda.org/article/longterm-financial-planning

http://www.alsa.org/news/vision-express/articles/april2016/9-tips-for-financial-planning.html?utm_source=natlnewsletter&utm_medium=email&utm_campaign=april2016

http://www.alsa.org/als-care/living-with-als/emergency-preparedness.html

http://www.alsa.org/als-care/resources/publications-videos/factsheets/cognitive-changes-family.html

http://emedicine.medscape.com/article/1170097-treatment

http://www.mayoclinic.org/diseases-conditions/amyotrophic-lateral-sclerosis/symptoms-causes/dxc-20247211

http://www.alsforums.com/forum/

http://www.alstdi.org/forum/

http://memory.ucsf.edu/ftd/community-support/support/dementia/multiple

http://www.alsphiladelphia.org/document.doc?id=2045 (Firefox)

Twenty-Eight

Management of Respiratory Symptoms in ALS

A mong the many medical problems encountered with ALS, perhaps one of the most serious ones regarding your quality of life and your survival time will be the development of *hypoventilation* (under-ventilation of the lungs), since it is associated with some of the worst symptoms experienced in ALS and is also the most common cause of death in ALS (respiratory failure). It is worth noting that the survival time of an ALS patient can be significantly influenced by how well hypoventilation is managed. Thus, the optimum management of hypoventilation ought to be of primary importance to someone diagnosed with ALS.

Fortunately, hypoventilation can often be well managed for years with the proper use of respiratory support equipment. Respiratory support for hypoventilation includes the use of non-invasive ventilation (e.g., BiPAP) and, less frequently, the use of invasive ventilation (e.g., tracheostomy ventilation).

The diaphragm is the primary muscle of respiration since it does about 80 percent of the work needed for inspiration. It is a large, thin, dome-shaped muscle located just beneath the lungs, separating the chest from the abdominal cavity. It is a voluntary muscle, which is innervated by phrenic nerves arising from motor neurons located in the cervical spinal cord. As the diaphragm's motor neurons die, its muscular function will grow weaker until one can no longer adequately breathe without assistance. These events will occur over time and will cause a decline in ventilation (lung air exchange), which will be mirrored by increasing respiratory symptoms of hypoventilation and decreasing pulmonary function values. As the diaphragm continues to weaken, affected patients will develop an increase in their blood carbon dioxide (CO_2) level and a decrease in blood oxygen (O_2) level. Fortunately, hypoventilation in ALS can usually be corrected for a time with the use of respiratory support equipment such as noninvasive ventilation (e.g., BiPAP). To better understand air exchange in the lungs, review the following website:

www.khanacademy.org/science/health-and-medicine/human-anatomy-and-physiology/lung-introduction/v/the-lungs-and-pulmonary-system

https://www.alshopefoundation.org/understanding-als/respiratory-management.php

Symptoms of Hypoventilation
The symptoms of hypoventilation may include any or all of the following symptoms:
- Shortness of breath when lying down and difficulty in getting a good night's sleep due to symptoms related to hypoventilation
- Shortness of breath during exertion and eventually at rest
- Daytime sleepiness
- Excessive yawning
- Frequent coughing episodes
- Ineffective cough and sneeze
- Decreased voice volume and difficulty talking due to shortness of breath.

- Persistent fatigue
- Diminished cognition
- Mental torpor
- Irritability
- Difficulty concentrating
- Loss of weight
- Symptoms of respiratory failure (agitation, confusion, rapid shallow breathing, racing pulse, gasping for breath ("air hunger"), etc.

Noninvasive Ventilation (NIV)

Noninvasive ventilation is usually the easiest and best initial option for the management of hypoventilation for most ALS patients suffering diaphragmatic weakness, and it is often successfully carried out with the use of a bi-level positive air pressure machine (e.g., BiPAP machine).

When one takes in a breath (inspires) while on NIV, the BiPAP machine senses your inspiratory effort and immediately delivers a volume of air under pressure to your nostrils and/or mouth by way of a mask or mouthpiece. When air under pressure arrives at your mask, it will travel down your trachea and bronchi to inflate your lungs, providing you with the volume of air needed for inspiration. At the end of each inspiration, the machine's air pressure precipitously drops, allowing you to exhale without much airway resistance. However, some pressure will be maintained in the airway in order to prevent it from collapsing during expiration. This cycle is repeated about a dozen or more times each minute in order to provide adequate lung air exchange (ventilation).

Some ALS patients may delay beginning BiPAP even though their physician recommended it simply because they find it uncomfortable, or perhaps they are in a state of denial. Such an approach is likely to have a negative impact on one's quality of life as well as one's survival time.

Studies over the past few decades have consistently revealed slower rates of decline of pulmonary function values and longer survival times in those ALS patients who begin treatment with NIV earlier in their course when their pulmonary functions decline. It appears wise to start on NIV when or before your pulmonary function values (e.g., FVC) fall to around 50 or 60 percent of predicted. NIV will not only relieve the symptoms of hypoventilation but could also benefit affected patients by resting their fatigued respiratory muscles and reduce excessive calorie burning by fatigued respiratory muscles (e.g., work of breathing). In addition, NIV may also slow the loss of pulmonary compliance, resulting in lung stiffness, which will make the lungs harder to inflate. Loss of lung compliance will increase the risk of atelectasis (collapse of parts of the lung), which could hasten the onset of respiratory failure in a hypoventilating ALS patient.

Noninvasive ventilation is often started to treat the nocturnal symptoms of hypoventilation (e.g., disturbed sleep, morning headaches, etc.). As your diaphragm continues to weaken, you may also benefit from the use of noninvasive ventilation during the day.

Many of the ALS patients that develop hypoventilation can be successfully maintained on NIV for years, just as I have. However, NIV is likely to eventually fail as one's lungs become stiffer or should other pathology develop (pneumonia, atelectasis, etc). Under such a circumstance, adequate ventilation may require that inspiratory volume be delivered at higher pressure to permit adequate ventilation. When NIV is no longer able to meet a patient's ventilation needs, then tracheostomy ventilation (TV) may be able to provide adequate ventilation because TV can inflate lungs at higher pressures than NIV, and its interface (the tracheostomy tube) is more secure and less likely to leak at a higher pressures, than would a mask.

Although respiratory support may slow the deterioration of pulmonary function and improve breathing, it will have no affect on the progressive death of motor neurons in ALS.

Interface for NIV

Perhaps the most common and annoying problem associated with the use of NIV (e.g., BiPAP) is finding a mask that is both comfortable and one that fits securely enough to prevent excessive air leaks. Part of the problem is that each of us has a different facial anatomy, and that masks are manufactured in a limited number of standard sizes and configurations. Although there are over a hundred different masks and nasal pillows available, it often takes time and effort to find one that is right for you. Fortunately, many patients will find an acceptable mask through a process of trial and error. Although custom-made masks are not yet available, I expect that the technology that exists today will be able to make custom masks available via 3-D printing in the near future (see www.metamason.com).

A pulmonary physician or respiratory therapist can evaluate your face and recommend a mask that is most likely to fit you. You may also need to make some modifications to your mask and/or find a way to protect your skin (e.g., Band-Aid, moleskin), should the mask cause significant discomfort due to pressure on your face.

When I started to use NIV, I began treatment with a full-face mask at night. Although it did alleviate nocturnal symptoms of shortness of breath, I found that it pressed so firmly on the bridge of my nose and that it caused skin irritation and pain. A friend helped modify my mask, and I began using Band-Aids or moleskin to cover pressure areas. After a while, I switched to a nasal mask, which I found to be far more comfortable than the full-face mask. I also needed to add humidification at night to prevent my nasal passages from drying out to the point that it would awaken me. A free standing Fisher Paykel humidifier proved perfect for the job.

You will need to clean your mask, hose, and humidifier regularly or risk creating a source of infection. I found it best to alternate between different interfaces regularly to avoid skin irritation. For example, each day I alternate between a nasal mask and a mouthpiece (see the discussion on mouthpiece ventilation below). I also use a different nasal mask at night. As your need for NIV increases, alternating interfaces a few times a day may prevent pressure points and irritation due to prolonged pressure caused by the use of a single mask.

Mouthpiece ventilation (MVP) uses a plastic mouthpiece as an interface, which offers a number of advantages over a mask or nasal pillows. With MPV, a BiPAP machine or ventilator's hose is connected to an L-shaped plastic mouthpiece, which is held in place in one's mouth and sealed against leaks with your lips. The mouthpiece is usually held in one's hand; however, a wheelchair support can also be used to hold the mouthpiece.

Note that *true MPV* is a mode found only on a ventilator (e.g., Trilogy), which is able to generate high enough pressures needed for breath stacking (described below). Nevertheless, the mouthpiece itself can be used in place of a mask with any BiPAP machine or ventilator. Although a BiPAP machine will allow for the use of a mouthpiece as an interface, it will not offer the benefits of breath stacking or those of a true MPV mode.

The use of NIV through a mouthpiece will not interfere with your ability to shower or eat, nor will it cause skin pressure or irritation. In addition, one size fits all. With the correct ventilator setting, true MPV mode will allow you to raise the volume of your voice, and it may also better ventilate you than a mask or nasal pillows, especially if you use the method of breath stacking regularly (see the MPV section below).

I began to use NIV at bedtime about six years ago when I first experienced shortness of breath while sleeping. During the past few years, I found that I required increasing respiratory support during the day, without which I would quickly become short of breath. I now mostly use true MPV during the day, and it has significantly improved my quality of life. Although it took me a while to get used to it, I have found MPV to be superior to all the other interfaces I have tried; however, MPV can only be used while one is awake.

If you are dependent on respiratory support, it is critical that you develop a backup plan in the event of equipment malfunction or a power outage occurs. Having a second BiPAP machine or ventilator and battery backup could prevent such a respiratory crisis.

The selection of a comfortable interface (e.g., mask) that doesn't leak excessively is central to the successful use of NIV.

Facemasks offer the benefit of covering both one's nose and mouth simultaneously, which can be particularly helpful in preventing air leaks from your mouth during sleep. The problem with using a facemask during the day is that it can interfere with speaking, eating, showering, and wearing glasses. Facemasks can also cause claustrophobia and interfere with your vision.

Nasal masks cover only your nose and will interfere less with speech (other than causing a nasal twang). A nasal mask will make it possible to eat while wearing the mask, increase a user's line of vision, and it may allow for the use of eye glasses. A nasal mask is more comfortable and less socially daunting than a facemask.

Nasal pillows are even less intrusive because they cover only the nostril openings while providing airflow through two short nipple-like tubes that fit into the nostrils. Many patients prefer this interface, as it can be quite comfortable. However, nasal pillows may not work well for an individual with a significant deviated nasal septum, obstruction of the nasal passageway, nasal mucosal irritation, or marked nasal congestion. Facemasks, nasal masks, and nasal pillows may also interfere with the use of voice recognition software. In contrast, mouthpiece ventilation can accommodate voice recognition software dictation fairly well.

Patients with ALS may find that a mask that had previously fit them well no longer fits securely. This may be caused by significant weight loss or atrophy of facial muscles, and in such a case, the interface will need to be upgraded.

Although you will probably begin NIV on a BiPAP machine, it would be advisable to try to get a portable ventilator such as the Trilogy as soon as your insurance will pay for it because it will offer you many more options than a BiPAP machine. For example, you can better customize modes and settings, including the use of true MPV mode. In addition, should you find that you require tracheostomy ventilation in the future, you will not need to wait weeks to receive a home ventilator—you will already have one.

I have also learned not to eat large meals in the evening since this can have a negative impact on my breathing.

Review the following websites for additional information on respiratory issues in ALS, equipment, and options:

http://www.alsa.org/als-care/resources/publications-videos/videos/living-with-als-ventilation2.html

http://www.cochrane.org/CD004427/NEUROMUSC_non-invasive-ventilation-for-people-with-amyotrophic-lateral-sclerosis-or-motor-neuron-disease

http://www.thelancet.com/journals/laneur/article/PIIS1474-4422(05)70326-4/fulltext?rss=yes

http://www.alsa.org/als-care/resources/publications-videos/factsheets/breathing-difficulties.html

http://www.massgeneral.org/als/patienteducation/earlyrespiratoryissues.aspx

http://www.alsphiladelphia.org/Doent.Doc?id=834

http://www.medscape.com/viewarticle/578915_2

http://alsn.mda.org/article/noninvasive-ventilation-cant-sustain-life-indefinitely-als

http://www.mnda.org.nz/pdf/How-MND-might-affect-your-breathing.pdf (Firefox)

www.youtube.com/watch?v=wUsAZ2QOfV4

www.youtube.com/watch?v=zxujj4_HdEI

www.youtube.com/watch?v=6ib4kPKgleo

www.articles.complexchild.com/april2010/00197.pdf (Firefox)

www.sleepapnoeablog.com/choosing-a-cpap-bipap-masks-for-sleep-apnoea/

http://www.ncbi.nlm.nih.gov/pubmedhealth/PMH0072457/ (Firefox)

http://www.easybreathe.com/blog/cpap-mask-problems-tips-avoid-9-common-problems/

www.cpap.com/cpap-masks.php

www.thecpapshop.com

https://www.fphcare.com/products/categories/humidifiers/

https://www.youtube.com/watch?v=58jWIeg_VIY

https://www.youtube.com/watch?v=GJyyVLC_JMg

Mouthpiece Ventilation (MPV)
The use of MPV seems to be underutilized in managing hypoventilation in ALS. Considering its many benefits, I think that MPV should be routinely offered as an option to those hypoventilating ALS patients who are capable of using it.

Nowadays, whenever I sit down to eat, I use MPV. It allows me far more freedom and convenience than eating with a mask. With MPV, I can easily alternate between eating, breathing, and talking. MPV also does not obstruct my face or line of vision, and engaging in conversation is far more comfortable. When showering, I place the Trilogy ventilator just outside the shower, on a shelf about four feet above the ground to avoid any possible contact with water. The Trilogy's hose and mouthpiece are then passed through a hole in the shower curtain, which allows me to continue to breathe comfortably while showering. Should your nasal passages become obstructed for any reason, a nasal mask or nasal pillows may not be able to function correctly, but MPV can easily overcome nasal obstruction.

To use MPV, you will need enough hand strength to hold the mouthpiece, or you can use a wheelchair support to hold it. You will also need enough oral muscle strength to create a good seal around the mouthpiece. If you suffer from swallowing dysfunction, then MVP might be contraindicated if it increases your risk of aspiration.

Of particular value is MPV's ability to facilitate *breath stacking*. Breath stacking is a method in which an individual takes two or three consecutive inspirations (breaths) without exhaling during those inspirations in order to increase inspiratory volume (vital capacity). Breath stacking begins with an inspiration. At the end of the inspiration, the patient temporarily holds his breath, and then takes a second breath without expiring the first breath, and then may take in a third breath while continuing to hold the first two breaths in order to maximally inflate the lungs. Such a breath-stacking maneuver will temporarily increase one's vital capacity (the total volume of air held in the lungs), which will benefit an ALS patient who is not capable of inhaling deeply enough to cough effectively. The increase in lung volume from breath stacking can be used to generate a far more forceful cough than would otherwise be the case.

It takes a little training and practice to master breath stacking. Once you get the hang of it, you will find it is quite easy to perform. However, this should only be attempted under a physician's supervision until you have been fully vetted.

Breath stacking can improve your ability to cough by increasing the amount of air inhaled into your lungs just prior to a cough. This technique can help an ALS patient with weak inspiration to cough up secretions, which might otherwise have accumulated in the airway; risking the development of atelectasis and/or pneumonia. Breath stacking can also improve air exchange in a hypoventilating patient and might even delay the onset of micro-atelectasis (e.g., collapse of the lung's alveoli), which could decrease lung compliance and worsen hypoventilation.

If lung compliance continues to decrease and lungs become stiffer, a point will be reached at which a bi-level positive pressure machine will no longer be effective. Further, BiPAP at high pressures can cause masks or nasal pillows to leak excessively as well as cause discomfort. In contrast, MPV can be used at relatively high pressure without causing excessive leaks or discomfort, which could be useful should one's lungs become stiffer.

The MPV mode (mouthpiece ventilation) offers a number of advantages over the BiPAP or the AVAPS modes of a BiPAP machine. The unique benefit of MPV in the treatment of hypoventilation in patients with neuromuscular disease has been published.[1]

When I began MPV, I observed that my blood oxygen saturation level rose from 94 or 95 percent to 96 or 97 percent, and I also felt better.

The following websites reviews of the many benefits of mouthpiece ventilation:

www.youtube.com/watch?v=OX4LTaELoPs

www.youtube.com/watch?v=UJjXdJpLJiw

---

[1] S. Kang, MD, and J. R. Bach, MD, "Maximum Insufflation Capacity," *CHEST*, 118(1) (2000): 61–65.

http://apps.elsevier.es/watermark/ctl_servlet?_f=10&pident_
articulo=90334211&pident_usuario=0&pcontactid=&pident_rev
ista=420&ty=41&accion=L&origen=zonadelectura&web=www.
elsevier.es&lan=en&fichero=420v20n04a90334211pdf001.pdf
(Firefox)

http://europepmc.org/abstract/med/24841239

www.youtube.com/watch?v=6ib4kPKgleo

http://casereports.bmj.com/content/2015/bcr-2015-209716.
abstract

Diaphragmatic Pacing (DP)

Diaphragmatic pacing (DP) is a newer and unique method of invasive respiratory support for managing hypoventilation of neurogenic origin, as would be the case with ALS. Those who have trouble tolerating noninvasive ventilation or just want to avoid the hassle of being tied to a BiPAP machine might consider DP as an alternative.

The DP device is made up of a few components. One is a pulse generator that stimulates electrodes implanted in the patient. The electrodes are attached to phrenic nerves that innervate the patient's diaphragm. When activated, the pulse generator stimulates diaphragmatic muscles to contract at a rate needed to support effective ventilation. The pulse generator is connected to an external device that controls the rate and power of the impulse generated. Both the electrodes and pulse generator are implanted into the patient. A small external controller device is carried on the patient, and it is connected to the implanted pulse generator.

Diaphragmatic pacing was approved for use in ALS in 2011 based on a study that indicated that it was safe and effective. However, a recent study[2] of diaphragmatic pacing involving

---

[2] *Lancet Neurology*, Volume 14, Issue 9, September 2015, Pages 883-892

seventy-four ALS patients at seven centers in England found that patients treated with diaphragmatic pacing did worse than those that received noninvasive ventilation. Specifically, 78 percent of patients in the DP group died during the study while only 51 percent of those on noninvasive ventilation died during the same study period. As a result, the study was discontinued after two years. During the study, ALS patients who had diaphragmatic pacing added to their noninvasive treatment survived an average of 11 months while those receiving noninvasive treatment alone survived an average of 22.5 months. Further, the DP group suffered 162 adverse events while the noninvasive group reported 81 adverse events. These findings are not in agreement with the data used by the FDA for DP approval.

Until these discrepancies are resolved through further investigation, I would be hesitant to consider diaphragmatic pacing as an alternative to NIV in the management of ALS.

http://ac.els-cdn.com/S1474442215001854/1-s2.0-S1474442215001854-main.pdf?_tid=32b23b28-6ec5-11e6-9088-00000aacb35f&acdnat=1472570572_24e355c7a27801f93cb843347ac10184 (Firefox)

http://www.sciencedirect.com/science/article/pii/S1474442215001520

http://www.alzforum.org/news/research-news/second-trial-diaphragm-pacing-als-shuts-down

http://alsworldwide.org/care-and-support/article/neurrx-diaphragm-pacing-system

https://www.youtube.com/watch?v=IInxqRQgVLw

https://www.youtube.com/watch?v=FDBEzup-ciQ

https://www.youtube.com/watch?v=1rYpFyurYng

Tracheostomy Ventilation (TV)
TV is considered to be invasive ventilation (IV) because it requires either intubation with an endotracheal tube or the surgical placement of a tracheostomy tube. View the following website for a demonstration of one method used to perform a tracheostomy:

www.youtube.com/watch?v=d_5eKkwnIRs&list=PLKSERGyYd7p
BB7k_iF8V_tghLSu3p66RU

The decision to begin respiratory support with tracheostomy ventilation is usually based on the fact that you have run out of better options to manage worsening symptoms of hypoventilation or you wish to begin TV to protect your airway from aspiration. Patients with bulbar symptoms might elect to forego NIV and start TV early in order to help prevent recurrent episodes of aspiration, or to stop violent coughing and choking attacks due to swallowing dysfunction. TV might allow an ALS patient to live a life relatively free of the symptoms of hypoventilation for years even though his or her diaphragm is no longer functioning or hardly functioning.

If an ALS patient suddenly enters into a state of respiratory failure, and arrives at the ER, the ER doctor will want to intubate such a patient and start him or her on a ventilator. Once intubated, an endotracheal tube can remain in place for only a relatively short period of time (a few days to a week or so) because of the risk of complications. While intubated, the patient will not be able to speak. Should one's respiratory condition improve to the point that NIV could be resumed then the patient might be extubated and be restarted on NIV.

If a patient can't be weaned off of an endotracheal tube, then TV (tracheostomy ventilation) will be recommended.

Optimizing respiratory support before a crisis develops might prevent an ER visit and the need for emergency intubation. A decision to undergo an elective tracheostomy made well in advance of a crisis could decrease the risk of errors and complications. It will also give you the option of choosing an excellent surgeon and a hospital to perform the procedure.

Starting tracheostomy ventilation on an ALS patient is a big deal since the requirements for caregiver management, nursing support, and resources will be great. Tracheostomy management will require a lot of skilled home caregiver time as well as immediate access to a knowledgeable caregiver or nurse twenty-four seven. For example, one's upper airways will need to be suctioned a number of times each day with a catheter under sterile conditions. The tracheostomy site will also need to be cleaned regularly to prevent infections. The considerable demands made on a caregiver will benefit from scheduling several shifts to share the workload.

TV can prolong an ALS patient's life by months, years or occasionally by decades; however, it will have no affect on the progressive death of motor neurons. All of these issues should be thought through well in advance and discussed with your physician, loved ones, and caregiver(s) before TV is needed.

A great concern for many regarding this decision is the thought of progressing to a state of wide spread paralysis while living in a "locked-in syndrome", a state in which you are just about completely paralyzed with little or no ability to communicate even though you remain fully conscious and alert while being maintained on a ventilator.

Considering this issue, it would be wise to develop a detailed contingency plan as part of your advance directives for discontinuing tracheostomy ventilation support should this be your wish.

It should be noted that you might be able to talk with tracheostomy ventilation, provided that the cuff has been partially deflated to allow air to flow over working vocal cords. Better yet, a valve can be installed in the tracheostomy tube that will allow air to flow over the vocal cords during expiration, which should facilitate speech. A fenestrated tracheostomy tube may also facilitate speech.

A tracheostomy should not painful once the surgical site has healed. Tracheostomy in an ALS patient with bulbar symptoms should also help prevent food, drink, or saliva from reaching an open airway. A tracheostomy will also facilitate suctioning out secretions in the trachea, which could prevent recurrent violent coughing episodes, obstruction of the airway, pneumonia, and/or atelectasis. Of course, the presence of a tracheostomy tube itself is an irritant that is also likely to induce the production of secretions, thus it will require regular suctioning.

Tracheostomy is not without its own potential for complications. For example, a tracheostomy could result in tracheal stenosis, fistulas, damage to the tracheal cartilage (tracheomalacia), infections, the sudden obstruction of the airway due to the accumulation of thick mucus, and/or damage to surrounding tissues. Nevertheless, tracheostomy ventilation could help support a good quality of life in an ALS patient for many years.

If you plan to have an elective tracheostomy, you will need to do a lot of advanced planning. For example, your physician will need to order a home ventilator and suction equipment as well as try to find a way to get a backup ventilator well in advance of its need. It turns out that some types of medical insurance, including Medicare, will pay for two ventilators if they are ordered at the same time and you have a power wheelchair. One ventilator is mounted onto the wheelchair, and the other is kept at the bedside for nocturnal use.

Finally, the expenses related to tracheostomy care should be taken into account. Although most of the equipment and supplies may be covered by insurance, the cost of home caregiver staffing for TV (twenty-four hours a day, seven days a week) can be extremely high, and this is unlikely to be adequately covered by medical insurance in the U.S. The actual direct patient care time for TV homecare is likely to be less than twelve hours a day; however, a competent caregiver will still need to be immediately available for the remaining hours of each twenty-four-hour cycle. This level of caregiver support will continue without cessation throughout holidays, weekends, or caregiver illness. You don't necessarily need to hire a respiratory nurse specialist to manage day-to-day tracheostomy care; however, you will need more than one person who is well trained, competent, highly reliable, and willing to take on this level of responsibility to provide the care you will need. Aside from a spouse or perhaps family members or a close friend who is willing to be trained, you will also want to hire additional caregiver support to provide relief for your primary caregiver.

You should be aware that the cost for a group of hired caregivers trained to provide total 24/7 TV care could cost well in excess of $120,000 a year if you do not have unpaid caregiver support. Alternatively, there are nursing homes that specialize in tracheostomy ventilation that might accept your insurance, but this may not be an acceptable solution for many individuals with regard to their quality of life. You may find following websites helpful in understanding tracheostomy ventilation:

https://www.youtube.com/watch?v=i5CbIJsGRAc

www.youtube.com/watch?v=gk_Qf-JAL84

www.youtube.com/watch?v=vywHHhXAK3c

http://thorax.bmj.com/content/early/2011/06/21/thx.2011.160481.full

www.youtube.com/watch?v=UVuPzhOWxRs

http://thespeakfoundation.com/wp-content/uploads/2015/08/Notes-from-Bach-presentation-at-2015-Speak-Foundation-Conf2.pdf

http://www.telegraph.co.uk/news/science/stephen-hawking/10029218/Stephen-Hawking-Being-on-a-ventilator-has-not-curbed-my-lifestyle.html

http://webmi.alsa.org/site/PageNavigator/MI_8c_videos.html

www.youtube.com/watch?v=UCYBGRj4Teo (Firefox)

www.alsfrombothsides.org/decision.html

http://blog.smw.ch/is-tracheostomy-still-an-option-in-amyotro phic-lateral-sclerosis/

http://www.alsphiladelphia.org/document.doc?id=1981 (Firefox)

Hypoventilation and Respiratory Failure
Respiratory failure in ALS is the result of worsening of air exchange within the lungs (hypoventilation), which due to weakness or paralysis of the diaphragm, pneumonia, atelectasis, or some combination of any of the three. During respiratory failure, blood flowing through the lungs fails to receive enough oxygen (O_2) while carbon dioxide (CO_2) is not adequately removed. In respiratory failure, blood CO_2 levels rise significantly above normal (hypercarbia, >50 mmHg CO2) and blood oxygen levels can fall far below normal (hypoxemia, <60mmHg O2,).

Normally, the lungs fill with oxygen-rich fresh air during inspiration, inflating the lung's tiny air sacs (alveoli) that are found along the end of the smallest bronchioles. Air sacs or alveoli are specialized air-exchange units that are surrounded by tiny blood vessels (capillaries). The alveoli allow the metabolic waste gas carbon dioxide to diffuse out of capillary blood and into the lungs while oxygen in the alveoli diffuses into the capillaries. During this process, oxygen passes through the alveoli and into the bloodstream, where it binds to hemoglobin in red blood cells. During expiration, the CO_2 that has diffused into the lung is expelled as you exhale.

A common complication of hypoventilation in ALS is the occurrence of atelectasis, a term used to describe a process in which part of the airway or lung collapses, which will cause a decrease of air exchange, worsen hypoventilation and could lead to respiratory failure. Atelectasis can result from blockage of the airway (e.g., bronchi, bronchioles) due to the accumulation of secretions or mucus plugs, or it may result from a collapse of airways due to low air pressure within the bronchial tree during expiration. When atelectasis occurs, affected alveoli will cease to function, and the lung's ability to exchange respiratory gases will decrease, perhaps allowing dangerously high levels of CO_2 to accumulate, which can result in respiratory failure. Atelectasis will also cause the lung's compliance to decrease, making the lungs harder to inflate. Moderate elevation of CO_2 levels could cause symptoms of head-aches, confusion, sleepiness, and/or lack of energy. If CO_2 rises to very high levels, it can cause an increase in blood pressure, cardiac arrhythmia or heart failure. A very high level of CO_2 can also result in disorientation, convulsions, coma, cardiac arrest and eventually death. For this reason, an emergency-room physician will want to quickly intubate such a patient and put him or her on a ventilator.

Respiratory failure in ALS can be acute in onset, or it may develop gradually. The sudden onset of respiratory failure might be the result of a potentially reversible process, such as pneu-monia, aspiration, mucous plugs, atelectasis, and so on. Should the underlying problem be resolved (e.g., pneumonia) then a patient could exit from respiratory failure and might be able to return to his or her previous respiratory management (e.g., NIV). On the other hand, if respiratory failure is the result of progressive micro atelectasis or another cause of decreased pul-monary compliance, then long-term tracheostomy ventilation may be required for continued survival.

https://americannursetoday.com/caring-patients-respiratory-failure/ (Firefox)

http://www.alsclinic.pitt.edu/patients/respiratory.php

https://www.nhlbi.nih.gov/health/health-topics/topics/rf/treatment

http://emedicine.medscape.com/article/167981-treatment

https://www.youtube.com/watch?v=UmKx7I0Broo

https://www.alshopefoundation.org/understanding-als/respira
tory-management.php (Firefox)

http://www.actamedicamediterranea.com/medica/2009/med
2009_pag53-55.pdf (Firefox)

Equipment, Modes, Settings, and Safety
If you are dependent on respiratory support, it is of critical
importance that you develop a backup plan in the event of equipment malfunction or loss of power. Maintain your equipment by
following the user manual instructions (read the manual!), and
your equipment is likely to function well for years. Use a bacterial filter between your machine and the hose leading to your
mask or mouthpiece to prevent the inhalation of environmental
bacteria produced by coughing and sneezing guests or family
members. Definitely insert a bacterial filter after your machine
has been serviced or before you begin using a "loaner"—a con-
taminated ventilator could end your life. Finally, have a battery
backup for your equipment in case of power loss. If you have a
ventilator, check its accumulated hours of operation in order to
know when it needs to be recalibrated or rebuilt. Although the
company servicing your equipment should do this automatically,
it's a good idea to check that this has actually been done.

Many of the newer bi-level pressure-assist machines (e.g.,
BiPAP) also have an AVAPS mode (average volume-assured pressure support) that can provide a specific volume of air to be
inhaled with each breath.

Each mode of ventilation has its advantages and disadvan-
tages. In the BiPAP (bi-level positive air pressure) mode, your
physician will prescribe pressure settings targeted to correct your
hypoventilation; a high level is set for inspiration (e.g., 14–20 cm

H2O or more) and a low level (e.g., 4–6 cm H2O) is set for expiration. These initial settings may need to be adjusted for both comfort and efficacy as your pulmonary status changes over time. An alternative approach is to use your machine in the AVAPS mode. In this mode, the bi-level pressure machine automatically adjusts the pressure required to deliver a set volume of air to be inspired with each breath (the tidal volume). A tidal volume (resting inspiratory volume) is selected for optimum ventilation based on your height or ideal weight, and can be further adjusted to meet individual needs. AVAPS offers an advantage over BiPAP since it makes automatic pressure adjustments to maintain a set tidal volume. If lung compliance decreases over time, a machine in the AVAPS mode will increase the inspiratory pressure needed to achieve the tidal volume desired up to the machine's maximum capacity. Theoretically, AVAPS should be advantageous for ALS patients suffering from hypoventilation and decreasing lung compliance, but I have yet to see a published study providing solid evidence that this is in fact the case. Nevertheless, I use the AVAPS mode at night, which I prefer over the BiPAP mode.

Study your BiPAP machine or ventilator's manual to understand its modes of operation and know your settings in order to be sure that everything is operating correctly. You may find the following websites helpful in understanding the topics in the section:

http://emedicine.medscape.com/article/1417959-overview#a1

https://en.wikipedia.org/wiki/Bilevel_positive_airway_pressure#Settings_and_measurements

http://thespeakfoundation.com/wp-content/uploads/2015/08/Notes-from-Bach-presentation-at-2015-Speak-Foundation-Conf2.pdf (Firefox)

www.youtube.com/watch?v=Jms3qM8069Y

www.youtube.com/watch?v=UwDtmYmz3UE

www.youtube.com/watch?v=zTR7cwEAeBA

www.iasrc.org/documents/filelibrary/powerpoints/2013_
conference/Heather_Meehan_1539A33002080.pdf (Firefox)

Cough Assist
A cough assist machine is a device that does exactly what its name
implies. Such a machine is particularly valuable in the management of an individual who suffers from an ineffective cough.
PALS often have difficulty coughing up airway secretions if their
respiratory and abdominal muscles are weak or paralyzed, and
they are unable to take in a deep enough inspiration to fill the
lungs with the amount of air needed to produce an effective
cough. As a result, pulmonary secretions can accumulate in the
respiratory tract. This will become a serious problem should
secretions block airways, induce atelectasis, or cause respiratory
tract infections such as pneumonia.

A cough assist machine (also known an insufflator-exsuf-
flator) works by pumping air (equal to a maximal inhalation)
under relatively high positive pressure into the airway, thus significantly increasing a lung's inspired volume. The cough assist
machine then suddenly reverses its action to produce an equally
great negative air pressure to cause a very rapid exhalation of air
from the lung that is meant to mimic an effective cough. This
rapid and forceful rush of air into and out of the lungs can help
mobilize airway secretion when a cough is weak. A cough assist
machine can change air flow pressures in the trachea and bronchi from +40 cm $H2O$ of inspiratory flow to −40 cm $H2O$ of
expiratory flow or greater in seconds, and in so doing it can help
you cough up secretions. Regular use of cough assist can also
temporarily increase lung inflation and as a result reduce the
risk of atelectasis and perhaps slow down the loss of pulmonary

compliance. For more information and to view a video, check the following websites:

www.youtube.com/watch?v=QHdqcRYIkmU

http://www.alsphiladelphia.org/document.doc?id=1983&frs id=5848 (Firefox)

A Cautionary Note

I have learned that it pays to check on my respiratory equipment each morning and night to be sure that all of the equipment is functioning normally. Check that:

- The settings are correct;
- The humidifier is filled and turned on;
- That filters have been changed and that the interface and hose have been cleaned.
- All hose connections are tight;
- Your mask is adjusted to fit you properly with each use;
- The ventilator's backup batteries are fully charged;
- The AC connection is secure and the machine is receiving electricity
- Your caregiver should also check all of the above.

Bulbar Pattern, Respiratory Symptoms, and Tracheostomy

ALS patients who develop recurrent bulbar symptoms such as coughing, choking, laryngospasm, and/or aspiration may consider elective tracheostomy ventilation in addition to the placement of a feeding tube in an effort to prevent the above symptoms and their complications. An elective tracheostomy might be a good choice in such a case if a feeding tube fails to resolve the above symptoms. More about feeding tubes can be found in a subsequent chapter. Additional information on bulbar symptoms and tracheostomy ventilation may be viewed at the following websites:

www.nature.com/nrneurol/journal/v4/n7/full/ncpneuro08
53.html

www.isno.nl/neuromuscular_info/disorders_and_diagnostics/
disorders/items/progressive_bulbar_palsy/Default.aspx?
Readall=true

http://www.ncbi.nlm.nih.gov/pubmed/22989611 (Firefox)

Oxygen Therapy

Hypoventilation in ALS *cannot* be corrected by the administration of oxygen, since hypoventilation in ALS is caused by insufficient air exchange resulting due weakness or paralysis of the diaphragm and other respiratory muscles and not due to lung pathology. Oxygen administration will not stop the accumulation of CO_2 or the development of respiratory failure in those suffering from hypoventilation. In fact, the administration of oxygen to a hypoventilating ALS patient is likely to suppress his or her respiratory drive (desire to breathe), which could actually cause a hypoventilating patient to decrease their respiratory effort and rapidly enter into a state of respiratory failure. Therefore, oxygen should NOT be administered to hypoventilating ALS patients UNLESS they are receiving some form of controlled ventilation support where one's respiratory drive is not necessary for ventilation (e.g., manual use of an Ambu bag or some form of controlled ventilation). Unlike a BiPAP machine, a ventilator in a controlled mode requires no patient inspiratory effort to function and under this circumstance and therefore respiratory support will not be affected by the administration of oxygen in such a case.

Nevertheless, ALS patients that present with "air hunger" or significant hypoxemia (low blood oxygen) can receive oxygen as long as they are being ventilated in a manner that doesn't require a patient's respiratory drive to trigger his or her source of ventilation.

PALSs receiving supplemental oxygen should also have their CO_2 level checked to be sure that signs of respiratory failure are not being masked by O_2 administration. In this situation, the administration of oxygen could obscure a worsening respiratory status, which could precipitate a sudden worsening of hypoventilation and bring on respiratory failure. Review the following website for more information.

www.alsphiladelphia.org/document.doc?id=835   (Firefox)

http://www.alstdi.org/forum/yaf_postst55122_oxygen-should-never-be-given-to-als-patients-even-in-conjunction-with-trilogy.aspx

http://www.tandfonline.com/doi/full/10.3109/21678421.2016.1172818

Measuring Your Blood Oxygen Saturation Level
PALSs receiving respiratory support should have the ability to measure their blood oxygen saturation level at home in order to objectively monitor their respiratory status. This can be easily carried out with a finger oximeter, which can cost less than fifty dollars. You simply place your finger into a small measuring device (the oximeter), and within two or three minutes, you will have a read out of your pulse rate and blood oxygen saturation level (SaO_2).

Normally, blood oxygen saturation levels will range between 95 and 100 percent. Should an ALS patient who is receiving respiratory support notice a worsening of respiratory symptoms, he or she should be able to quickly check his or her blood oximetry levels. If oximetry levels are falling and your pulse rate is rising, then your state of hypoventilation would appear to be worsening. This would indicate the need to quickly consult with your physician and/or the need to go to the ER. Should oximetry values fall into the low 90s or less and remain there, it would indicate that your respiratory support is definitely not providing adequate ventilation and that your respiratory status needs to be quickly evaluated and corrected because you are at risk for respiratory failure.

If your oxygen level is frequently low, ask your pulmonologist to evaluate your current situation and to also review your BiPAP machine or ventilator settings to be sure that they are optimized. See the following websites for more information on oxygen measurement:

www.youtube.com/watch?v=9PSXruEjBlY

www.nonin.com

http://www.ncbi.nlm.nih.gov/pubmed/15539719

Pulmonary Function Testing
Your ALS center will undoubtedly perform pulmonary function tests on you regularly in order to evaluate any change in your respiratory status. Many patients who are free of respiratory symptoms at the time of their diagnosis will gradually experience a decline in pulmonary function test (PFT) values, and this will predict the future onset of the clinical symptoms of hypoventilation in an ALS patient.

The rate of decline of one's PFT values will have some correlation with survival time; the more rapid the rate of decline, the shorter the survival time. Decline in PFT values in ALS usually reflects a weakening of one's respiratory muscles. A rapid decline in a patient's PFT values is a sign of a significant worsening hypoventilation, and if severe, it could indicate impending respiratory failure.

The pulmonary function tests that are commonly used to evaluate a PALS include the FVC (the forced vital capacity, which is the volume of air that can be maximally expired over a period of six or more second following taking a deep breath). The maximum inspiratory and expiratory pressures (MEP, MIP), which usually mirror respiratory muscle strength. The SNIP test is a very sensitive test for diaphragmatic weakness and is based on nasal inspiratory pressure.

Once a patient's FVC falls below 50 percent of predicted, the odds favor that such a patient is or will soon be experiencing the symptoms of hypoventilation. Starting such a patient on noninvasive ventilation would be a very good idea because it will treat the symptoms of hypoventilation as well as slow down its rate of progression of hypoventilation, rest the diaphragm, and extend survival time. The correlation between respiratory symptoms and PFT values can vary greatly; therefore, PFT test results need to be correlated with clinical symptoms and physical findings for a meaningful interpretation.

A significant decrease in MIP (maximum inspiratory pressure) strongly correlates with diaphragmatic muscle weakness and is typically observed in ALS patients suffering from hypoventilation. Review the following websites for more information:

http://www.ncbi.nlm.nih.gov/pmc/articles/PMC4240929/ (Firefox)

http://jnnp.bmj.com/content/early/2016/03/24/jnnp-2015-312185.full

http://amyandpals.com/interpreting-lung-function-tests/

http://www.shortnessofbreath.it/materiale_cic/781_3_3/6737_lung/article.htm

http://cdn.intechopen.com/pdfs-wm/26551.pdf   (Firefox)

http://web.rwjms.rutgers.edu/nmalsweb/newsletter/respiratory.htm

http://www.ncbi.nlm.nih.gov/pubmed/21745123 (Firefox)

http://www.ncbi.nlm.nih.gov/pubmed/25522696 (Firefox)

http://qjmed.oxfordjournals.org/content/94/9/497

Nocturnal Hypoventilation in ALS

While in deep sleep, all voluntary muscles *except the diaphragm* completely relax as if they were in a state of hibernation. During deep sleep, abdominal organs tend to move upward and press against the diaphragm, making it more difficult to inspire if your diaphragm is weak. This phenomenon occurs when an individual lies down flat, and the abdominal organs are no longer pulled down by gravity as would occur in the erect position. Under normal circumstances, this would not affect ventilation, since a healthy diaphragm is strong enough to fully move downward during inspiration in spite of resistance caused by one's abdominal organs.

However, a sleeping ALS patient's weak diaphragm may lack the strength needed to move downward far enough to achieve a normal inspiration when abdominal organs press against it. Furthermore, during deep sleep, relaxed accessory muscles of respiration will not assist in inspiration. Under such a circumstance, a weak diaphragm will limit one's inspiratory volume, which will result in hypoventilation. Increasing one's respiratory rate might initially compensate for a decrease in inspiratory volume; however, at a certain point, fatigued respiratory muscles will no longer be able to compensate for the loss of normal inspiratory volume, and this will result in worsening hypoventilation.

http://www.atsjournals.org/doi/full/10.1164/ajrccm.161.3.9805008#.V2g85WNpbww

http://www.futuremedicine.com/doi/abs/10.2217/nmt.12.28

http://erj.ersjournals.com/content/19/6/1194

Respiratory Crisis

Individuals with ALS who suffer from hypoventilation should anticipate that one day they might experience a serious decline in air exchange and enter into a state of impending or frank respiratory failure. Such a situation could be brought about by a worsening of hypoventilation due to increasing diaphragm dysfunction, a pulmonary infection (e.g., influenza or bacterial pneumonia), aspiration, obstruction of the trachea or bronchi by thick secretions, atelectasis, a decrease in lung compliance, or by equipment failure.

Monitor your respiratory state at home with an oximeter if you are short of breath. This may help you identify a worsening respiratory state well before you actually enter into a crisis. Should your O_2 saturation level suddenly decline, quickly check whether your equipment is working properly. If your lungs are full of mucus, a cough assist machine or breath stacking could help you cough up obstructing mucus and avert a crisis. If this works, your SaO_2 should improve following treatment. Sometimes nebulization of saline, with or without a bronchodilator, just prior to the use of a cough assist machine can really help bring up bronchial secretions.

In any case, you should have a plan in place to identify and manage the development of a respiratory crisis so that it will be attended to in a timely manner. This would include having a method for transporting you to an emergency room while remaining on respiratory support equipment. Have a cough assist machine at home, and practice its use.

It would also be a good idea to have the antiviral medication *Tamiflu* on hand during the flu season in order to be able to quickly begin treatment if your doctor suspects that you have contracted influenza. Influenza can be a killer in a hypoventilating ALS patient.

If you feel that you are deteriorating rapidly, call 911 for emergency assistance, and get transported to the emergency room. Pneumonia need not be a terminal event in ALS. If the EMT wants to administer oxygen, remind him if *you are on assisted ventilation* that the administration of O_2 alone could suppress your respiratory drive and quickly push you into respiratory failure.

Patients suffering from shortness of breath while receiving respiratory support that is been managed well may benefit from low doses of morphine as a palliative treatment for the disturbing symptoms of hypoxemia.

Call your ALS physician so that he or she has the opportunity to advise you as well as speak to the emergency room physician in advance of your arrival in order to alert him or her of you specific needs.

Should you arrive at the emergency room in respiratory failure, you may have waited too long to call for help, and you might find yourself quickly intubated and placed on a ventilator. In such situations, one might soon be urged to accept tracheostomy ventilation especially if the staff has difficulty in intubating you or weaning you off the ventilator. Part of crisis management in such a situation would include having written advanced directives as well as a HCPOA. To do otherwise could leave you unprepared to make needed decisions, and in such a case, you will run the risk of having decisions that you may not want made for you by the medical staff. Advanced directives should be carried with you into the emergency room.

http://www.mndassociation.org/wp-content/uploads/PX017-MND-in-acute-urgent-and-emergency-care.pdf   (Firefox)

Coughing and Choking
Recurrent attacks of intense coughing and/or choking in ALS are frequently associated with swallowing dysfunction. Swallowing dysfunction may permit saliva, drink, and/or food to be aspirated into the airway. Such events are likely to trigger prolonged bouts of coughing and/or choking. Coughing attacks may result from secretion build up in the airways. Severe episodes of coughing often persist because a patient's cough may be ineffective and

unable to clear the airway. Recurrent coughing attacks are not only likely to lead to exhaustion but could increase a patient's risk of aspirating additional food, drink, or saliva. When mucus containing bacteria and/or viruses is aspirated, it could move deep down into the airways to cause pneumonia. The accumulation of thick mucus could also block airways to cause atelectasis. In this situation, the use of a cough assist machine could help mobilize secretions and mucus, and help cough them up. Breath stacking can also help you expel mucus by assisting in the production of a stronger cough.

The use of a suction machine and catheter might be helpful in the removal of secretions and debris at the back of the throat near the entrance of the airway or via a tracheostomy.

Should you choke while eating, the Heimlich technique could dislodge a chunk of food obstructing the upper airway. If choking is a recurrent problem, then mastering the Heimlich technique by your caregiver(s) and having suction equipment available could be lifesaving. To view the Heimlich technique video, check the following website:

www.youtube.com/watch?v=7CgtIgSyAiU

Coughing and choking can also be due to due to postnasal drip. I have found that sipping water and sucking on a lozenge can soothe the pharynx, and shorten the duration of a coughing episode.

The production of an effective cough begins with a deep inspiration followed by closure of the epiglottis, glottis, and the vocal cords to seal off the airway's entrance. At the moment the upper airway is tightly closed off, the chest wall and abdominal muscles contract forcefully, compressing air in the lungs. As the air pressure in the lungs peak, the epiglottis, glottis, and vocal cords suddenly open, and a burst of compressed air explodes out of the airways and throat. The outward rush of air is meant to produce an effective cough and can reach speeds of one hundred miles an hour, carrying along with it mucus and/or debris present in the airway. At the end of each cough, one rapidly inspires again to refill the lungs with enough air for the next cough, and this cycle will be repeated until the cough reflex subsides.

Drinking lots of water can help loosen up thick, tenacious mucus. Good hydration will enhance the efficacy of oral expectorants such as Guaifenesin (glyceryl guaiacolate). In addition, lying prone on your bed with your upper body hanging over the side of the bed can allow a caregiver to rapidly percuss your back and help mobilize secretions. Alternatively, an inflatable vest attached to a machine that produces high-frequency chest wall vibrations can also help loosen chest mucus and support expectoration.

If you suffer from allergy or sinusitis, get them treated. Just because a PALS has it difficult to manage cough it does not mean that it is related to bulbar symptoms or is a result of airway secretions. For example, recurrent coughing may be due to cough variant asthma, which would benefit from nebulized bronchodilator (albuterol) or other asthma medication; a chronic cough could be due to COPD. Symptoms may be due to a neurogenic cough, which requires a different approach. Therefore, a difficult to manage cough should be carefully evaluated buy a pulmonologist and perhaps an ear nose and throat specialist who can explore the differential diagnosis. Rarely, a PALS with severe bulbar dysfunction who has both a feeding tube and tracheostomy in place and yet continues to suffer repeated aspiration may considered a laryngectomy.

Check out the following websites for additional information:

http://www.ncbi.nlm.nih.gov/pubmed/9730998 (Firefox)

http://www.alsfrombothsides.org/choking.html

http://www.mndassociation.org/forprofessionals/mndmanagement/respiratory-symptoms-in-mnd/cough-management/

http://www.alsa.org/als-care/resources/publications-videos/factsheets/respiratory-challenges.html

http://alsn.mda.org/article/all-choked

http://alsworldwide.org/care-and-support/article/congestion-relief

http://jnnp.bmj.com/content/68/5/601.full

https://www.youtube.com/watch?v=kFyRbLPilyE

http://laryngopedia.com/sensory-neuropathic-cough/

Laryngospasm
Laryngospasm occurs in a minority of PALS, and is characterized by a sudden partial or full closure of the upper airway due to a spasm of the vocal cords and/or the glottis. Laryngospasm often causes stridor (a high-pitched, harsh breathing sound, that is most prominent during inspiration) and/or the inability to speak. When laryngospasm is severe, you may not be able move much air into or out of your airway, cough, speak, or even breathe. Episodes of laryngospasm can be triggered when food, drink, or saliva reach an unprotected open airway, which is not a rare occurrence in ALS should bulbar symptoms be present. Irritants, sinus drainage, gastric reflux, spicy food, alcohol, or even a panic attack can also trigger laryngospasm. Attacks of laryngospasm usually resolve spontaneously, often within minutes. In the worst case, a prolonged episode could cause a short period of loss of consciousness. If attacks occur often, treatment with liquid lorazepam (Ativan, Intensol) administered under the tongue or alprazolam (Niravam orally disintegrating tablets) may relieve symptoms. See the following websites for additional information:

http://archneur.jamanetwork.com/article.aspx?articleid=798356

http://lindseykc.blogspot.com/2013/12/unexplained-choking-laryngospasm-panic.html

http://alsn.mda.org/article/all-choked

https://www.alshopefoundation.org/understanding-als/symptom-directed-therapy.php

https://www.youtube.com/watch?v=7RohF5PAggY

https://www.youtube.com/watch?v=nPtdkqOLLP4

https://www.youtube.com/watch?v=3KV2D5w9hVw

Twenty-Nine

Management of Leg, Foot, Arm, Hand Weakness and Paralysis

Muscle weakness in ALS often begins in the lower extremities, making one susceptible to tripping and falling. As leg muscles grow progressively weaker, you eventually will have trouble walking and begin to fatigue easily. When this occurs, an affected individual will usually find a rollator useful because it offers stability while walking or standing and can reduce fatigue due to overexertion of weak muscles. The distance an ALS patient can walk will decrease over time as weakness advances, until one can no longer walk. This process may occurs slowly over a period of years; however, in the minority of patients, weakness can advance to wide spread paralysis very rapidly over a period of a year or so. When you can no longer walk, a wheelchair or power wheelchair will offer you safety and mobility while preventing fatigue due to exertion. A Hoyer lift can assist a weak patient with safe transfers into and out of a wheelchair, chair, or bed.

A PALS's hands may become weak, and he or she may soon have trouble turning a doorknob, holding a knife and fork, turning the pages of a newspaper, writing, typing, or brushing one's teeth. In such a situation, adaptive devices such as thick-handled eating utensils, armrests, page turners, foot and/or hand orthotics (braces), etc. can help retain function for as long as possible.

Range-of-motion (ROM) exercises and stretching involving all extremities and joints can help maintain flexibility and prevent or moderate contractures.

Adaptive clothing will make it easier to dress and undress.

A mobile arm support may help you type or eat should your arms and/or shoulders become weak.

A foot brace can help control foot drop. Padded booties can prevent heel pain and pressure at night. Should you advance to the late-stage of ALS, most of your voluntary muscles will suffer marked weakness and/or paralysis. At that point, you will become increasingly dependent on a caregiver for your daily needs, and you also likely to require various types of equipment and devices for safety, communication, comfort, function, and mobility at some point.

Going through catalogs at the following websites may help you find the adaptive equipment you seek:

www.pattersonmedical.com

www.rehabmart.com/category/Daily_Living_Aids.htm

www.easierliving.com/all-products/

www.alimed.com

www.assistireland.ie/eng/Products_Directory/Orthoses/Hand_Wrist_Splints_and_Braces/Hand_and_Wrist_Positioning_Splints/

www.assistireland.ie/eng/Products_Directory/

www.alimed.com/alimed/default.aspx

www.ncmedical.com

www.spinlife.com

http://www.alsa.org/als-care/resources/als-insight/articles/
staying-one-step-ahead.html

http://emedicine.medscape.com/article/1170097-clinical

https://books.google.com/books?id=z8nXD17NdeoC&pg=
PA172&lpg=PA172&dq=managing+disability+in+mnd&sour
ce=bl&ots=VB0FyTER68&sig=BLOp1VXQSF-7_jla7-Q8-6lfA
yE&hl=en&sa=X&ved=0ahUKEwi41uzb-7LPAhVDFj4KHZi-
dArUQ6AEISzAF#v=onepage&q=managing%20disability%20
in%20mnd&f=false

http://imnda.ie/wp-content/uploads/2014/09/MND-guide
lines-on-Physiotherapy.pdf

Thirty

Muscle Cramps, Spasticity, and Fasciculation

Muscle Cramps

An early sign of ALS is often the onset of recurrent muscle cramping. Muscle cramps (e.g., calf muscle cramps) can begin years before your diagnosis of ALS is made, and may be severe enough to wake you at night. In ALS, cramping often originates as a spontaneous sustained intense muscle contraction resulting from the loss of a muscle's motor-neuron innervation. Cramping may result from muscle fatigue experienced by weakened muscles during exertion. Cramping can also be brought on or worsened by dehydration. Cramp pain is due to a temporary interruption of a muscle's circulation and local oxygen supply during a prolonged intense muscle contraction. Severe muscle pain will continue until the muscle relaxes and local circulation is restored. Cramping of one's hands may be relieved by manually extending fingers to stretch out cramped muscles. Stretching calf muscles may also help terminate a leg cramps. Adequate hydration may also diminish the frequency of muscle cramps. Moist heat applied to a cramped muscle may also help diminish cramping as will a hot bath. Medical treatment for cramps includes the use of muscle relaxants such as Flexeril or Valium, and recently a cardiac drug (mexiletine) was found to reduce cramping in ALS. Quinine is no longer recommended because of concerns related to its potential cardiac toxicity. Good hydration and avoiding the overexertion of weakened muscles will help prevent cramps. Baclofen (Lioresal) and Neurontin (gabapentin) may also help manage cramps. However, benefits are highly variable, so finding what works for you will depend on trial and error of both medications and dosage. Muscle cramping will diminish and eventually cease as weakness gives way to paralysis and muscle atrophy.

http://www.news-medical.net/news/20160301/Cardiac-drug-combats-muscle-cramps-in-ALS.aspx

http://www.ncbi.nlm.nih.gov/pubmed/26332705   (Firefox)

http://www.ncbi.nlm.nih.gov/pubmedhealth/PMH0041586/ (Firefox)

http://www.ncbi.nlm.nih.gov/pubmed/22513921 (Firefox)

http://alsn.mda.org/news/als-mexiletine-helped-muscle-cramps-did-not-show-other-benefits

Spasticity

Muscle spasticity (muscle stiffness or tightness) in ALS presents as an increase in muscle tone or a prolonged sub maximal muscle contraction resulting from UMN damage or the death of upper motor neurons.

Spasticity can vary from mild muscle stiffness, to resistance to movement, to limb rigidity. It can interfere with the normal smooth contraction of voluntary muscles, which allow for well-controlled body movement(s). This could lead to jerky, clumsy, imprecise or uneven movements. Spasticity is associated with an increase in deep tendon reflexes (hyperreflexia), which can be observed on physical examination. Marked spasticity can also be painful, because prolonged muscle contractions can lead to cramping. Spasticity can affect almost any group of muscles. It may occur for a brief period or persist for quite a while.

Muscle spasticity can affect any voluntary muscle, including those of the legs, arms, hands, neck, jaw, and/or trunk, causing them to stiffen, even to the point of marked rigidity. Treatment includes a trial on any of the following medications: Baclofen, Dantrium, or Zanaflex.

Spasticity that is severe enough to require treatment will only occur in a minority of patients with ALS. Should limb stiffness result in significant pain, impaired mobility, or present great difficulty with patient care (e.g., dressing), then pharmacological treatment would be warranted. One can begin treatment with baclofen (Lioresal), gradually increasing the dose until spasticity lessens or intolerance occurs. Side effect can include weakness and fatigue. Controlled spinal canal infusion of baclofen has been used successfully for difficult to manage spasticity. Other medications that may offer benefit include Zanaflex, Valium, Klonopin, and Ativan. For more information review the following website:

http://www.mndcare.net.au/Living-with-MND/Symptom-management/Movement-and-joints/Spasticity.aspx

http://my.clevelandclinic.org/health/treatments_and_procedures/hic_Intrathecal_Baclofen_Therapy_for_MS

Fasciculation
Fasciculation is observed as a recurrent twitching of a muscle. It usually occurs spontaneously, that is without any obvious trigger. Fasciculation can continue for minutes or go on for hours; however, it is not usually painful. Nevertheless, fasciculation can be annoying especially if it occur during sleep and wake you up.

Thirty-One

Management of Bulbar Dysfunction in ALS

The muscles involved in speech and swallowing are under the control of motor neurons located in the brain stem. If these neurons are damaged or die, the muscles under their control will weaken, become uncoordinated or eventually paralyzed, resulting in various degrees of dysfunction. Bulbar pathology can lead to symptoms of coughing, choking, difficulty while eating and drinking due to swallowing dysfunction, and/or present with difficulty in speech.

More than a dozen muscles, eight in the tongue alone, are involved in coordinating the actions needed for swallowing and speech. Therefore, it is no wonder that damage to the motor neurons that control the nerves innervating these muscles will lead to the symptoms described above. If the airway is not closed off at or before the moment food or liquids are swallowed, they might enter the airway to cause choking, laryngospasm, paroxysms of coughing, aspiration, bronchospasm, or even blockage of the airway. Aspiration of food or liquid into the airway can result in pneumonia, atelectasis, respiratory failure, or even sudden death due to asphyxiation.

Should food or liquid come in contact with the airway, an ineffective cough might not be able to clear the airway of foreign material. Patients affected with bulbar symptoms may also find that they cannot swallow their saliva at a rate that prevents saliva from accumulating in the oral cavity to cause drooling.

Swallowing thin liquids such as water can be particularly difficult for patients with bulbar dysfunction because it can move swiftly to the back of the throat before the epiglottis moves back to close off the airway. Changing the consistency of liquids by adding thickeners can improve swallowing function in such a case. A speech pathologist and/or a dietitian at your ALS center could help you improve eating and drinking when you have bulbar symptoms. When bulbar dysfunction is combined with an ineffective cough, a patient is likely to suffer aspiration and will be at high risk for the development of pneumonia.

Since choking on food can lead to complete obstruction of the airway, your caregiver needs to be prepared for such an emergency by practicing the Heimlich maneuver. By quickly applying a strong upward thrust to the abdomen and diaphragm, the resulting compression could create enough air pressure in the stomach and lungs to force an obstructing chunk of food out of the way.

Thick secretions such as those produced by postnasal drip can also cause choking and gagging in patients with bulbar dysfunction. Drinking lots of water during the day and using expectorants such as glyceryl guaicolate (Guaifenesin) in adequate amounts could help loosen secretions, which could then be more easily coughed up. If you have a nasal allergy, treatment could decrease the production of excess mucus. Decongestants (e.g., Sudafed (pseudoephedrine) can also be helpful in decreasing postnasal drip.

If you have bulbar symptoms, try to cut up your food into small bite sized pieces before chewing in order to reduce the chances of choking. Avoid hard-to-chew foods. Sip a bit of liquid while chewing to moisten your food.

The moment you notice that the food you are swallowing is sticking in your throat, sip some liquid to help it pass into the esophagus. Avoid dry foods or sticky or adherent foods that tend to get stuck in the throat or cause swallowing problems, such as nuts, crackers, pretzels, potato chips, and so on. Stay focused on what and how you are eating, while you are eating, to be sure that food is well chewed and moisturized before attempting to swallow it. Limit the quantity of food you place into your mouth at any one time, and avoid talking and distractions while swallowing if you have a swallowing dysfunction. Drink liquids slowly, and thicken them if need be to slow down their passage to the back of the throat. Attention to detail in this matter can save you a lot of suffering and perhaps prevent a crisis.

Supplement meals with drinks of high caloric content (e.g., Boost Plus) in order to maintain sufficient nutrition and keep weight on, if that is an issue.

If you suffer from symptoms of coughing, gagging, or choking while eating, you *should only eat when your caregiver is present,* one who is competent to perform the Heimlich maneuver. Sit up straight while eating to be sure that it will be easier to swallow correctly.

If you suffer from repeated episodes of aspiration, choking, or severe coughing while eating, this is an indication that you need a feeding tube, also known as a PEG or a RIG (see chapter 32).

The following websites contain additional information related to bulbar dysfunction:

http://www.massgeneral.org/als/patienteducation/speechandswallowingissues_ALS.aspx

www.alscareproject.org/respresearch/RespiratoryComplications.pdf (Firefox)

http://www.nature.com/nrneurol/journal/v4/n7/full/ncpneuro0853.html

www.unm.edu/~atneel/shs531/dys_ALS.pdf (Firefox)

http://www.alsphiladelphia.org/document.doc?id=827
(Firefox)

http://www.nysslha.org/i4a/pages/index.cfm?pageid=3560

http://www.hindawi.com/journals/nri/2011/714693/

http://thorax.bmj.com/content/early/2016/08/12/
thoraxjnl-2016-208919.full

http://www.alzforum.org/news/conference-coverage/
help-speech-swallowing-and-salivation-problems-als

www.youtube.com/watch?v=s6TEaAZJ9Ao

http://www.mndassociation.org/wp-content/uploads/2015/02/
mnd-bulbar-slt-dietitian-05nov14.pdf (Firefox)

Thirty-Two

A Feeding Tube

Management of significant swallowing dysfunction in ALS usually includes the placement of a feeding tube into the stomach. A feeding tube, which is also known as a *percutaneous endoscopic gastrostomy tube, a **PEG** or a radiologically inserted gastrostomy tube, a **RIG***, will facilitate the passage of food and drink directly into the stomach, bypassing the mouth and throat. In this way, a tube feeding can reduce the risk of choking and/or aspiration while providing adequate nutrition. The feeding tube itself is made out of a polymer and is surgically inserted through the abdominal wall and into the stomach. It is fixed in place in the stomach, and the external entrance of the tube is closed off when the tube is not in use.

www.youtube.com/watch?v=YjkZ6mQJ4JU

A RIG, does not involve the use of a gastroscope since is performed by an interventional radiologist.

https://www.youtube.com/watch?v=trZ0p3jrWl4

A dietitian can create a diet consisting of semiliquid food that is nutritionally balanced to provide adequate calories, vitamins, hydration, and even medications. This semiliquid food can then be passed through the feeding tube by either using gravity feed or by pushing it through with the help of a large syringe.

Receiving nutrition via a feeding tube can prevent or even reverse weight loss and malnutrition if started early in the development of symptoms weight loss.

Waiting too long to place a feeding tube can create a number of problems. As ALS advances, the diaphragm can weaken, allowing the stomach to move up beneath the rib cage, which can make the placement of a PEG or RIG much more difficult. In addition, if your FVC % falls below 50% of predicted your risk for complications increases when pacing feeding tube, which should give you good reason to place it sooner rather than later if you have bulbar symptoms or are losing weight. Although feeding tubes have been successfully placed in PALS with FVCs far lower than 30%, however I still think it would be advisable to place the feeding tube by the time one's FVC reaches 50% if you anticipate the need for it in the future because it is an your best interest to lower your risks.

Surgical methods for placement of a feeding tube are available should no other method work. In the event the stomach it has moved into a position that it is no longer possible to perform a gastrostomy feeding tube, then a feeding tube can be connected to a portion of the small intestine to create a jejunostomy feeding tube. However, this procedure carries a higher risk of complication than does a gastrostomy feeding tube.

Delaying placement of a feeding tube and/or waiting until significant weight loss or malnutrition has occurred may lead to an irreversible trend, which is likely to shorten one's survival time.

A nurse or dietitian can teach a patient or caregiver how to use and maintain a feeding tube. Premixed formulas for feeding tubes are available. Alternatively, you can create a diet recommended by your clinic's dietitian and place it into a blender to achieve the proper consistency for administration.

Although the use of a feeding tube should eliminate the bulbar symptoms of choking from food and drink, it will not stop the accumulation of saliva in one's mouth, which could continue to cause the symptoms of choking and/or aspiration. Saliva production can be reduced with the methods mentioned in following section.

If you have the choice the method of placement used for your feeding tube, there is evidence that a RIG may have a higher success rate and lower rate of complications than a PEG, so a RIG so would be my choice if a feeding tube were needed. Nevertheless, the great majority of feeding tubes are successful and without complication. Finally, PALS should be highly selective regarding who performs the procedure and where it is being performed in order to select a physician who has lots of experience with performing the procedure on PALS, along with good results.

The following websites contain additional information:

http://www.alsa.org/als-care/resources/publications-videos/factsheets/feeding-tubes.html

http://www.massgeneral.org/als/patienteducation/feedingtubes.aspx

https://www.ncbi.nlm.nih.gov/pubmed/23286755

www.youtube.com/watch?v=VQJQ7Dx0K48

http://www.als.ca/sites/default/files/files/PEG%2520FactSheet.pdf (irefox)

https://www.youtube.com/watch?v=trZ0p3jrWl4

http://www.miami-als.org/faq/swallow.shtml

https://www.youtube.com/watch?v=aAMHjKg4jN0

http://www.alsphiladelphia.org/doent.doc?id=828

http://alsworldwide.org/care-and-support/article/feeding-tube-decisions

http://onlinelibrary.wiley.com/doi/10.1002/mus.25051/abstract

https://www.ncbi.nlm.nih.gov/pmc/articles/PMC4069302/ (Firefox)

http://mndaust.asn.au/Get-informed/Information-resources/Living_better_for_longer/WEB-MND-Australia-Fact-Sheet-EB8-Considering-gastr.aspx

https://www.researchgate.net/publication/227824988_Application_of_percutaneous_endoscopic_gastrostojejunostomy_in_a_case_of_amyotrophic_lateral_sclerosis_associated_with_the_superior_mesenteric_artery_syndrome

http://emedicine.medscape.com/article/1821257-overview#a4

https://www.ncbi.nlm.nih.gov/pubmed/19922142

Thirty-Three

Drooling

D rooling can be a significant problem for those with bulbar symptoms because affected individuals may not be able to swallow their saliva at a rate sufficient to prevent it from pooling in the mouth. Excess saliva will tend to dribble out of the mouth, causing skin irritation as well as social discomfort. More importantly, excess accumulation of saliva can lead to aspiration, severe coughing episodes and respiratory complications.

Accumulation of saliva can be mechanically removed from the mouth every so often with a suction machine. A hand towel or absorbent paper towel can also help clean up excess secretions. A barrier cream applied periodically to the skin around the mouth may prevent skin irritation and erosion caused by drooling. However, these are often inconvenient or satisfactory solutions. Attempts to slow down the production of saliva can be made with the use of medications that tend to dry the mouth, such as atropine tablets or scopolamine patches.

The use of medications whose side effects include dry mouth, such as antidepressants, can also help decrease the production of saliva. For persistent symptoms, medication such as Robinul may have a greater effect on drying the mouth. Check with your physician regarding side effects and compatibility of these medications with your current medications and medical problems.

Unfortunately, drying medications may also cause the thickening of bronchial secretions and/or the formation of mucus plugs.

Injections of Botox into the salivary glands have been used for the treatment of severe symptoms of drooling when they are unresponsive to the medications.

Finally, localized radiation to the salivary glands has also been used to decrease the production of saliva in particularly recalcitrant cases. It should be noted that excessive reduction of the production of saliva can lead to oral mucosal lesions as well as dental problems associated with a dry mouth.

http://www.alsa.org/als-care/resources/publications-videos/factsheets/saliva.html

http://alsn.mda.org/article/managing-saliva-als

http://emedicine.medscape.com/article/879271-treatment

http://www.mndcare.net.au/Living-with-MND/Symptom-management/Swallowing/Dysphagia/Saliva-management.aspx

Thirty-Four

Nasal Obstruction

What will you do if your nose is blocked and you are dependent on a nasal mask for NIV? Nasal passages may become obstructed due to thick secretions, a cold, or an allergy. Swelling of your nasal mucosal or swollen nasal turbinate's may cause nasal obstruction and postnasal drip. If you are using a full facemask, and your nose is blocked, you can just open your mouth to breathe, bypassing the nasal passageway. However, if you are using a nasal mask or nasal pillows for BiPAP, it will be difficult or impossible to receive air when nasal passages are blocked. If your problem is a result of thick nasal mucus blocking the passage, you could try using a saline nasal spray or saline sinus rinse to loosen and remove secretions. If need be, you can follow this treatment with a nasal decongestant such as Afrin (oxymetazoline) or even a topical nasal steroid (e.g., Flonase (fluticasone) to keep the nasal passageways open. Having these medications always available is a necessity for those dependent on nasal BiPAP. In the event that your nasal passageways continue to be obstructed due to swelling, you might consider the use of an oral decongestant such as pseudoephedrine if it doesn't interfere with your other medical conditions. If your problem is associated with allergies, then you could receive treatment with topical or oral antihistamines, decongestants, mast cell inhibitors, nasal steroids (e.g., Nasocort, Flonase, etc.) and/or receive specific allergy treatment with immunotherapy. If nasal symptoms persist consult an allergist.

The use of BiPAP can cause a sore, dry nose, a dry mouth or a parched throat. The best management of this problem begins with humidification. Your BiPAP machine should come with a humidifier. If it does not, you could add one.

For example, a Fisher & Paykel humidifier can be added to any BiPAP machine or ventilator. In addition, the room in which a BiPAP machine is being used should be maintained at humidity levels of between 30 and 40 percent during dry winter months so that your respiratory mucosa does not dry out as a result of the constant flow of air from your BiPAP machine. Saline gels are also available over-the-counter and can protect the anterior mucus membranes of the nasal passageway.

If you are using nasal BiPAP, and your nose continues to be obstructed, you can always switch to mouthpiece ventilation and continue on noninvasive ventilation at least while you are awake.

Finally, nasal congestion can be associated with a copious postnasal drip, which can lead to episodes of severe coughing, choking and even laryngospasm.

Thirty-Five

Weight Loss

A complication commonly associated with ALS is excessive weight loss and in some cases malnutrition. Malnutrition will cause a decline in your energy level, can result in listlessness, further weaken muscles, and can impair your immune system. Certainly muscle wasting is a direct result of the death of motor neurons and accounts for a portion of one's weight loss in ALS. However, loss of appetite and/or difficulty in eating due to swallowing dysfunction often plays the most significant role in weight loss. In fact, inadequate nutrition is likely to accelerate the loss of muscle mass apart from muscle atrophy due to ALS. In addition, an increase in caloric consumption due to overworked fatigued muscles may also play a role in weight loss. It should be noted that significant weight loss is strong indicator of a shortened survival time in ALS.

Depression and anxiety can also result in loss of appetite and inadequate caloric intake. Progressive difficulty in chewing and swallowing will make it increasingly difficult to receive adequate oral nutrition.

Should weight loss become a problem, a feeding tube can be implanted into the stomach in order to receive needed nutrition when you can't gain weight on your own.

Waiting too long to insert a feeding tube when you are unable to maintain your weight is likely to cause significant damage to your health (e.g., malnutrition, dehydration, constipation, weakened immune system, etc.).

Those suffering from anxiety and depression are likely to benefit from psychotropic medications could help improve one's appetite. A novel approach to improvement of appetite in ALS is the legal use of medical marijuana in any one of its many forms.

Finally, a dietitian can devise a diet with high caloric content. For example, high caloric supplements in the form of drinks such as Boost Plus taken three or more times a day can increase one's caloric intake by a thousand or more calories a day. This approach helped me regain thirty-five pounds of the weight I had lost.

http://alsn.mda.org/news/als-experts-keep-weight

https://bmcneurol.biomedcentral.com/articles/10.1186/1471-2377-13-84

http://web.rwjms.rutgers.edu/nmalsweb/newsletter/weightloss.htm

http://www.alsa.org/assets/pdfs/brochures/nutrition.pdf (Firefox)

http://www.alsa.org/als-care/living-with-als/maintaining-adequate-nutrition-2015.html

http://neurology2.ucsf.edu/brain/als/pdfs/healthy_nutrition_for_als.pdf (Firefox)

https://consumer.healthday.com/cognitive-health-information-26/lou-gehrig-s-disease-als-news-1/early-signs-that-high-calorie-diet-may-help-with-lou-gehrig-s-disease-685308.html

https://www.sheffield.ac.uk/news/nr/weight-management-helps-mnd-survival-1.468878

http://www.mndassociation.org/forprofessionals/mndmanagement/nutrition-and-enteral-feeding/

http://www.alsclinic.pitt.edu/patients/NutritionalIssues.php

Thirty-Six

Falling and ALS

Once diagnosed with ALS, you should expect to experience a falling incident to occur sooner or later, as your lower limbs grow weak. PALS are at great risk for serious injury during a fall because they are often too weak to slow down or soften a fall. Hard falls can result in fractures, torn muscles, dislocations and/or head trauma. This should provide weakened ALS patients a strong incentive to begin using a walker, a rollator, or a wheelchair once lower body muscular weakness becomes apparent.

Some patients will begin using a cane for stability; however, from my point of view, the use of a cane is an inadequate solution as a mobility aide in ALS because you will become progressively weaker and increasingly unstable over time and a cane just won't do. Should weakness increase, a cane's support might unexpectedly prove inadequate for support and lead to fall. While a cane offers a single point of support, a rollator provides three points of support, which include the right and left sets of wheels and the patient's feet, together they form a tripod, which offers greater stability than a cane. In addition, a rollator allows you to use your upper body strength to further strengthen your support. Therefore, a rollator provides a margin of safety far greater than would a cane as well as a greater ease of use than a walker. Considering the stakes involved, it would appear that the use of a rollator should be the first line of defense when one's stability begins to falter whether standing or walking. However, should your hands or arms weaken you may have reason for not using a rollator. When legs further weaken, the next level of protection could be the use of a transporter wheelchair and eventually, you might decide to move onto a power wheelchair for safety, comfort, autonomy, and the conservation of energy.

Individuals who develop foot drop are at particularly great risk for falling. In this situation, your forefoot flops down to make contact with the ground before your heel does and this can cause you to trip forward. Wearing an *ankle-foot orthosis* (a brace or AFO) can keep you from tripping in such a case. This type of foot brace will maintain your foot in a natural position so that your forefoot will not make contact with the ground before your heel does. In this way, it can prevent you from tripping over your toes.

Should weak PALS begin to trip or fall, it is unlikely that they will be able to easily regain their balance because of muscle weakness. As a result, such a patient is likely to fall suddenly and fall hard. This is particularly risky when trying to go down a flight of stairs or when stepping off of a curb. The key to dealing with this risk is anticipation and prevention of accidents.

Recognize your risks, and be willing to ask for and accept assistance when needed. Those that insist on trying to maintain their mobility without assistance or the use of adaptive and/or mobility devices will sooner or later suffer a fall. The only question is how much damage will occur and whether that damage will be repairable.

If you are unsteady and/or have weak lower extremities, it might be a good idea to wear a gait belt and have someone assist you when wand to get up, transfer or walk. A gait belt around your waist will allow a caregiver to hold on to you and support you while walking or transferring. Finally, having a Hoyer lift and practice using it should be part of your plan before you have fallen or realize that you are at risk of falling. Check out the following websites for more information:

www.youtube.com/watch?v=SWvEU8FYMFc

http://alsn.mda.org/article/take-falls-seriously-prevent-further-injuries

http://www.massgeneral.org/als/patienteducation/fallprevention.aspx

https://www.youtube.com/watch?v=w8c1DN_3W_A

http://www.walker-facts.com/How-To-Use-a-Wheeled-Walker.asp

www.youtube.com/watch?v=6YmAyzzKwAY

www.youtube.com/watch?v=rRrdRfs9caQ

www.youtube.com/watch?v=SaGHn0JOpkQ

www.youtube.com/watch?v=4bhfjCCcjyo

Should you fall, your caregiver can help reposition you out of an uncomfortable position with the help of a gait belt. Once comfortable, a lift and sling can be used to lift you up and then lower you into a wheelchair or other safe and comfortable place. During the lift, tell your caregivers if anything is hurting you so that he or she can address the issue quickly. Visit the following websites for more information on this subject:

www.youtube.com/watch?v=p_kOsMPduGY

www.youtube.com/watch?v=-Xun0_yoqew

www.youtube.com/watch?v=O98wKlkRSO8

www.cdss.ca.gov/agedblinddisabled/res/VPTC2/4%20
Care%20for%20the%20Caregiver/How_to_Use_a_Hoyer_Lift.
pdf (Firefox)

http://www.umich-als.org/resources/mobility-and-independence/

Thirty-Seven

Sitting

Under normal circumstances, one does not think much about sitting as being an issue. However, as ALS symptoms advance, you are likely to find yourself sitting for most of your waking hours. Considering this, you will need to come up with a plan that allows you to remain comfortable when sitting for prolonged periods and also find ways to rise from a chair when your leg and core body muscles are weak.

As you weaken, choose to sit in chairs that are relatively elevated or ones that can assist you in rising. Armrests around a chair will allow you to use your upper body strength to assist you in rising. A toilet surround will serve the same purpose. A caregiver can also assist you in rising and arising could also be made be easier with the use of the gait belt.

If you are sitting for many hours each day and have lost muscle mass and subcutaneous tissue from your buttocks, the bones of your pelvis and sacrum can press down on the soft tissues and skin trapped between your bony prominences and the chair's surface, and this is likely to cause you considerable discomfort and risk damaging your skin.

Sitting on a cushion filled with moldable air cells that conform to your anatomy will redistribute the pressure so that you will "float" on a cushion of air, providing comfort as well as skin protection. I recommend the ROHO air cushion for this purpose. They come in various sizes to meet just about every need. I now sit in a wheelchair for more than twelve hours a day, and I suffer no discomfort thanks to the ROHO. The ROHO model I use comes with a device to check the cushion's air pressure (called the "Smart Check"). This alerts me to whether I need to adjust the air pressure in order to maintain the perfect pressure for maximal comfort. Letting the cushions air pressure fall too low will result in bottoming out and lead to discomfort. Attention to these details is really important. For those you can't move, excessive seat or mattress pressure can lead to great discomfort as well as pressure sores. New technology using pressure mapping of your seating or mattress can to help your seating specialist choose the right cushion or mattress for you.

Check the following websites for more information:

www.youtube.com/watch?v=WNQQLQ7l0Wc

www.youtube.com/watch?v=ho2ScIV8AhI

http://www.nrrts.org/directions/DIRECTIONS_2013no6%20CC.pdf (Firefox)

http://www.nrrts.org/directions/DIRECTIONS_2013no6%20CC.pdf

http://seatingmatters.com/motor-neuron-disease-als/

https://www.youtube.com/watch?v=38Jwp2iKsUo

http://www.rehab.research.va.gov/mono/wheelchair/ferguson-pell.pdf

http://www.mobilitycorner.com/wheelchair-cushion-selection.html

https://roho.com/support/how-to/

https://mobilitymgmt.com/articles/2010/07/01/pressure-mapping.aspx?admgarea=features

http://www.rehabpub.com/2016/02/using-pressure-mapping-seating-positioning/

http://www.rehabpub.com/2013/12/pressure-mapping-reveals-the-complete-picture-for-seating-and-positioning-solutions/

Thirty-Eight

Sitting to Standing

A s muscle weakness and paralysis advance, it will become increasingly difficult to get up from a chair, sofa, toilet or to even get out of bed. Therefore, try to sit on higher chairs with armrests. When possible, raise your seat height by placing a cushion on the chair's seat. You can elevate your bed's height by using a thicker mattress or by placing risers or blocks under your bed's legs. A hospital-type bed can be elevated mechanically or with power.

If you find that you spend a lot of time in a chair, and find that it is becoming increasingly difficult to rise, a power recliner that has a built-in riser can replace your chair. Such a chair's a remote control will elevate the chair while tilting the seat forward until you are almost in a standing position. I used such a chair for years until I switched to a power wheelchair. To see such a chair in action, check the following website:

www.youtube.com/watch?v=5J6UtW_Yc_4

With the passage of time, you may become too weak to get out of a chair unassisted. Under this circumstance, a caregiver can help you to rise by using one of the following methods: wear a gait belt around your waist, which will allow your caregiver to grip the belt while pulling you into a standing position. Alternatively, the caregiver can stand in front of you while you are seated, placing one of his or her legs between yours, lean over to grip you and hold of you in a bear hug and then pull you up and forward and up into a standing position. Once you are standing and facing your caregiver, he or she can pivot you into an adjacent chair or wheelchair. The same technique can be used to pull you out of a wheelchair and then lower you onto a bed. Performing either of these methods safely requires strength and skill.

Another transfer technique is the use of a transfer board, which is demonstrated among the websites below.

A sit-to-stand lift can also be used for patient transfers when a patient can partially bear some of his weight while standing. A video of this equipment can be found among the websites below.

When you can no longer safely get up or stand, transfer with a caregiver's assistance, or use a sit-to-stand lift, then it is time to begin using a lift (e.g., a Hoyer lift). Check the following sites for transfer techniques:

www.youtube.com/watch?v=Em0qwlXxuXs

www.youtube.com/watch?v=fXXXUnpM-Ss

http://www.thewright-stuff.com/ways-to-make-transfers-easier-for-als-month/

https://www.youtube.com/watch?v=CtrmDpsY9BY

https://www.youtube.com/watch?v=SDBilvn3ddA

https://www.youtube.com/watch?v=olT9mJmLsR8

https://www.youtube.com/watch?v=I5LQH6I963I

https://www.youtube.com/watch?v=SDBilvn3ddA

https://www.youtube.com/watch?v=59snvMqC5iY

http://medmartonline.com/arjohuntleigh-sara-3000-power-standing-lift?utm_source=google_shopping&gclid=CJ2V5s-MlM4CFYgfhgodji4KAw#

https://www.youtube.com/watch?v=IN-blhbxIhQ

https://www.youtube.com/watch?v=_8vjCmUx8cY

http://www.spinlife.com/critpath/match.cfm?categoryID=229

http://www.alsa.org/als-care/resources/als-insight/articles/nov2014-hoyer.html

https://vimeo.com/45069922

https://www.youtube.com/watch?v=DinUBHOBlWU

Thirty-Nine

Lifts and Transfers

Although a caregiver can assist you in getting up, walking, and transferring, at a certain point, physical assistance alone will not be adequate or safe. When weakness and paralysis have advanced to the point that you have become "dead weight" and difficult to safely maneuver; then both you and your caregiver will be at risk for injury during a transfer.

A solution for this problem is the marvelous invention of the lift (e.g., the Hoyer lift). A lift is either a manual or motorized hydraulic crane that is used to safely lift a patient up for transfer. A lift is controlled by either a hydraulic hand pump or by an electric motor.

A lift raises a disabled person from either a seated position or from a lying (supine) position so that he or she can be safely moved out of or into a chair, toilet, or a bed. A lift can also safely raise a weak or paralyzed person off of the floor for transfer.

A patient lift consists of four or five components. The device has a horseshoe-shaped base (legs) that can be widened to fit around most chairs, and is also low enough to roll under a bed. The hydraulic crane on the lift can move up or down to lift a patient up or lower them for transfer. A cradle or horizontal spreader bar is attached to the head of the crane. Each end of the horizontal bar contains two or three hooks that are used to attach a sling.

A fabric sling is placed beneath or around a person in preparation for the lift. The sling will support a person during the lift process, very much like a hammock. The Hoyer's arm is lowered, and the sling's straps are attached to the Hoyer's spreader bar. As the lift's spreader bar rises, it will pull on the straps of the sling. As tension is applied to the sling, it will envelop the person, lifting and supporting the back, buttocks, and thighs as it elevates an individual. The person is slowly and gently raised into a sitting or horizontal position until the desired height is reached for transfer. This procedure can be used to safely lift a heavy person with little physical effort. Even a small person can transfer a big person with a minimum of physical effort.

There are many manufacturers of lifts. The Hoyer lift is a name commonly used to describe any lift, but it actually is a brand name. Not all lifts are the same; therefore, you will need to be specific in considering your needs. Review the lift's specifications to be sure it meets your exact needs. For example, I only have five inches of clearance beneath my bed, so the height of my lift's front leg has to be less than five inches in order to get under the bed. I also made sure that the lift could be lowered enough so that it could be attached to a sling underneath me should I be lying flat on the floor. The lift also had to be able to elevate me high enough so that the sling could clear the top of my mattress in order to place me in bed. I chose a powered model so that my wife could easily operate it, although it is best that two people operate a lift during the transfers. My lift (Hoyer Advance-E), weighs only sixty-nine pounds, is easy to transport, and even folds up. You may need two or more types of slings, one for transferring and another for toileting and showering. There is even a sling designed for positioning an immobile person in bed.

There are many different types of slings, and you will need to consider which design best meets your needs. Some slings are padded for comfort; others are made of mesh to dry quickly and meant for use in the shower or toilet. A U-shaped universal sling is likely to meet the needs of most whereas a rectangular whole body sling may be best for raising a patient up from the floor or out of bed. Some slings are designed to offer head and neck support. Go online, and study the various designs to familiarize yourself with your options. You should be able too also get good advice regarding these matters from your physical therapist or occupational therapist. Read the lift's manual carefully in order to use it safely and to I had know what to do should it suddenly stop functioning a during lift. Various slings and lifts can be viewed at the following websites:

https://www.phc-online.com/Hoyer_Sling-Instruction_a/147. htm

https://www.youtube.com/watch?v=Aib_EZFaM_I

www.spinlife.com/critpath/match.cfm?categoryID=320

www.spinlife.com/critpath/match.cfm?categoryID=109

www.spinlife.com/critpath/match.cfm?categoryID=110

Until now, I have focused on Hoyer-like lifts because they are commonly used and are mobile. The costs of some lifts are covered by insurance. However, there are also special lift systems that can be mounted onto a ceiling track (an overhead lift), allowing the lift to move in any room with a connected ceiling tract, including the bathroom. This might be a good option if you have very little floor space in which to maneuver a lift on wheels. There are also special-purpose lifts that can be attached to a wall or set up over a bathtub. However, such lifts are expensive and are not commonly covered by medical insurance such as medicare.

When lifting a patient, carefully check that all the sling's loops are attached securely and that there is no damage to the sling's material or loops. Align the sling so that it fits comfortably, that no wrinkles or areas that cause excessive pressure are present, and that the sling has been applied symmetrically. When a sling comes into direct contact with a patient's bare skin, the pressure it exerts during the lift at the point of contact can be painful on occasion. To correct this problem, a soft microfiber towel or better yet, a rubber pads (cut from a yoga mat) can be placed between the sling and the patient's skin at the pressure points, if padding is needed for comfort during a lift.

A Hoyer lift should be acquired sooner rather than later once you have been diagnosed with ALS. The ability to quickly and safely lift a patient who has fallen can greatly contribute to one's sense of security as well as avoiding the need to have someone try to manually lift you by pulling on your extremities and posing a risk of injury to both you and the person being lifted. The use of a lift in such situations may also spare you the need to call 911 and wait for help to arrive while you lie on the floor in pain. A physical or occupational therapist should train you before attempting to use a lift. The following websites demonstrate the use of a lift present some of the options link using a lift and slings:

www.wikihow.com/Use-a-Hoyer-Lift (Firefox)

www.youtube.com/watch?v=fu5sXHaL2fQ

https://www.youtube.com/watch?v=LyAZDXg3QPA&list=PLjts UVM8BgeYAAvVoYzbYidtPNVNz-Xb5

www.youtube.com/watch?v=U_FULpuroas

www.atitesting.com/ati_next_gen/skillsmodules/content/ ambulation/viewing/Transfering-mechanical-lift.html

www.youtube.com/watch?v=O98wKlkRSO8

http://www.thiscaringhome.org/spec_concerns/vid_7_usingahoyerlift.php

https://www.phc-online.com/How_to_use_Hoyer-Lift_a/146.htm

http://www.patientliftsystems.net/hoyer-lifts/

www.spinlife.com/Hoyer-Advance-Patient-Lift-Power-Patient-Lift/spec.cfm?productID=77308##tabSpecs (Firefox)

www.spinlife.com/category.cfm?categoryID=108

www.spinlife.com/Hoyer-Advance-QuickFit-Padded-Sling-Universal-Slings/spec.cfm?productID=86434

https://www.youtube.com/watch?v=iP4byYGfWaU

https://www.youtube.com/watch?v=udiMgef4HhA

Forty

Mobility

O nce you have had the time to absorb and accept the diagnosis of ALS, you will need to prepare for advancing physical limitations.

Start by getting the adaptive and mobility equipment in order to help you retain as much control as possible over your independence, safety, and comfort. If you begin to unnecessarily limit your lifestyle because of unwillingness to use adaptive or mobility equipment, then you will suffer more than need be. Your best alternative is to adapt to your limitations in a way that allows you to pursue your interests, needs, and desires.

Some people might be embarrassed to use a wheelchair in public, as I was the first time I sat in one. However, if you need to use adaptive equipment in order to maintain access and independence, then the benefits clearly outweigh any difficulty or embarrassment. Within a short time, I adjusted to my new situation and I was no longer embarrassed or self-conscious about sitting in a wheelchair or wearing a BiPAP mask in public.

A rollator or a transporter wheelchair can be needed and they can be placed in a car's trunk when you need to travel.

A power wheelchair, on the other hand, is very heavy and requires a wheelchair-accessible van for transport. Once you are in a van, it can take you and your power wheelchair to any place the van can reach, providing you almost unlimited accessibility.

If you live in an urban environment, you may be able to use the services of a wheelchair-accessible taxi. Recently, the car service, Uber, began providing wheelchair-accessible van service in major metropolitan areas. In my area, you can also rent a wheelchair-accessible van for a day, a week, a month, or longer. Your ALS local chapter may be able to provide wheelchair access transportation for doctor's visits.

Most urban and many suburban areas will provide transportation that is wheelchair accessible by way of Para transit. Finally, you may be able to purchase a new or used wheelchair-accessible van. Veterans may be able to get a van through the VA.

PALS with significant disabilities have been able to travel abroad, go on cruises, and so on because accommodations for wheelchairs are commonly available. Check out the following websites for more information:

http://www.alsa.org/als-care/resources/publications-videos/factsheets/mobility-and-als.html

https://mobilitymgmt.com/Articles/2010/05/01/ALS.aspx

http://www.alsa.org/als-care/resources/publications-videos/videos/mobility.html

https://www.youtube.com/watch?v=BtnrFAdCZfE

https://www.youtube.com/watch?v=XSW6yoQ4Q3Y

Forty-One

Wheelchairs

When should you get a power wheelchair? The answer is quite simple: when your mobility is compromised and your QOL has been negatively impacted because you are *not* using a wheelchair. For example, if you are using a rollator, and are still falling, then you need a wheelchair. Should you find that walking with a rollator is limiting your willingness to engage in activities, causing you fatigue, or limiting your mobility and/or preventing attendance at desired events then you definitely need a wheelchair.

When I was diagnosed with ALS, one of my greatest fears was losing my independence. I pictured myself sitting in a wheelchair and being pushed around. At that time, I knew very little about the management of ALS or how to deal with disability. Most of my concepts regarding disability turned out to be incorrect. Nothing could better highlight this issue than the use of a wheelchair. With a power wheelchair, I am free to navigate independently, leave my home, and exit and enter my building unassisted. I am now free to ride around the neighborhood if I choose to do so. I can enter and exit a wheelchair-accessible van, which gives me the ability to go pretty much everywhere. Since most public venues provide wheelchair access, you will have lots of choices and considerable independence if you choose to exercise them. Best of all, I have great mobility within my home and immediate surroundings and I can sit for the whole day in my power wheelchair without discomfort.

Some might feel that using a wheelchair is somehow equivalent to giving up one's independence. Actually, the opposite is true—a wheelchair will allow a disabled person to maintain or even regain much of his or her independence that would have been otherwise lost. Power wheelchairs offer incredible advantages. For example, they can tilt ("tilt in space") to redistribute your body's weight, relieving the constant pressure on your bottom or back. In addition, many power wheelchairs come with accessories such as articulated power leg supports that can elevate your legs comfortably. A power back will allow the chair back to recline into a comfortable position. A power-elevation feature will raise the chair up to a height that is convenient for certain tasks and conversation. A few new models even have a standing mode (e.g., Permobil F5 VS), making it possible for someone with weakness of their lower extremities to be supported in a standing position while maneuvering in the wheelchair. Such a wheelchair will redistribute your weight; eliminate pressure on your back, thighs, and butt; and can improve your ability to work and/or allow for better social interaction and function because you can interact standing rather than seated. In addition, the standing position we reduced risk of developing osteoporosis as a result hope not bearing weight. If it had been available when I was first diagnosed, this would be the type of wheelchair that I would have liked to receive. Check with a wheelchair specialist and your physician as to which model would be right for you.

It is now clear to me that a power wheelchair is an extremely important piece of equipment that will improve the quality of your life during the middle and/or late stages of ALS.

Since ALS is almost always relentless in its progression, muscle wasting will increase over time and reduce muscle mass and subcutaneous tissue, making you more vulnerable to discomfort as well as at risk for the development of pressure sores when sitting most of your waking hours. Fortunately, wheelchair seat technology has advanced to the point is that solutions for this problem are available today (e.g., ROHO dry-flotation system).

A power wheelchair will prevent unnecessary muscle fatigue and the excessive burning of needed calories, since you can move around with very little physical effort.

As you become more disabled, a power wheelchair's function can be extended with the use of various electronic assistive control functions. For example, if you have difficulty operating a wheelchair, a caregiver control module can be attached to the back of the chair and that will allow your caregiver to fully operate your chair. Low effort micro switches and assistive devices to help you function can be added to the wheelchair.

When ordering a power wheelchair, you should order all the accessories that you might need in the future. This would include ordering a ventilator tray that attaches to the wheelchair, allowing you to take your BiPAP machine or ventilator along with you as you move about. Even if you have decided that you are not going to accept tracheostomy ventilation, a ventilator tray can also accommodate a BiPAP machine with batteries so that you can use noninvasive ventilation while in your wheelchair. Adding a ventilated tray could increase length of the wheelchair making it more difficult to maneuver. This problem should be kept in mind when choosing your wheelchair, looking for model that would allow for compact mounting of a ventilator.

A power wheelchair needs to be custom fitted by a professional wheelchair specialist to meet your needs. For example, when I went to order my power wheelchair, a specialist in wheelchair technology at a rehabilitation center first evaluated me. She measured the seating dimensions of my body so that I could comfortably fit into the wheelchair. She also advised me which accessories might be needed and explained how they would be of benefit. In order to select which model, make, and design could best meet my needs I was asked how I planned to use the chair in my daily activities.

When should you order a wheelchair? The best answer is to order it long before you need it. A long lag time (months) is often encountered because of the time needed for insurance approval and fabrication, often several months.

At first, I bought a transporter wheelchair for occasional use. However, at a certain point, it no longer met my needs. Soon thereafter, I was able to borrow a power wheelchair from the MDA/ALS Association's loan closet. I began to go on long "walks" with my family using the power wheelchair. Soon thereafter I was able to order a custom power wheelchair and was happy to find out that Medicare covered this expensive piece of equipment. I had to wait months before it arrived. I can imagine what a mistake it would have been to delay ordering it.

It is important to know what accessories can be ordered for your power chair. I recommend talking to your OT, PT, and wheelchair specialist and then going online to find out what options are available for your future needs so that you can make good choices.

Wheelchairs come in front-wheel-drive, mid-wheel-drive, and rear-wheel-drive models. Which one should you order? Mid-wheel drive has the smallest turning radius, which would be an important feature if you have limited space in which to maneuver. However, it may not perform as well out of door or on irregular surfaces. On the other hand, mid-wheel-drive wheelchairs are very stable on inclines because they have both front and rear casters. My wheelchair is a front-wheel-drive model, which can easily overcome a threshold of an inch or two in height and has great pulling power for getting up ramps. Front-wheel drive can also easily get around tight corners. Stability and ease of control seem to be a rear-wheel-drive model's advantage, but their wider turning radius will make maneuverability in tight spaces more difficult. However, some people find that rear-wheel-drive power wheelchairs are easier to control outdoors.

Power wheelchairs that are approved by insurance companies are usually models that are meant for indoor use. They rarely can be safely navigated on an incline of more than 6°.

Although they can be used out of doors on a firm flat surface such as paved street or a sidewalk, they may be unstable on an irregular surface and put the occupant and the wheelchair at risk for being tipped over. If you wish to use a power wheelchair "off-road", then choose an off-road model, which can be found on the Internet. However, an off road model equipped with all the amenities you desire are rarely covered by insurance. View a demonstration of off-road models that are far less likely to tip over on rough terrain review the websites below.

Check out the following websites for more information regarding choosing a power wheelchair:

http://neurology2.ucsf.edu/brain/als/PDFs/Wheelchair_FAQs.pdf (Firefox)

http://web.alsa.org/site/PageNavigator/wheelchair_reimbursement.html

https://www.youtube.com/watch?v=C82VdIKq4dQ

www.youtube.com/watch?v=NNTfbJ-L02c

www.youtube.com/watch?v=PpGPK6r9vqI

http://www.permobilus.com

http://www.permobilus.com/wheelchairs.php

https://www.youtube.com/watch?v=VhXmD8yHtro

http://quest.mda.org/article/tilt-or-not-tilt-benefits-tilt-space

www.youtube.com/watch?v=qQ9JxXCoZCI

www.youtube.com/watch?v=IAa6oPavuCk

http://www.nrrts.org/directions/DIRECTIONS_2013no6%20 CC.pdf (Firefox)

https://www.youtube.com/watch?v=3zuAoSc1rTU

http://www.goodshepherdrehab.org/sites/goodshep-herdrehab.org/files/documents/POSTURE-SEATING-WHEELCHAIR%20-%20updated.pdf (Firefox)

https://mobilitymgmt.com/articles/2010/07/01/power-chair-drive.aspx?admgarea=features

https://motionspecialties.com/article/choosing-electric-wheelchair-what-consider

http://www.schepens.harvard.edu/images/stories/nire/mobil-ity-training.pdf

http://www.wheelchairnet.org/WCN_ProdServ/Docs/PWTG/PDF/PWTG%20Excerpts.pdf

https://www.youtube.com/watch?v=0HkUWlmjZE4

http://www.offroadtrackchair.com

Forty-Two

Transportation and Traveling with a Wheelchair

Initially, I used a portable transporter wheelchair to get around when walking and the use rollator became too fatiguing. When I needed to travel by car, the transporter wheelchair could be folded and put into the car's trunk. When I arrived at my destination, I just took out the transporter chair and used it with someone's help. You will also find that wheelchairs are often available for use in museums and at other public venues; however, it is best to order one in advance of your visit. Most airlines will provide you with the use of a wheelchair to get around in the airport terminal if you make the request in advance.

Once you begin using a power wheelchair, which weighs a couple of hundred pounds, you will need to use a specialized wheelchair-accessible van if you wish to sit in the power wheelchair during transport.

You can buy or rent a minivan that has been modified to accept a power wheelchair. Around urban centers such as Philadelphia, wheelchair-accessible taxi minivans are available. You can even carry portable wheelchair ramps with you in a van, which might allow for entry to locations whose threshold would otherwise be too high for your power wheelchair to pass over on its own. Renting a wheelchair-accessible van is another possibility in major metropolitan areas. Check the following websites:

http://www.als.ca/sites/default/files/files/Traveling%2520 with%2520ALS.pdf

http://kdsmartchair.com/blogs/news/43644419-accessible-transportation-with-uber-and-lyft-for-wheelchair-users

http://www.powerwheelchairguide.com/traveling-with-your-power-wheel-chair/

http://www.wheelchairtraveling.com/air-travel-with-a-power-wheelchair/

https://www.transit.dot.gov/regulations-and-guidance/civil-rights-ada/questions-and-answers-concerning-wheelchairs-and-bus-and

http://www.accesstravelcenter.com/wctaxi.html

http://www.als-ny.org/index.php?page=for_patients&sub= insurance

http://web.alsa.org/site/PageNavigator/wheelchair_ reimbursement.html

http://alsn.mda.org/article/wheelchair-control-upgrades-keep-you-moving

Forty-Three

Purchasing a Minivan for Your Power Wheelchair

You can buy a minivan that has been modified to accept a power wheelchair. Such a minivan will not require any special driving skill or license other than what you would ordinarily need to drive a car. Minivans are as comfortable to drive as a car.

There are two types of wheelchair-accessible minivans. The rear-entry van is equipped with a rear ramp for entry into the vehicle. The back hatch door opens, and a ramp extends out to the pavement. You simply align yourself with the ramp and drive in. The driver then secures your wheelchair, and off you go. Buckle your wheelchair's seatbelt, and wear a neck brace if your neck muscles are weak and whiplash is a risk. Your wheelchair should be equipped with a headrest.

The other minivan variant is the side-entry van, where the van's sliding side door allows access by a ramp or lift. Check the van's entry height to be sure you can pass while seated in your wheelchair. Some vans have a raised roof and a lowered floor, offering greater headroom for easier entry.

Rear-entry vans benefit power wheelchair users because little maneuvering is required aside from rolling in and rolling out.

Therefore, the agility of the wheelchair and its occupant is not much of an issue with these vans. Side-entry vans require that the power wheelchair to turn while entering the van so that the chair faces forward toward the front of the vehicle. In addition, side-entry vehicles require considerable free available space along the side of the vehicle when parked so that a lift or ramp will not be blocked by another vehicle should one park adjacent to your van.

When a ventilator is added to the back of a power wheelchair, its length will increase and its turning radius will be reduced, which will limit maneuverability within the van. This last issue needs to be taken into consideration when choosing an accessible van. You will also need to measure the height your wheelchair from the floor to the top of your head while seated. You need to know this measurement so will know in advance whether you can easily enter a specific minivan.

If the cost of a new van is not within your budget then a used one may be found at a much lower cost. Alternatively, you may be able to rent a wheelchair-accessible van, use a wheelchair-accessible taxi or use Para transit. Check the following sites for more information:

www.youtube.com/watch?v=emjE4t6yoEA

https://www.braunability.com/help-me-decide-wheelchair-vans/ (Firefox)

https://www.silvercross.com/accessible-vans/6-tips-to-selecting-the-right-wheelchair-van/

http://www.disabled-world.com/disability/transport/private/right-van.php

https://usodep.blogs.govdelivery.com/2014/08/14/choosing-the-right-wheelchair-van-for-your-family/

http://www.mobilityworks.com/wheelchair-lifts/how-to-choose-a-wheelchair-lift.php

http://www.mobilityworks.com/resources/getting-started/wheelchair-vans.php

https://www.classicvans.com/specialty-van-information-center/mobility-and-wheelchair-vans/side-versus-rear-entry.html

Forty-Four

Home Modification

Accessibility to one's home is not something one usually thinks about. However, once you are diagnosed with ALS, you will need to consider this issue. As symptoms advance, you may not be able to climb a flight of stairs, cross a threshold, or even enter your home with a power wheelchair. The year before I was diagnosed with ALS, we lived in a three-story home built in 1912 that would have been impossible to negotiate with a power wheelchair. As luck would have it, we moved to an apartment the year before I was diagnosed with ALS. Although our apartment required some modification to allow me to enter the bathroom with a wheelchair, the modifications needed for accessibility were not great.

You will need wheelchair accessibility to your home and enough space for maneuverability, especially in your bedroom, bathroom, and common rooms. Doorways and hallways will need to be wide enough to allow a power wheelchair to easily pass and turn. Your shower should permit access to a roll-in shower chair, and your toilet should allow access for an over-the-toilet commode wheelchair. Finally, your home should be able to accommodate a Hoyer lift. Clearance beneath your bed should be adequate for use of a lift's legs. Room enough will also be needed to maneuver a mobile Hoyer lift, if not, then consider a ceiling lift.

Home modification often begins with changes to the bathroom to permit accessibility for adaptive equipment and safety for a disabled PALS. It may also require enlarging the space around your toilet to permit a wheelchair commode to roll over the toilet. While you are still able to walk, it would be good idea put up grab bars and/or hand rails wherever your stability is at risk. Ask a physical therapist or occupational therapist to evaluate your home and advise you regarding what modifications would best meet your current and future needs. You should consider all the equipment you will be using in the future and modify your home so that nothing will impede the use of that equipment. For example, should you need to use a Hoyer lift, consider removing rugs in the area of its use so that nothing impedes its operation. I needed to install a ramp that allowed a lift and a wheelchair to enter the bathroom.

A wheelchair will not be able to enter or exit a home even if it has a single step at its entrance and exit without some modification. In some cases, modification may be as simple as placing a portable ramp over the steps to create an incline that will allow the wheelchair to enter. At other times, a long ramp or a mechanical lift will be required to provide wheelchair accessibility.

If you find that the modifications you need to be prohibitively expensive, consider relocating to an apartment or a single-level home that meets your accessibility requirements.

Since getting up and down stairs in a wheelchair is likely to be impossible, you might consider relocating your bedroom and toilet to the first floor of your home, where wheelchair access will be possible. Alternatively, a chairlift may give you access to a higher floor but that not solve the problem of the wheelchair. Installing an elevator that is wheelchair accessible is an option in multilevel homes; however, this may not be economically or structurally feasible for many. You may find the following websites useful:

http://www.als-ny.org/index.php?page=for_patients&sub=accessability

http://www.adaptiveaccess.com/home_changes.php

https://lifecenter.ric.org/index.php?tray=content&cid=2246 (Firefox)

http://www.post-gazette.com/news/health/2012/12/24/Anticipating-limitations-from-ALS-family-begins-renovating-home/stories/201212240218

www.youtube.com/watch?v=BNm2zFZreiI

www.youtube.com/watch?v=Vny70ftdesU

www.youtube.com/watch?v=C_z5vrJDAC0

www.christopherreeve.org/site/c.mtKZKgMWKwG/b.4453201/k.1B08/Caregivers.htm#

www.youtube.com/watch?v=_uKd6yvbZzg

http://www.garaventalift.com/en.html

In summary, the use of adaptive equipment and home modification can greatly improve your quality of life, provide safety, and make life easier for you and your caregiver especially during the late stage of ALS. A problem related to the use of adaptive equipment, at times, may lie not with the equipment or the device but with a person's reluctance to acquire and use the equipment to his or her advantage. Some ALS patients delay the acquisition of necessary equipment or home modification until the day they suddenly find that they are stuck because they have neglected this issue. The point is that you need to prepare for expected ALS-related problems well in advance of their occurrence in order to avoid unnecessary delays, discomfort, limitation, and/or the risk of injury. Finally, if you don't know about home modification or adaptive equipment that would be perfect for your needs, it is unlikely that you will acquire them by the time they are needed. This is why this book can help you because it will give you a heads up regarding what might occur in the future and present you with many options to manage the problems caused by ALS.

Forty-Five

Constipation and ALS

Constipation is a common problem for people with ALS as a result of decreased physical activity, inadequate diet or hydration, and the presence of weakened abdominal muscles. A sedentary person who eats a modest diet with little bulk or fiber is more likely to become constipated than not. Food is mostly digested in the small intestines and rapidly passes to the large intestines in a semiliquid form. When it reaches the large intestines, water is absorbed from the bowel's content and it is rendered semisolid in consistency. However, if the bowel's content remains in the colon for an extended period, too much water will be extracted, leaving a hard stool that may be difficult to pass.

To prevent such a situation, it is best to develop a regular routine for attempting bowel movements in order to avoid prolonged transit time in the colon. Stay as physically active as possible, and try to drink lots of fluids. Add fiber to your diet, and develop the habit of going to the toilet at the same time every day. Take a stool softener if you have hard stools. If you are straining excessively during bowel movements or should bowel movements become infrequent, then you are suffering from constipation.

Constipation is not a minor problem for a disabled ALS patient. Weak abdominal muscles may not be able to generate enough pressure to facilitate defecation, particularly if a stool is hard. Should constipation persist over an extended period, a bowel obstruction could occur. This would constitute a medical emergency that could require digital removal of hardened feces, multiple enemas, or if that proves unsuccessful then surgery may be required to relieve the obstruction. An ALS patient suffering from hypoventilation and muscular weakness will be at increased risk for operative and postoperative complications should bowel surgery be required.

The management of constipation begins with establishing a diet that has adequate bulk, hydration, and fiber necessary to support normal bowel movements. Aside from adequate hydration, the use of suppositories and/or saline enemas can be useful in reestablishing regularity. Eating cereal with lots of fiber and dried fruit such as prunes can help establish regularity. I like Uncle Sam Cereal, to which I add dried fruit.

The daily use of supplemental fiber (e.g., Konsyl, Metamucil, etc.) can also add bulk to the stool and should enhance bowel movement. Stool softeners such as Colace (docusate) will promote the absorption of moisture into a stool to soften it. Glycerin suppositories may also be helpful in stimulating defecation.

Enemas should only be used occasionally for significant difficulty with constipation. Regular use of enemas could lead to dependency and risk loss of efficacy over time.

The frequent use of stimulant laxatives is also associated with dependence and loss of effectiveness with chronic use; therefore, they should be used sparingly. However, use of an osmotic laxative such as Miralax can help regulate bowel movement with a lower risk dependency, especially if used intermittently.

While I was in college, I worked as a waiter in a resort hotel during the summer. Early each morning, geriatric guests would descend en masse to the dining room to drink a glass of hot water and prune juice. When I inquired about this ritual, I was told that it was their magic potion for regular bowel movements.

http://alsn.mda.org/article/regaining-simple-pleasure-regularity

https://www.als.ca/sites/default/files/files/Constipation%2520-%2520English.pdf (Firefox)

https://www.nlm.nih.gov/medlineplus/ency/article/000230.htm

https://www.patientslikeme.com/symptoms/show/2-constipation?condition_id=9

http://www.healthline.com/health/fecal-impaction#Overview1

http://www.alsphiladelphia.org/document.doc?id=1938 (Firefox)

http://www.ncbi.nlm.nih.gov/pmc/articles/PMC3348737/ (Firefox)

http://www.mayoclinic.org/diseases-conditions/constipation/basics/complications/con-20032773

Forty-Six

Infection Prevention

The highly contagious influenza virus is a killer, especially in a weakened ALS patient who suffers from hypoventilation and an ineffective cough. All PALS and their caregivers should receive annual flu immunizations and insist that all members of the household do the same. Receiving a timely pneumonia immunization would be wise and it would also be a good idea to have your pneumococcal antibody titers checked to be sure the immunization was effective. If somebody in your home is ill with respiratory symptoms, they should be told to wear a mask and wash their hands frequently in order to limit the spread of contagion. Make it a habit to check that everyone who comes in contact with you, handles your food, or touches you has first washed his or her hands thoroughly. The use of hand sanitizers can also help prevent the transmission of bacteria and viruses after hand washing. Always use bacterial filters on respiratory equipment since it will lower your risk for pulmonary bacterial infection. Audit the cleaning and maintenance of all of your respiratory equipment including all filters. You can find your equipment's maintenance manuals online if you're unsure of maintenance schedules.

Be vigilant regarding the development of skin lesions and infections, and treat them promptly. Make it a policy to inform all friends and relatives not to visit you when they have a respiratory illness or if they have a potentially contagious condition. In the event that you or a household member develops symptoms of influenza, contact your physician to see if treatment with anti-viral medication (e.g., Tamiflu) should be started. This medication needs to be started within forty-eight hours of symptom onset; therefore, it would be wise to keep a supply of it at home during the flu season.

Prompt management of infections can be lifesaving in ALS. Be alert to the onset of a cough, discolored mucus, fever, and/or chills—each a possible sign of pneumonia.

If identified early and treated quickly, bacterial pneumonia need not be a terminal event in ALS. At the first sign of an infection, contact your physician so that treatment can be administered promptly. You should always have a cough assist machine available at home to help speed the resolution of infected lungs.

Swollen feet are a setup for skin infections. A scratch on skin that is stretched over a swollen foot could allow bacteria to invade and cause cellulitis. Pressure from sitting or lying immobile for long periods could lead to a pressure sore or infection. Therefore, you and your caregiver should examine your skin regularly for any signs of damage or emerging infection. A scratch or cut should be cleaned and quickly treated with a topical antiseptic or topical antibiotic and covered with a Band-Aid or other dressing. Areas of the feet with poor circulation will also have a tendency to become infected by bacteria or fungus. Topical antibiotics or antifungals should be applied appropriately when this occurs.

Another problem seen in disabled individuals is the occurrence of urinary tract infections. Symptoms usually include a sense of burning during urination, difficulty urinating, frequent urination, and unexplained symptoms of fever and/or chills. Should this occur, quickly ask your physician for a urine analysis in order to make a correct diagnosis, and begin antibiotics before the situation gets out of control and puts you in the hospital. View the websites below for more information:

http://alsworldwide.org/care-and-support/article/avoiding-pneumonia

http://alsn.mda.org/article/protection-and-prevention-are-keys-comfortable-skin

http://www.ncbi.nlm.nih.gov/pubmed/17453635 (Firefox)

http://www.ncbi.nlm.nih.gov/pubmed/21506896 (Firefox)

http://www.healthline.com/health/aspiration-pneumonia#Overview1

https://jamilzogheib.wordpress.com/2016/07/01/how-to-prevent-pneumonia-in-als-patients/

http://web.alsa.org/site/PageServer?pagename=ALSA_Ask_January2012

http://alsworldwide.org/care-and-support/article/avoiding-pneumonia

http://www.alsa.org/als-care/resources/publications-videos/factsheets/flu.html

Forty-Seven

Management of Discomfort

Although the death of motor neurons and their nerves do not directly cause pain or discomfort, patients with ALS are susceptible to pain and discomfort related to muscle cramps, muscle contractures, pressure on body parts, coughing paroxysms, headaches, trauma from falls, sprains, or malpositioning, and so on. Malpositioning of a body part of a paralyzed patient could cause pain to joints, muscles, tendons, or skin. Muscles and tendons can be stretched or torn if pulled upon, and joints can easily be hyperextended or dislocated in an individual when muscle support is weak and if muscle atrophy, contractures or join adhesion are present.

Capsulitis (frozen joints, joint adhesions) are likely to occur as a result of immobility. Contractures may develop in unused or underused muscles and lead to limited of range of motion of one's joints. An attempt to move an extremity or rotate a joint beyond its limited range of travel is likely to cause pain.

Shortness of breath due to weakness and/or paralysis of respiratory muscles can also lead to great distress due to shortness of breath and complications related to hypoventilation. Individuals with bulbar symptoms are at risk for suffering repeated episodes of violent choking or coughing as a result of aspiration. Even lying down in bed at night can cause pain as a result of your body's weight compressing skin and subcutaneous tissue if you are not able to move or turn to relieve the pressure. Such a circumstance could lead to great discomfort or the development of a pressure sore. Bedsores may be prevented under such circumstances by the use of specially designed pressure-relieving mattresses as well as frequent repositioning (see chapter on mattresses). However it is interesting to note that bedsores are not common in ALS.

ROHO cushions can allow a severely disabled person to sit all day in comfort if the cushion's air pressure has been properly adjusted.

At a certain point, I found that I would awake within an hour of falling asleep because of a sharp pain in my heels. Apparently my heel tissue was being compressed between the mattress and the weight of my foot and leg as I lay on my bed. As it turns out, this is a common problem for immobile patients. The solution was to put on specially designed pad-ded boot, which prevented my heel from coming in contact with the bed,. This approach completely eliminated the prob-lem. In this case, I discovered boots designed for this specific problem while reviewing online disability supply catalogs. The information needed was not found by accident but by search-ing for it—reading widely, researching issues on the Internet and systematically pursuing solutions. After looking through a number of catalogs, I finally found the exact boots I needed, and since then they have prevented heel compression and also have prevented plantar contracture while sleeping. View the website below for more information:

http://www.braceshop.com/braces-and-supports/foot-braces/ heel-achilles-braces.htm

Check the following websites for more info:

www.spinlife.com/ROHO-Shower/Commode-Specialty- Cushion/spec.cfm?productID=252

https://www.als.ca/sites/default/files/files/10%2520Facts%25
20about%2520Pain%2520and%2520ALS.pdf   (Firefox)

http://alsn.mda.org/article/pain-als-what-research-shows

http://seekingalsanswers.com/range-of-motion-therapy/

http://www.ncbi.nlm.nih.gov/pmc/articles/PMC2117693/
(Firefox)

http://www.hindawi.com/journals/nri/2011/403808/

Forty-Eight

Dental Care

A LS does not directly affect one's teeth or gums. However, weak hands and/or bulbar symptoms can interfere with dental hygiene if it prevents you from brushing your teeth and flossing. Weakness and paralysis may also make it difficult or impossible to sit in a dental chair at a certain point in order to receive dental treatment. Since you know that ALS is a progressive disease, you should make it a point to receive all the dental care you need as soon as you are diagnosed with ALS, while getting into a dental chair is not yet a problem.

Neglected dental care may lead to painful dental and gum disease. Bacteria from dental and gum disease can cause a loss of teeth and could also be a source for the aspiration of bacteria.

If you live in an urban environment, you may be able to find a dentist who specializes in treating patients with disabilities who will be able to accommodate you. In addition, a dental hygienist may be able to come to your home as part of a dental maintenance program.

My daily routine consists of thoroughly brushing my teeth with an electric toothbrush and flossing each morning and after meals. Flossing or use of a WaterPik regularly has worked well. So far, this has prevented any dental problems over the years of my illness. A dental hygienist now comes to my home for a cleaning. Recently, as my hands have become weaker and my caregiver now assists me with brushing and flossing so that they are carried out properly. See the following websites for more information about this subject:

www.alsa.org/als-care/resources/publications-videos/factsheets/fyi-oral-care.html

www.youtube.com/watch?v=FuhZ4CFLixU

www.youtube.com/watch?v=ztMcZ1fK1ig#t=450.149579369

http://www.dentaleconomics.com/content/dam/de/print-articles/Volume%20104/Issue%206/1406cei_Parson_RDHpdf.pdf (Firefox)

http://alsn.mda.org/article/keeping-it-clean-toothbrushing-tips

Forty-Nine

General Medical Care

It is important to have your primary-care physician perform regular medical checkups, immunizations, screenings and manage chronic medical problems that are not related to ALS. Chronic conditions such as diabetes, hypertension, heart disease, and so on require regular follow-up. Underlying problems such as hypertension, if not properly managed, could lead to a stroke or a heart attack. Poorly managed diabetes could lead to leg ulcers, heart disease, infections, coma, and damage to your kidneys and/or brain. Just because you have ALS and a good neurologist does not preclude the need for having a good internist or general physician.

If you are in the late stage of ALS, then you will be at risk for medical problems associated with decreased mobility. For example, the development of blood clots secondary to deep vein thrombosis (DVT) are not a rare occurrence in an immobile patient. If you have symptoms of pain, swelling, or persistent tenderness in your calf muscle, then you need to be quickly evaluated for deep vein thrombosis. Should a blood clot break off and make its way to your lungs, you will suffer a pulmonary embolism and be at risk for sudden death.

If you are found to be at risk for deep vein thrombosis, your primary-care physician will probably recommend the use of a blood thinner. The use of pressure hose (TED stockings) and range-of-motion exercises and massage involving your lower extremities can also lower the risk of developing deep vein thrombosis. The important thing is to prevent blood clots from forming and alert your doctor the moment you notice any pain or swelling in your calf.

Keep your ALS doctor and other physicians informed about all of your medications, diagnoses, and study results. When in doubt about what to do, call someone on your ALS team or your general physician for advice. Finally your GP or internist can be your backup in the event of an emergency, so find a good one who has hospital privileges and a decent hospital.

Finally, if you have a medical problem that needs attention (e.g. Sinus disease or medical problem that requires surgery) take care of it as soon as possible while you can still tolerate treatment and or surgery and avoid the increased risks.

http://www.ncbi.nlm.nih.gov/pubmed/24727309 (Firefox)

Fifty

Exercise and ALS

During the early stage of ALS, exercise will be particularly beneficial because it can help maintain the strength and health of unaffected muscles and prevent their premature deterioration due to muscle disuse. With regard to this matter, the goal for individuals with ALS is not to try to build muscle mass but rather to maintain muscle health and function for as long as possible.

In the early stage, muscle strength is often adequate to permit moderate exercise in a safe manner. When functioning muscles are not used, they tend to weaken, lose bulk, and to some extent begin to atrophy independent of one's ALS.

However, over-exercising weakened muscles to the point that you feel "muscle burn", cramping, or muscle fatigue could risk further damaging affected muscles.

Therefore, exercising with ALS requires a balance between appropriately working unaffected muscles while not overexerting weakened muscles to the point that they become fatigued.

Mild to moderate exercise will also benefit your cardiovascular system. Further, regular exercise can have a positive effect on your psychological state.

Active range-of-motion exercises, stretching, isometrics, swimming, using exercise machines, and riding a stationary bike are usually safe forms of exercises. Moderate or limited exercise every day or every other day can be beneficial if it is followed by a period of rest. This will allow muscles to avoid undue fatigue by giving them time to recuperate. Try to continue to walk for as long as you can in a way that does not increase your risk of falling. Vigorous exercise such as weight lifting cannot stop the process that is killing your motor neurons, nor can it reverse the damage already caused by ALS. The real benefit of exercise will come from preserving functioning muscle and joint health as well as reaping the benefits of cardiac exercise. Review your exercise program with your ALS team so that together you can decide on what exercises will be safe as well as beneficial.

In the early stage of ALS, you may be able to exercise for twenty or thirty minutes every day or every other day without becoming exhausted. Swimming is a great exercise, and so is walking, as long as it can be done safely. The use of exercise equipment in the gym can allow you to exercise specific muscles without pushing your limits. This may only be possible during the earlier stages of ALS, so take advantage of the opportunity while it exists.

As ALS symptoms advance, your physical mobility will become increasingly limited. Nevertheless, you can continue to exercise with isometrics or active range-of-motion exercises and stretching. When this is no longer possible, your caregiver or physical therapist can perform passive range-of-motion and stretching exercises. Range-of-motion exercises can delay or limit the development of contractures and loss of joint flexibility; therefore, it should be performed daily when you have mobility issues.

Review the following website for more information:

www.alstdi.org/news/exercise-does-a-body-good-but-what-about-pals/

http://www.alsa.org/als-care/caregivers/caregivers-month/exercise-and-fitness.html

https://www.youtube.com/watch?v=8-2wwzMTyRc

http://www.ncbi.nlm.nih.gov/pubmed/23728653 (Firefox)

http://www.cochrane.org/CD005229/NEUROMUSC_
therapeutic-exercise-for-people-with-amyotrophic-lateral-sclerosis-
or-motor-neuron-disease

http://alsworldwide.org/care-and-support/article/exercise-
helpful-or-harmful-in-als

Fifty-One

Physical Therapy and ALS

Every ALS clinic or center will have a physical therapist (PT) as part of the team. As muscles begin to weaken, a PT can recommend appropriate exercises to help you maintain muscle strength as long as possible. They will teach you stretching and range-of-motion exercises (ROM) in order to maintain function and prevent contractures. A PT can also recommend devices (e.g., orthotics, mobility devices, adaptive devices, etc.) that will allow you to optimize your ROM, function, mobility, safety and comfort.

Physical therapists are also knowledgeable about splints and braces, positioning, lifts, and transfers, which you will need to employ as your physical limitations increase and mobility decreases.

A PT can recommend methods to manage weakness and paralysis. For example, should you be unable to dorsiflexion (upwardly flex) your foot due to foot drop, such a problem could cause you to trip. In this circumstance, your PT could recommend a foot brace (ankle-foot orthotic or AFO) that can manage foot drop by supporting your foot in a level and slightly upwardly flexed position while walking. This device can prevent your foot from flexing downward (plantar flexion) while walking to cause you to trip and fall.

In addition to PT, your ALS center's occupational therapist (OT) might recommend various hand or wrist braces, which can help you to maintain function and proper alignment of your hand and wrist. A brace could allow you to oppose your thumb and fingers in order to better grasp objects when hands weaken. Paraffin baths and stretching exercises for my hands and fingers were recommended by my OT, which definitely helped delay the loss of hand function and the development of contractures.

An ankle-foot brace could also prevent your foot from twisting or misaligning into an uncomfortable position (e.g., inversion or eversion of the foot ankle), as muscles grow weaker. The PT might also recommend various devices that can enhance your mobility, reduce fatigue and prevent falls (e.g., a rollator).

Your physical therapist or occupational therapist can also recommend devices that can help you with everyday tasks, from buttoning your shirt to writing with a penholder or opening a door, when muscle weakness interferes with such tasks.

http://www.massgeneral.org/als/patienteducation/physicaltherapy.aspx

http://www.alsclinic.pitt.edu/patients/pt_ot_therapy.php

http://www.physicaltherapy.com/articles/amyotrophic-lateral-sclerosis-physical-therapy-2943

Fifty-Two

Range-of-Motion
Exercise

A s ALS advances, muscle weakness will evolve into paralysis and loss of mobility. In the early stages of ALS, your physical strength and mobility will be at their best. At this point, you should be able to perform active exercise that includes a full range of motion of your joints.

As muscles atrophy, they can contract, limiting your range of joint movement. Every joint in your body has a normal range of motion (ROM), and the goal of ROM exercise is to preserve that range as much as possible during the progression of muscle weakness and paralysis. In order to maximally maintain range of motion, you will need to attempt to move all of your joints every day through their normal range of movement (travel) or as far as possible without causing significant pain. If this is neglected, the result will be muscle and joint stiffness, contractures, limited range of motion and pain as limbs are moved and contractures overly stretched. Your physical therapist can train you to perform active range-of-motion exercises, which can help maintain muscle tone and joint flexibility. When you no longer have the ability to perform active range-of-motion exercises, your caregiver can be trained to perform passive range-of-motion exercises, which does not require your assistance.

A physical therapist or your caregiver can help maintain joint mobility, prevent contractures, loss of range of movement, prevent pain related to contractures, and in some cases prevent deformity.

ROM exercises are performed slowly and steadily so as not to cause pain or injury. The physical therapist can gently move a joint through resistance that is due to muscle spasticity rather than a contracture. However, if you are in pain, then you should tell your caregiver or physical therapist that you have reached your limit and that they should not flex or extend the joint any farther without reevaluating why you are experiencing pain.

ROM exercises should be performed daily. Repeat each movement ten times followed by a period of rest. Each set of exercise can be repeated depending on need, tolerance, and available time. When a point of resistance is met during a movement, it should be held for ten or twenty seconds. No prolonged discomfort should be felt if ROM is performed correctly. When resistance is encountered because of contraction, then gentle stretching should be attempted—but not to the point that it causes significant pain.

Each exercise should be performed slowly and carefully while the joint is supported with two hands throughout the exercise. The following websites provide more information on passive range-of-motion exercises:

www.youtube.com/watch?v=ouOtMnigomI

www.youtube.com/watch?v=myoazlf9pdc

www.wikihow.com/Perform-Passive-Range-of-Motion

www.youtube.com/watch?v=vHYKR3GWMZk

www.alsworldwide.org/assets/misc/RANGE_OF_MOTION_ EXERCISES_WITH_PHOTOS_copy.pdf   (Firefox)

Fifty-Three

Fatigue

Fatigue is a significant and common symptom in ALS. Fatigue may result from over exertion of weakened muscles, lack of sleep, hypoventilation, malnutrition, depression, or any combination of these. In part, fatigue can be a result of having to make a greater physical effort than normal to perform physical tasks because of muscular weakness. Working weakened muscles will fatigue them more quickly and they may consume more calories than would be the case with healthy muscles. In addition, PALS suffering hypoventilation may require greater caloric consumption due to an increased in work of breathing associated with working weakened respiratory muscles. Hypoventilation can also cause hypoxemia, which will disturb sleep and contribute to fatigue. Increased blood CO_2 levels due to hypoventilation could also make a person feel tired and/or sleepy. Furthermore, not being able to achieve a good night's sleep because of the effects of hypoventilation, loss of REM sleep, and elevated levels of CO2 can soon lead to daytime fatigue and exhaustion.

To counteract fatigue, you will need to learn to conserve your energy by becoming more efficient in performing activities, not overly stressing weak muscles, resting fatigued muscles (e.g. wheelchair), correct hypoventilation with respiratory support equipment, receive adequate nutrition (e.g., placement of a

PEG if it is required), and/or begin treatment if you suffer from anxiety or depression.

Use mobility devices such as a rollator, transporter chair or power wheelchair to save energy. Taking frequent breaks during physical activity will allow muscles to recuperate. Don't take on physical tasks that unnecessarily expend energy if someone else can do them for you. Don't rush, take your time, and gauge your actions so that they are in line with your ability and energy level.

If your pulmonary function studies reveal that your diaphragm is weakening and you suffer hypoventilation, then begin respiratory support as soon as possible.

A caregiver can definitely help lessen your expenditure of energy and increase your ability to function, while reducing fatigue.

Since excessive weight loss or malnutrition can significantly contribute to fatigue, aggressively increase your caloric intake (e.g., Boost Plus) if this is needed. If you are unable to maintain weight on your own, you should consider the use of a feeding tube in order to get the nutrition you need.

If you find that getting out of bed or transferring is exhausting, have your caregiver use a Hoyer lift. In this way you'll save energy as well as lower your risk of falling during the transfer while conserving energy.

Acquire devices that put less physical strain on you and allow you to conserve energy. For example, if you have trouble getting out of a chair, then get an easy chair that elevates you into a standing position. Sit on your rollator when not walking so that you don't waste energy or suffer fatigue muscles by standing. Use a wheelchair for longer outings such as going to a museum.

http://alsn.mda.org/article/fighting-fatigue

www.alsa.org/als-care/resources/publications-videos/factsheets/fyi-fatigue.html

http://www.alsphiladelphia.org/NetCommunity/Document.
Doc?id=818 (Firefox)

http://www.ncbi.nlm.nih.gov/pmc/articles/PMC3944139/
(Firefox)

https://www.patientslikeme.com/symptoms/show/7-
fatigue?condition_id=9

http://web.alsa.org/site/PageServer?pagename=ALSA_Ask_
March

http://www.mndcare.net.au/Living-with-MND/Symptom-
management/Fatigue.aspx

Fifty-Four

Foot Edema

E dema or swelling of feet, commonly occurs in the late stage of ALS when an affected individual can no longer walk and may need to sit in a wheelchair for most of the day.

Foot edema can lead to complications that include pain, discomfort, difficulty in putting on shoes, and will be at risk for skin damage and infection. Since the skin on one's swollen feet will be stretched and the foot that also may suffer poor circulation, it would be rendered more vulnerable to wounds and infection.

While walking, contracting leg muscles normally pumps venous blood back into circulation. Non-contracting leg muscles (due to paralysis) will permit the accumulation of venous blood to pool in leg veins, which will increase local vein pressure. As a result, venous pressure in your lower extremities will build up and force fluid out of the tiny blood capillaries in one's feet and legs into the surrounding tissue, where it will accumulate as foot and/or leg edema.

Treatment of foot edema in ALS begins with elevation of one's feet. To be effective, keep your feet at or above the level of your heart. In addition, wearing pressure hose (a type of elastic sock also known as TEDs or compression stockings) can help prevent accumulation of foot edema. It is best to put on the pressure hose each morning when your legs have been elevated during the night before edema has had a chance to accumulate. The use of diuretics will offer no benefit in this matter unless a PALS's has another cause for foot and leg edema (e.g., congested heart failure)

Having your legs massaged as well as performing range-of-motion exercise involving your feet and legs may be of benefit.

Recalcitrant cases of foot and leg edema in a paralyzed patient might benefit from edema pumps, which are inflatable cuffs that encircle the lower legs and rhythmically inflate and deflate to pump venous blood back into circulation.

Finally, daily inspection of your feet and legs will help detect cuts, sores, and abrasions that can be treated immediately.

http://www.alsfrombothsides.org/swelling.html

http://amyandpals.com/why-all-the-swelling/

www.compressionpoint.com

https://www.amazon.com/s/ref=nb_sb_noss_2?url=search-alias%3Daps&field-keywords=teds

www.parentgiving.com/shop/flowtron-excel-dvt-compression-pump-3695/p/

http://www.alsphiladelphia.org/document.doc?id=1932 (Firefox)

http://www.mayoclinic.org/diseases-conditions/deep-vein-thrombosis/basics/definition/con-20031922

Fifty-Five

Management of Neck Weakness

As limb muscles weaken and paralysis advances, neck muscles may also weaken, to the point that you may begin to have difficulty with maintaining your head in an erect position. Your head may begin to fall forward (head to drop) or fall to one side or the other. One way to deal with this problem is the use of a neck brace or a head support brace, which can help maintain correct alignment of your head.

More than a dozen different types of neck braces are available. When you first notice head position problems due to neck-muscle weakness, you can try to use a soft neck collar for support. I found these to be uncomfortable as well as offering inadequate support. The next level of support to consider is the use of a rigid neck collar or brace, which can be effective but may be quite uncomfortable for prolonged support. The reason that such collars are often uncomfortable is that the weight of your head tends to fall mostly onto the area where your chin and the top of the rigid collar meet.

The neck brace that I found to be somewhat more comfortable turned out to be a relatively inexpensive one called the *Vista collar* (www.aspenmp.com/products/upper-spine/

vista/). It is well padded internally and it is also height adjustable, allowing for some customization of fit. It can be bought on www.amazon.com. Another alternative is the headmaster collar, which I found to be relatively comfortable for limited periods of use. The headmaster collar is less restrictive and quite adjustable. To view the headmaster collar, check the following websites:

http://jnnp.bmj.com/content/74/5/683.full

www.necksolutions.com/headmaster-collar.html

www.allegromedical.com/browse/browseProducts.do?searchPhrase=headmaster

Head control can also be accomplished with a head-control support system that is mounted onto your wheelchair. The device is attached to the back of your power wheelchair, and it can cradle your head in a way that prevents your head from falling forward with the use of an integrated headband. The Savant headrest is one brand that I have used and found to be helpful. However, it limits head movement to a point that I found very annoying whenever I try to move my head. Accessories for this headrest will allow for axial movement (rotation).

Some head-support systems can be seen on the following websites:

www.pattersonmedical.com/app.aspx?cmd=getProduct&key=IF_921117923

http://www.pridemobility.com.au/default/assets/pdf/Brochures/cat_Head_Solutions_Catalog_2015-16(1).pdf (Firefox)

http://www.aspenmp.com/products/upper-spine/vista/

https://www.youtube.com/watch?v=jgxv4L9CZbg

www.youtube.com/watch?v=O-FNgncJBuE

www.necksolutions.com/savant-wheelchair-headrest.html

http://www.alscareproject.org/management/muscle-weakness.pdf   (Firefox)

Perform range-of-motion exercises for the neck in order to prevent neck-muscle contracture. I have also found message therapy to also be helpful. Consult with your ALS center's physical therapist and occupational therapist for advice about the best management options.

Fifty-Six

Skin Care

As you grow weaker, lose weight, develop paralysis, your skin will be at increased risk for damage.

A diminished capacity to move will prevent independent relief of discomfort secondary to pressure on one's skin, which can also be due to body-part misalignment. Such a situation can cause pain as well as skin damage.

When I developed significant weight loss, my subcutaneous tissues thinned a lot. I found that sitting for long periods of time became increasingly uncomfortable. Since ALS does not affect your sensory nerves, you will feel pressure and pain just as anyone else. However, if you can't move to relieve the pressure so you will be at risk for significant discomfort as well as devitalization of tissue due to diminished blood flow to the compressed soft tissues. As skin and soft-tissue circulation becomes compressed for long periods, it can result in the development of a pressure sore or ulcer.

Fortunately, discomfort due to pressure can be prevented with the use of a ROHO-type dry-flotation cushion for seating or the use of a pressure-relieving mattress when in bed. Soft pads, pillows, and foam support can also be used to prevent pressure discomfort on dependent body parts. As a patient's mobility diminishes, a caregiver should regularly reposition the individual to prevent discomfort and the risk of skin breakdown.

The skin of a PALS may become irritated, sheared, stretched, compressed, and/or damaged because one's lack of muscular control and ones inability to move in order to relieve pressure or prevent skin shear. Daily showers or baths can help maintain good skin hygiene and prevent infections. Use of moisturizing lotions can help maintain skin hydration to prevent dryness and cracking. Apply moisturizers such as Eucerin immediately after bathing to help lock in moisture. Pat the skin dry with a soft towel after bathing and keep skin folds and intertriginous areas (where skin folds trap moisture) clean and dry in order to prevent irritation, skin fold maceration, and/or infection. Antihistamines can help control itching, hives and dermatographism (a type of pressure induced hive).

In addition, the loss of subcutaneous fat in ALS will increase the skin's vulnerability to compression damage. Diminished subcutaneous fat might explain pressure sensitivity in ALS.

Apply antifungal cream to skin folds that show any signs of a fungal rash and use topical steroid cream for persistent itchy rashes. Topical antibiotic cream should be used on scratches, abrasions, and cuts. Special Care Cream (Bard) is particularly helpful in treating irritated and damaged skin. A physician should evaluate skin inflammation or infection for evidence of cellulitis.

Clothing should be soft, loose, nonrestrictive, and non-occlusive in order to prevent skin irritation and infections. Silk undergarments may diminish irritation from materials that wrinkle or from irritating materials.

http://alsn.mda.org/article/protection-and-prevention-are-keys-comfortable-skin

http://www.mayoclinic.org/diseases-conditions/bedsores/basics/prevention/con-20030848

http://www.ncbi.nlm.nih.gov/pmc/articles/PMC3694869/ (Firefox)

Fifty-Seven

Prevention of Complications in ALS

Once diagnosed with ALS, it would be wise to begin to put together a comprehensive plan to help prevent or mitigate complications by learning what to expect and putting in place methods for preventing and managing potential complications. Consider each of the following scenarios, and acquire the equipment and knowledge you need to prevent complications and accidents.

Since falling is a very great risk in ALS which is probably universally experience by PALS, it would be a good idea to begin using a rollator or walker the moment you become aware of the presence of lower-body weakness, unsteadiness, or the development of foot drop. For more information on rollators and how to use them visit the following websites:

www.youtube.com/watch?v=w8c1DN_3W_A

www.walker-facts.com/How-To-Use-a-Wheeled-Walker.asp

If you notice the onset of foot drop, prevention of tripping would include the use of an ankle-foot orthotic (AFO). Inspect your home for obstacles such as irregular flooring, carpets, or furniture that might cause you to fall or obstruct your access. Install grab bars and railings where needed. Part of your approach should be to get over any sense of embarrassment about the use of adaptive equipment. Accept that you need to use adaptive and mobility equipment in a timely manner in order to manage your risk.

Always use a lift when transfer creates a potential risk, especially when a PALS needs to be lifted up from the floor. Prevent contractures by the daily performance of range-of-motion exercises. Maintain body parts in alignment as paralysis advances to prevent contractures and discomfort. Acquire the necessary respiratory support equipment and use it as prescribed to manage hypoventilation, prevent respiratory failure and to extend your survival time. The use of pressure-relieving cushions and mattresses as well as regular repositioning could prevent the development of pressure sores and discomfort.

Massage calf muscles and visit your doctor at the first sign of deep vein thrombosis.

Be attentive to the risk of skin shear while being transferred or repositioned. Have your caregiver check your skin following bathing and while dressing in order to identify sites of irritation, inflammation, edema, or the beginning of a pressure sore. Complications associated with ALS include pneumonia, atelectasis, choking, malnutrition, respiratory failure, infections, daytime sleepiness, diminished cognition, foot and hand edema, aspiration, loss of communication ability, muscle contractures, frozen joints, bedsores and other complications resulting from long term immobility.

If you're having trouble maintaining your weight or suffer from significant bulbar dysfunction that risks aspiration then get a feeding tube sooner rather than later.

Acquire and use a cough assist machine when needed. Your caregiver needs to be trained in the Heimlich maneuver. Practice the management of potential emergencies. Be alert to the signs of pneumonia and other serious infections. Contact you physician at the first sign a fever, chills, signs of urinary tract infection, coughing up discolored mucus or should you experience any worsening of respiratory symptoms.

Review the following websites for more information:

http://www.mayoclinic.org/diseases-conditions/amyotrophic-lateral-sclerosis/basics/complications/con-20024397

http://www.alscareproject.org/management/immobility.pdf (Firefox)

www.youtube.com/watch?v=wyicm4dBH8M

www.youtube.com/watch?v=qTVM74sRdhY

www.youtube.com/watch?v=rkBWcIrJnK8

http://emjreviews.com/wp-content/uploads/Sialorrhoea-How-to-Manage-a-Frequent-Complication-of-Motor-Neuron-Disease.pdf (Firefox)

Fifty-Eight

Backup

A s the symptoms of ALS progress, you will become increasingly dependent on various pieces of equipment to maintain function, prevent discomfort, and to enjoy as good a quality of life as is possible. Some of your equipment will require power (e.g., BiPAP, powered Hoyer lift). If you suffer a power outage, your electrical equipment will not work because of a loss of electricity or when batteries cannot be recharged. Loss of heating or air conditioning could be a disaster for a person with limited mobility, especially during freezing winter months or hot summer days. Therefore, you will need to create a backup plan that will ensure access to electricity during a power outage. If that is not possible, then develop an exit strategy in order to temporarily relocate to an area where adequate heating, cooling, and power are available.

To prevent a crisis, consider acquiring a home generator and/or have battery backup for essential equipment. Occasionally a generator will fail to start, but batteries that have been maintained in a charged state will be ready on a moment's notice. Having two or more *heavy-duty deep-cycle marine batteries and an inverter* could provide emergency power for most of your critical equipment for hours, giving you time to either restore your power or to move to a safe location.

Make an inventory of each piece of essential equipment, and develop a plan to prevent or manage a future crisis for each item.

For example, should you lose power, and you are on BiPAP or are ventilator dependent, what is your backup plan? If you have a power wheelchair, and it suddenly ceases to function, what is your plan? Should your Hoyer lift malfunctions, what will you do? And so it goes as you become increasingly dependent on equipment that is needed to maintain your quality of life. If your caregiver becomes ill and can't come to work, what is your backup plan?

In my case, where possible, I have duplicate equipment, including battery backup power, a relocation plan, and a backup for my caregiver. In the event of a long-term power blackout, I plan to relocate until power is restored. This might not be an ideal solution, but it is better than not having planned an alternative.

Creating adequate backup begins with understanding your degree of dependency and vulnerability as well as possible alternatives. Certainly among the issues that require planning will be a plan to manage your financial state as symptoms progress. You will need to learn what your insurance will cover, what qualifications and documentation will be needed. You'll also need to begin budgeting as soon as you are diagnosed so that you will have a realistic financial plan to manage increasing expenses. In particular, the costs of a caregiver will need planning, since this expense is usually not adequately covered by medical insurance unless you have a long-term home health care policy. You are also likely to benefit from the advice of a social worker or an experienced nurse coordinator who might be able to help guide you through the best utilization of available resources.

Keep your ALS physician's telephone number handy in case of an emergency. Prepare a list of the equipment and medications you need to take with you should you need to visit an emergency room (e.g. BiPAP) or should you need to quickly relocate for some reason. Notify your ALS doctor if you need to visit the emergency room before you leave home so that he or she can advise you and also prepare the emergency room physician for your visit.

http://alsn.mda.org/article/do-you-have-backup-power

http://www.mndassociation.org/wp-content/uploads/PX017-MND-in-acute-urgent-and-emergency-care.pdf (Firefox)

http://quest.mda.org/article/going-emergency-room-tips-people-neuromuscular-diseases

http://www.mndassociation.org/forprofessionals/for-acute-urgent-and-emergency-care-staff/

Fifty-Nine

Contractures

As motor neurons die, the muscles they innervate will weaken, lose mass, wither (atrophy), become fibrotic, and shorten. As muscles shorten, they will pull on their tendons, which are attached to the bones that make up a joint. As a result, a bone attached to a shrinking muscle will be pulled in the direction of the contracture. For example, as the muscles of the hand and forearm atrophy, they will shorten and pull on the tendons attached to the bones of the fingers, causing them to flex. As a result, the fingers flex toward the palm to form a fist. Contractures most often occur during the late stage of ALS. Contractures will not only interfere with the use of hands, arms, legs, and feet but can also cause pain when you are moved or pulled upon in an attempt to open a contracted hand or move a contracted extremity. This is a good reason for practicing ROM on a daily basis so as to prevent the formation of contractures or frozen joints.

In some instances, splinting a finger, a wrist, or a hand, and so on can maintain a joint into a neutral alignment in order help prevent a contracture from forming or worsening as well as to maintain comfort.

Using a brace or a splint to maintain normal alignment of body parts can also be beneficial because it will prevent discomfort. Treatment for contractures is based on prevention through physical therapy, which includes range-of-motion exercises, stretching, and use of splints or braces.

Should paralysis occur, affected muscles will atrophy and will become infiltrated by connective tissue. A lack of movement of a joint predisposes the joint space to fill with connective tissue and adhesions, rendering it non functional. The longer a joint's immobility persists the greater the risk that it will become fixed in place due to adhesions and evolve into a "frozen joint", as often occurs with the shoulder joint.

Underuse of muscles that are still functioning can only lead to further weakness and continuing loss of muscle mass, which will accelerate the loss of function. This will create a vicious negative cycle leading to increasing weakness and the development of or the worsening of contractures, joint adhesions and further loss of function. Attempts to move affected limbs and/or joints can lead to sharp pain if contractures are overly stretched or frozen joints are moved. Gentle daily range of motion exercise and stretching, preceded by the application moist heat, may help deal with contracture management and decrease pain over the long term. Ibuprofen or aspirin may also help with pain associated with contractions and capsulitis.

Review the following websites for additional information:

http://physical-therapy.advanceweb.com/Article/Managing-Contractures-in-Long-Term-Care.aspx

www.ncbi.nlm.nih.gov/pmc/articles/PMC3482407/ (Firefox)

http://cdn.intechopen.com/pdfs-wm/46071.pdf (Firefox)

http://ptjournal.apta.org/content/91/1/11

http://www.mndscotland.org.uk/information/tips/exercising-and-managing-contractures/

https://www.orlandoortho.com/orthopaedic-subspecialties/ hand-and-wrist-surgery-orlando/contractures/ (Firefox)

www.ncmedical.com/categories/Contracture-Management_12839517.html

http://www.nature.com/sc/journal/v40/n1/full/3101241a.html

www.alimed.com/contractures/

http://www.braceshop.com

Sixty

Orthotics

The word *orthotic* is derived from Greek, and it means to straighten out or to align. An orthotic is a device usually made out of plastic or some other firm material that is externally applied to a body part (e.g., hand, wrist, elbow, knee, ankle, etc.) in order to maintain or support an extremity in correct alignment. It may also help support function when a defect exists due to muscle weakness or paralysis. For example, an ankle-foot orthoses (AFO) can be applied to a leg and foot to prevent foot drop. Review the following website for examples of various foot-drop braces:

www.alimed.com/afo/

Orthoses can also be used to stabilize an extremity by supporting a limb or joint in a comfortable position that is correctly aligned.

For example, a wrist-hand orthotic (WHO) can be used to support the wrist and hand when they are too weak to maintain alignment or are needed for support to perform a specific function (e.g., eating). A hand positioner can also be helpful in preventing hand and finger contraction.

A wrist brace is a functional orthotic that supports a weak wrist. A type of orthotic wrist brace can support a thumb so that it can oppose the index finger improving function when hand muscles are weak. Check out the following websites for examples of various orthotics used on the upper extremities:

http://www.alsa.org/als-care/resources/publications-videos/factsheets/orthotic-devices.html

http://www.ballert.com/index.php/orthotic-prosthetic-services/21-ballert-op/75-amyotrophic-lateral-sclerosis

https://www.youtube.com/watch?v=SKRhXSZw0D0

http://www.ncbi.nlm.nih.gov/pmc/articles/PMC4235924/ (Firefox)

http://www.omicsonline.org/open-access/upper-extremity-orthoses-use-in-amyotrophic-lateral-sclerosismotor-neuron-disease-a-systematic-review-2329-9096-1000264.php?aid=43786

www.breg.com/products/elbow-wrist-bracing/wrist

www.rehabmart.com/product/wrist-drop-orthosis-30902.html

Orthoses can be custom fabricated and fitted by an orthotic specialist, or they can be acquired in a prefabricated state.

Splints can be made out of any material that is firm enough to support a limb or joint in a specific position. Even strips of aluminum covered with foam are used as fixed supports and can be bent into the shape needed.

Mobile Arm Support

A mobile arm support is an adaptive mechanical device that offers hand, arm and shoulder support to provide assistance with movement and function. The device can be mounted onto a wheelchair or to a table. It can help individuals with a weak arm and/or shoulder muscles to assist hand and arm movement to carry out various activities (e.g., eating, computing, etc.), thus offering a person with upper-extremity muscular weakness greater independence and functionality.

www.ncmedical.com/item_1569.html

www.youtube.com/watch?v=5Oa5nytqm9E

www.youtube.com/watch?v=BxNoek3R86M

www.youtube.com/watch?v=XG2MfL-d_wQ

www.rehabmart.com/product/jaeco-elevating-multilink-mobile-arm-support-9872.html?gclid=COOm0t3Kk8wCFdBZhgodadEIxQ

www.medifab.co.nz/products/arm-supports-feeding

http://www.ncbi.nlm.nih.gov/pmc/articles/PMC4433000/ (firefox)

Sixty-One

Positioning

Correctly positioning a PALS who lacks the ability to move means that you are placing his or her limbs, trunk, and/or head in a position that is comfortable and properly aligned with the rest of the body. Correct positioning will prevent prolonged pressure, twisting, or tension to a body part. When a body part falls out of alignment or remains immobile for an extended period, it is likely to result in discomfort, pain, and risks injury. For example, a weak or paralyzed patient sitting in a wheelchair could fall forward, causing his or her body to be out of alignment as well as suffer injury. The use of a seatbelt could help such a patient maintain correct posture while sitting if one's trunk muscles are weak, and it could also prevent one from falling out of a chair. An octopus-like positioner can also help hold a paralyzed person in a correct position while seated. Check the following website to see this device:

www.medifab.co.nz/products/wheelchair-accessories/octopus-head-positioning-system

Weak neck muscles may cause your head to fall forward or tilt toward a shoulder, producing tension on muscles, tendons, and ligaments that will result in misalignment. This might be remedied with a neck brace or better yet a head-support system while sitting in a wheelchair or with the use of pillows or other soft supports. Such methods can help align the spine and neck into proper position with the rest of the body.

While in bed, the head, neck, and spine should be properly aligned, as should all limbs, including feet and hands. Alignment should be maintained each time a patient is repositioned.

While in a wheelchair, one's lower limbs should also be examined for proper alignment, ensuring they are in a comfortable position with the aid of pads, cushions, or pillows. In some cases, splints or orthotic braces may be helpful.

Any site exposed to prolonged pressure due to immobility should be intermittently relieved with a soft pillow, cushion, pad, along with repositioning or any other method to relieve persistent pressure. Check the following websites for more information on this subject:

https://moodle.gprc.ab.ca/videos/nursing_videos/mosby_4th_edition/Basic/skill/D002.html   (click on "agree" and then on "procedure video")

http://www.archealth.com.au/post/2840655-head-positioning-and-control-in-neurological

www.atitesting.com/ati_next_gen/skillsmodules/content/ambulation/equipment/positioning.html

www.youtube.com/watch?v=_syZv5sTnsw&list=PL77a4Xnd1I6zW–nnNi8wQpDyw4KuMt3q

www.pattersonmedical.com/app.aspx?cmd=searchResults&sk=splints

www.pattersonmedical.com/app.aspx?cmd=get_subsections&id=57929

www.youtube.com/watch?v=XZNtrYEN_uw

www.youtube.com/watch?v=AIRZImY1ORg

www.youtube.com/watch?v=esUDO_lZj2I

www.youtube.com/watch?v=gnyiwPXSxkI

Sixty-Two

Paraffin Baths

Fingers, hands, and arms are vulnerable to loss of function as joints stiffen and muscles shorten. When that happens, it will be a tremendous blow to your independence. Therefore, maintaining hand and finger function for as long as possible should be a top priority in ALS. As soon as you notice that you are beginning to experience stiffness or limitation in the range of motion of your fingers would be a good time to begin treatment with paraffin baths to relax muscles and tendons, followed by range-of-motion exercises and stretching. The heat of a paraffin bath will be retained for a while when bandages are applied to your hands to hold flexed fingers in a fist. (Sensi-Wrap Self-Adherent bandages). After submersion, the patient's hand is removed from the paraffin bath after a short period while the bandages retain the baths heat. The bandages are then slowly removed after a while. The heat treatment allows muscles and tendons to be more easily stretched during range-of-motion exercises. In this way, you may be able to prevent or delay the formation of contractures involving hands and fingers and extend their duration of function.

In addition to using paraffin baths to maintain hand function, evaluate the benefits of using a wrist brace, splints, mobile arm support as well as adaptive devices can help maintain arm, hand and finger function. The following websites has examples of hand adaptive devices that can help with dysfunction:

www.rehabmart.com/bodypart/Hand.htm

www.ncmedical.com/categories/Grips–Holders_12839993.html

http://www.pattersonmedical.com/app.aspx?cmd=get_subsections&id=57604

Review the following websites for more information:

www.youtube.com/watch?v=I5I2frg1bzM

www.youtube.com/watch?v=ZCrt5RHDk-E

www.youtube.com/watch?v=uDbRKElrDoI

www.therabathpro.com/products/tb6.php

https://www.youtube.com/watch?v=YMGhxvZD8g4

Sixty-Three

Pain Management in ALS

The death of motor neurons does not directly cause pain, since motor neurons have no sensory function. However, PALS often suffer pain resulting from complications related to muscle weakness and paralysis (e.g., falling) secondary to death of motor neurons, immobility (.e.g., pressure sores), cramps, contractures, psychopathology, bulbar symptoms, and/or hypoventilation.

Pain may be associated with soft-tissue compression secondary to immobility or from traction on tendons, muscles, or joints. Those with limited range of motion and/or contractures may suffer significant pain when limbs, digits, or other body parts are extended or flexed, when an affected joint is rotated or when a body part is positioned out of alignment. Misalignment of body parts can occur when a patient is assisted during transfer or following repositioning. Pain may be a result of skin shear.

If a PALS has too little muscle strength to protect a joint or if the joint is affected by adhesions, it will not be hard to inadvertently cause pain in an affected shoulder, elbow, or finger when force is applied. This may occur following a fall or when someone tries to pull a PALS up in order to lift them up from the floor or out of chair or bed. Repositioning a patient may cause a shearing injury or friction burn if care is not taken.

PALS often suffer pain from cramping muscles or spasticity, which has been reviewed elsewhere. When a cramp occurs, it is best to stretch out the muscle. See the sections in this book on muscle cramps and spasticity for treatment options.

As carbon dioxide (CO_2) rises above normal levels as a consequence of hypoventilation it may cause severe headaches. Such headaches will not respond to analgesic medication but will respond to improvement in ventilation. Suffering from shortness of breath can be diminished with the use of low-dose morphine if respiratory support proves unable to adequately relieve such symptom.

Pain due to swollen extremities requires elevation of the extremity and application of compression stockings. Pain due to arthritis, bursitis, inflammation, or trauma can be treated with nonsteroidal anti-inflammatories (e.g., ibuprofen). Pain due to pressure or traction on limbs may require repositioning, an orthotic device, splint, or cushions for support. Pain from prolonged pressure (e.g., sitting) can be prevented with the use of a ROHO type cushion or similar pressure-relieving devices as well as repositioning including a wheelchairs tilt in space function.

In some situations, the legal use of medical marijuana may be beneficial in the control of pain.

Finally, neuropathic pain in ALS may be a result of inflammation involving the microglia of the brain.

Treatment for neuropathic pain may include a trial on Neurontin (gabapentin) or Lyrica (pregabalin).

Finally, morphine, sedatives antianxiety medicine such as Valium can be used to manage end-of-life discomfort and anxiety.

Addition information can be found on the following websites:

www.hindawi.com/journals/nri/2011/403808/

alsn.mda.org/article/pain-als-what-research-shows

https://parkinsonsacademy.files.wordpress.com/2014/04/
mnd-pain-pathway1.pdf (Firefox)

http://www.mndassociation.org/forprofessionals/
mndmanagement/pain/

http://hospitalnews.com/pain-management-in-patients-with-als/

www.medicaljane.com/2014/11/12/amyotrophic-lateral-
sclerosis-als-and-medical-marijuana/

www.als.ca/sites/default/files/files/10%2520Facts%2520about
%2520Pain%2520and%2520ALS.pdf (Firefox)

https://www.als.ca/sites/default/files/files/Pain%2520
Management.pdf (Firefox)

http://www.medicinenet.com/neuropathic_pain_nerve_pain/
article.htm

www.alsphiladelphia.org/doent.doc?id=825 (Firefox)

Sixty-Four

Adaptive Clothing and Dressing

A daptive clothing is clothing designed to accommodate people with disabilities so that they can dress and undress independently or at least with less difficulty. Adaptive clothing will also help caregivers dress disabled individuals who can no longer assist as well as those with limited range of motion.

For example, pants equipped with zippers that open from the waist to the thigh, will make it relatively easy to dress or undress an individual with little or no mobility. Once the pants are pulled up in place, the zippers can be closed, and you are good to go. Adaptive clothing will often make use of Velcro, zippers, or snaps as fasteners.

I have found that using knit clothing, including silk underwear that is a size or two larger than normal, to be the most comfortable and the easiest to use. Silk is reported to be particularly comfortable for sensitive skin. When limb mobility is limited, using oversized shirts can make it easier to dress and undress.

To review your clothing options, just type the words *adaptive clothing* into your Internet browser, and you'll find many catalogs with hundreds of choices and innovations, all of which can make a disabled person's life easier.

In addition, many assistive devices are available to help you dress. For example, the use of a buttoner can help you button and unbutton your shirt should you find that your fingers are no longer able to do the job alone. Shoes using Velcro fasteners allow you to easily remove them without the need to untie laces. Review the following websites for more information on this subject:

http://www.alsa.org/als-care/resources/publications-videos/factsheets/dressing-with-ease.html

http://www.als-ny.org/index.php?page=for_patients&sub=adaptive_clothing

www.youtube.com/watch?v=Kf8NDBpKqmA

www.silverts.com

www.buckandbuck.com

www.pattersonmedical.com/app.aspx?cmd=get_subsections&id=57591

http://www.wisegeek.com/what-are-the-pros-and-cons-of-silk-underwear.htm

Sixty-Five

Dressing and Undressing When You Can't Assist

At some point during the late stage of your illness, you will no longer be able to stand up or assist with dressing and undressing. When this occurs, you will be completely dependent on your caregiver for help. With the proper equipment, methods, help, and adaptive clothing, once you get the hang of it, dressing and undressing will not be difficult; just time consuming. I have outlined below the method I use every day.

Equipment needed:
- Hoyer lift
- Wheelchair
- Adaptive clothing

Method:
- Assume that you are in bed in the morning. Following range-of-motion exercises, your undergarments are removed.
- A Hoyer sling is placed around you. Microfiber towels or padding are placed between the sling and your skin where the sling's pressure is likely to occur during the lift.

- The caregiver raises you with the lift, pivots the lift so that it and you are parallel to the bed, and you are transferred onto a shower/commode chair.
- The shower/commode chair is then rolled into the bathroom and positioned over the toilet.
- When you are finished, you can be rolled into the shower.
- Following bathing, you are dried. While you are seated, your underwear and pants are put on and pulled up to thigh level. At this point, a T-shirt can also be put on.
- While still in the shower chair, you are rolled to the bedside just beneath the cradle of the Hoyer lift.
- While in the chair, a lift sling is once again placed on you and connected to the lift.
- The lift raises you up, pivots, and positions you over the bed. When positioned correctly, you are lowered onto the bed. The sling is temporarily left in place beneath you while dressing.
- Without removing the sling, your caregiver rolls you onto one side and moves your underwear and pants up into their proper positions and closes the zipper on the exposed side.
- You are then rolled onto your other side, and the same maneuver is repeated.
- The sling beneath you is examined for correct positioning and connected to the lift's cradle.
- The lift then raises you off the bed, and while you are suspended in the sling, then pivots so that it is parallel to the bed.
- A wheelchair or power wheelchair is then moved into place beneath you, and you are lowered into the wheelchair. Now you are free to go about your day.
- At bedtime, the process is reversed, beginning with placing the sling on you while sitting in your wheelchair.
- The lift is connected to the sling, which lifts you up out of the chair and then lowers you onto your bed in preparation for changing your clothes or going to sleep.

- Once in bed, the caregiver rolls you onto your side, unzips your pants down to the knee, and lowers the pants on that side. Then you are rolled over to the other side and the maneuver is repeated. From that point, the knees are flexed, and the pants can be completely removed.

Before using this method review it with your physical or occupation therapist. View the following websites for more information:

http://www.alsa.org/assets/pdfs/fyi/fyi_dressing.pdf (Firefox)

www.youtube.com/watch?v=iIQkzTYPxdU

www.youtube.com/watch?v=VScDoIQE25Y

www.youtube.com/watch?v=eI4wBjavIBk

https://www.youtube.com/watch?v=ZwGRdn-7kVg

www.caregiverproducts.com/dressing-aids.html

Sixty-Six

Toileting

As weakness advances, a disabled individual might find it difficult to get on or off a toilet unassisted, or be able to perform adequate hygiene. The situation might be remedied by replacing your toilet with a higher toilet, or your toilet seat can be exchanged for one that adds two or three inches to the toilet's height. One can also install a "surround," a device that encircles the toilet and allows a person to grip the arm rests and use his or her upper body strength to assist in getting up. Installing a riser between the base of a toilet and the floor is another alternative that can add a couple of inches to the height of an existing toilet.

Alternatively, a Hoyer lift with a toilet sling can be used to lower a disabled person onto the toilet seat when he or she is too weak to assist.

Adding a bidet to replace the toilet seat will allow an individual to wash the perianal area with little effort when weak hands can't help with cleaning.

At a certain point, using a portable shower/commode wheelchair will be very helpful, because an individual using this device can be wheeled directly over the toilet. Afterward, the shower/commode wheelchair can then be wheeled into a wheelchair-accessible shower to facilitate washing. If you find your shower commode seat to be very uncomfortable you can use a ROHO shower/ commode cushion to relieve seat discomfort. View the following websites for more views of equipment and methods that might be helpful:

https://www.youtube.com/watch?v=dtFY0Pnougk

www.youtube.com/watch?v=cRyny3LFuEU

http://www.alsfrombothsides.org/toileting.html

http://www.home-med-equip.com/catalog/rolling-commode-chairs.html

www.spinlife.com/search.cfm?keyword=commode+wheelchair&x=0&y

http://www.pattersonmedical.com/app.aspx?cmd=get_subsections&id=57691

www.youtube.com/watch?v=FAIERP2RTzc

http://alsassistivetechnology.blogspot.com/2012/04/toileting-ideas.html

alsassistivetechnology.blogspot.com/2012/12/toilet-hygiene-and-use-of-bidets-for.html

alsn.mda.org/article/ups-and-downs-hygiene-slings

www.liftseat4home.com/als

www.youtube.com/watch?v=IhPzV1A_v8Y

https://www.youtube.com/watch?v=dpYTUksh1xk

https://www.youtube.com/watch?v=d98YZblkkQI

https://roho.com/product/products/specialty-products/
rohor-shower-commode-cushion/

Sixty-Seven

Bathing and Showering

During the early stage of ALS, you can sit on a shower seat or bench and use a handheld showerhead to safely shower. This diminishes the risk of slipping and falling. Install grips and rails at the points of entry and exit, and to wherever you need to stand in the shower. If you are at risk for falling don't try to stand up without the assistance. At a later date, should your legs become too weak to stand, you can use a shower wheelchair that can be rolled into the shower, and your caregiver can shower you while you sit in the chair. If your shower's threshold is too high to permit rolling in a shower wheelchair, then there are alternatives (e.g., ShowerBuddy). The ShowerBuddy consists of rails that are high enough to clear your shower's threshold. A rolling shower chair attaches to the rails, and a release mechanism allows the chair and its occupant to be rolled on the rails into the center of the shower without much effort or risk. A similar device can be used to roll a shower/commode chair between a toilet and an adjacent bathtub for washing. In the late stages of ALS, an individual's paralysis may be extensive, and a shower chair may be difficult to use. At that point, a caregiver could give a PALS a sponge bath in bed. Following bathing, and individual's skin should be carefully examined for sores, fungal or bacterial infections, skin breakdown, abrasions, and so on in order to be quickly treat the problem.

A moisturizer should be applied to dry skin to prevent itching and irritation. Finally, one should recognize the high risk of falling in the shower with its wet slippery floor and extremely hard surface and take the appropriate precautions to manage this risk.

View the following websites to see the ShowerBuddy and other useful devices demonstrated along with additional information regarding this subject.

www.alsa.org/als-care/resources/als-insight/articles/feb2014-bathtime.html

www.youtube.com/watch?v=XY1YN-s2x74

www.youtube.com/watch?v=arNizdjOSi8

www.spinlife.com/critpath/match.cfm?categoryID=114

www.amazon.com/Duro-Med-Heavy-Duty-Sliding-Transfer-Adjustable/dp/B000NGUD94

http://showerbay.com/about-the-shower/

http://www.alsphiladelphia.org/document.doc?id=1929 (Firefox)

www.wikihow.com/Give-a-Sponge-Bath

http://www.mycarehomemedical.com/tilt-n-space-shower-chair-pvc-bath-chair-wheels-193tishb/

Sixty-Eight

Sleep Disturbance in ALS

There are many reasons why an individual with ALS may have difficulty in getting a good night's sleep. Causes for sleep disturbance can include symptoms related to hypoventilation (common), difficulty in tolerating BiPAP, poor positioning, pressure on skin and soft tissue, pain, positional discomfort, anxiety, agitation, depression, cramps, spasticity, restless leg syndrome, bulbar symptoms, and so on. A sleep study and a pulmonary function study will help define whether hypoventilation and/or sleep apnea are disturbing your sleep.

Certainly a common cause of disturbed sleep in ALS is related to hypoventilation that causes hypoxemia (low blood oxygen) and elevated CO_2. Hypoxemia will arouse or awaken an affected individual, preventing a deep restful sleep (e.g., one associated with random eye movement (REM)). Fortunately, hypoventilation can usually be corrected with noninvasive ventilation and elevation of the head of the bed for a period of time.

Undergoing a complete pulmonary function study as well as a full overnight sleep study will help define both hypoventilation as well as sleep apnea. Either or both of these conditions could be the cause of sleep disturbance in a PALS. Treatment for this problem is usually successful with he use of noninvasive nocturnal ventilation with BiPAP. Even If sleep apnea were present without evidence of hypoventilation then BiPAP would still be a better treatment option than CPAP since hypoventilation is likely to occur at some point in the future since BiPAP can manage both sleep apnea and hypoventilation of the neuromuscular origin.

Restless legs syndrome can also disturb sleep.

Positional discomfort caused by traction, contraction, or by a misaligned torso, limb, or neck is likely to disturb sleep. Repositioning, with pillows, splints, braces, or cushions, may help solve such a problem.

Cramps and/or muscle spasticity can awaken you from a sound sleep. Treatment for cramps has been addressed in a previous section.

If you suffer from back pain while lying flat on a bed then an adjustable bed or hospital bed can elevate your feet, back and/or head and prevent or diminish pain by relieving tension on your back.

Pain may occur during sleep as a result of plantar flexion (flexing the forefoot forward and downward), which is a common problem in individuals with foot drop. This can be remedied with the use of a contracture boot, which will keep your foot properly aligned throughout the night. See the following websites for additional information:

http://valleysleepcenter.com/als-and-sleep/

alsn.mda.org/article/what-everyone-als-should-know-about-breathing

www.ncbi.nlm.nih.gov/pubmed/21217159 (Firefox)

http://erj.ersjournals.com/content/19/6/1194

http://www.webmd.com/brain/restless-legs-syndrome/restless-leg-syndrome-treatment

www.mountain-sleep.com/index.php/sleep-disorders/plmd-rls

http://www.ncbi.nlm.nih.gov/pubmed/20669314 (Firefox)

http://emedicine.medscape.com/article/1188327-treatment

www.futuremedicine.com/doi/abs/10.2217/nmt.12.28

www.youtube.com/watch?v=u1xwx6v6DDE

www.youtube.com/watch?v=dea5naYp1Y8

www.youtube.com/watch?v=3VAHOOMEWIE

A caregiver should reposition an immobile patient every few hours while in bed in order to relieve pressure and prevent discomfort. The use of padding, foam wedges, or pillows can prevent pressure pain by providing support during repositioning. The use of splints, braces, pillows, Multi Podus boot (for heel pressure, plantar flexion, inversion/eversion, toe pressure, etc), or cushions can also help prevent discomfort due to misalignment of extremities, heel pain, plantar flexion. etc.

Elevation of one's feet at night will help diminish discomfort due to foot edema while in bed. Even the pressure of a blanket or a sheet on one's skin can cause discomfort for an immobile individual trying to sleep. To prevent this problem, a blanket elevator could be placed between the blanket and a patient's skin. When problems such as these arise, a little bit of investigation or innovation can usually bring forth a solution. Check out the following websites for additional information:

https://www.youtube.com/watch?v=u1xwx6v6DDE

www.pattersonmedical.com/app.aspx?cmd=searchResults&sk=s plints

www.pattersonmedical.com/app.aspx?cmd=get_subsections
&id=57929

www.parentgiving.com/shop/aluminum-blanket-support-
4982/p/7887/?gclid=CLHy2fnIr8sCFYUXHwodOMEPSA

Finally, symptoms of anxiety and/or depression often accompany the diagnosis of ALS, and this can certainly keep a patient awake at night. Such symptoms can be treated with psychotropic medication, psychotherapy, and perhaps with meditation, all of which have been reviewed in a previous section.

Sixty-Nine

Beds and Mattresses

An adjustable bed will permit elevation of the foot and head sections to assist in repositioning a patient as well as to provide comfort. Raising the foot section could help relieve foot edema. Passive range-of-motion exercises will be more easily carried out in a hospital bed or twin bed, especially if its height can be raised.

An elevated hospital bed will also provide the ground clearance needed for entry of a Hoyer lift's legs.

Since hospital beds have wheels, they can be easily maneuvered for transfers and provide good access to caregivers for physical therapy and repositioning. The cost of a hospital bed is usually covered by insurance. Your medical insurance may only cover a simple mechanical model; however, motorized models will put less strain on your caregiver. Bed guardrails that allow an individual to grip onto them and can prevent falling when getting out of bed. Review the following websites for information about hospital beds:

http://www.als-ny.org/index.php?page=for_patients&sub=hospital_bed

http://alsn.mda.org/article/adjustable-beds-are-boon-both-patient-and-caregiver

www.spinlife.com/critpath/match.cfm?categoryID=593

http://www.phc-online.com/Lateral_Rotation_Mattress_s/13465.htm

https://roho.com/category/products/therapeutic-mattresses/

http://www.phc-online.com/Hospital_Bed_Mattress_s/139.htm

Mattresses
In the late stage of ALS, a PALS's mobility in bed is likely to be increasingly limited or altogether lost at a certain point, which is a set up for discomfort and a risk for the development of bedsores.

It is a fact that bedsores are much easier to prevent than to cure. Specially designed mattresses can accommodate a PALS's points of pressure by allowing bony prominences to sink into the mattress without bottoming out. This will reduce compression of skin beneath an affected individual, which will be a great help in preventing devitalization of skin and subcutaneous tissues.

Today, there are many high-tech mattresses that are specifically designed to prevent compression, discomfort and bedsores. These include alternating-pressure mattresses, ROHO-type mattresses, low-air-loss mattresses, mattresses that rotate patients in bed, and mattresses that combine a number of these features. Some mattresses can be used as an overlay on top of your current mattress while others can be integrated into your bed. A patient can lie on a dry-flotation-type mattress (ROHO) in which the patient's skin and subcutaneous tissues will not bottom out because they are supported by air-filled cells that can conform to a patient's anatomy. The ROHO mattress requires no compressor and is therefore silent and will work normally during a power outage. It is also a lot less expensive than mattresses that require an air compressor. One type of ROHO overlay mattress is about 3 ½ inches thick and weighs only about 6 pounds.

A low-air-loss mattress is one that allows a constant low air leak through the mattress's porous material, which will help support an individual on a cushion of air and also prevent the accumulation of moisture on skin that is in contact with the mattress. An air compressor continuously inflates these types of mattresses to offer great skin protection. Review the websites listed below for more information:

www.youtube.com/watch?v=kCF71gV2B9M

www.youtube.com/watch?v=3VAHOOMEWIE

www.spinlife.com/critpath/match.cfm?categoryID=375

www.spinlife.com/critpath/match.cfm?categoryID=374

www.youtube.com/watch?v=_N8dFq1NJDU

www.youtube.com/watch?v=V14YyCEZhrE

www.youtube.com/watch?v=T52OUXyeXmg&nohtml5=False

http://www.phc-online.com/Lateral_Rotation_Mattress_s/13465.htm

https://roho.com/category/products/therapeutic-mattresses/

http://www.phc-online.com/Hospital_Bed_Mattress_s/139.htm

https://www.youtube.com/watch?v=RBSsG2ZM4Fo

Seventy

Communication and Assistive Technology

PALS that do not suffer bulbar symptoms should have little trouble with speech (unless they also have FTD or are chronically shorter breath); therefore, difficulty with verbal communication should not be a problem for many unless they cannot generate sufficient breath for vocalization, have tracheostomy that is interfering with vocalization or one has some other respiratory problems. Should you have no problem would speech but have difficulty typing because of muscle weakness or paralysis then voice recognition software can assist you with written communication and computer control. For those who do have difficulty with speech, manual input (typing) into a computer can be converted into synthesized speech for communication.

Those presenting with bulbar symptoms are likely to have difficulty speaking along with the development of symptoms muscular weakness and paralysis. Since ALS is a progressive disorder, at some point, individuals with bulbar symptoms could lose hand function along with their ability to speak. Either or both of these events could occur at any point during the progression of your illness, especially during the late stage of the disease.

Should you have difficulty in speaking, assistive technology devices (e.g., eye gaze) may allow you to input whatever you want into computer and your text can be converted into spoken language or used for written communication. Assistant technology will allow you to navigate your computer, surf the Internet, communicate, perform research, connect with the world and enjoy entertainment. Review the following websites into a for more information:

http://www.alsa.org/als-care/augmentative-communication/

www.nuance.com

www.youtube.com/watch?v=ImlKOA1MhlI&list=PLMg-Kor9g9wIb8ApzNWHm5gpbbaAeBlqh

www.youtube.com/watch?v=lP7QYSAFyfw

https://support.apple.com/kb/PH21511?locale=en_US

Voice recognition software can also be used to navigate the computer (Apple's accessibility, dragon naturally speaking). In fact this book is being written by way of voice recognition software.

If the volume of your voice is low it can be increased by the use of voice augmentation devices through voice amplification. Review the following websites for more information.

ndipat.org/blog/be-heard-with-voice-amplification/

https://www.voice-amplifier.com (Firefox)

If you are having trouble typing because of a weak wrist or weak hand control, adaptive devices such as an arm, wrist, hand supports including the use of Mobile Arm Supports could help you.

A "universal cuff" can be slipped over your hand to hold a pencil or similar device to help you operate your computer's keyboard more precisely if your hand control is weak.

If you can neither speak nor use your hands then other assistive technology can help you to communicate.

For example, a keyboard can be made to appear on the screen of your computer and you can activate any key simply by looking at that key (eye gaze assistive technology), or through the movement of a body part over which you still have control. Alternatively you could use accessibility switches or a head mouse for computer control. The use of patient's brain waves to control a computer (Brain Computer Interface, BCI) is now being studied and such devices are likely to be available in the foreseeable future. In fact, I recently participated in a study involving BCI. A cap containing electrodes was placed on my head. With BCI you look at a computer screen that reveals flashing letters and numbers. When I focused on a specific letter or a number and silently counted each time it flashed, the character or number on which I focused would appear typed out on the screen. Although this is truly amazing, its operation is extremely slow. At this time, the use of eye gaze or a head mouse seems to be far superior to BCI.

With the help of assistive technology individuals with late stage ALS may be able to remain productive and communicative through their computer. For example, you can control a computer and type with the use of a head mouse. A small position indicator is placed on your forehead and its tracked movement can be used for computer input. Sensors mounted on the computer can follow your head movement to carry out your computer commands. Alternatively, your eye gaze will be tracked to control a computer or type input. Sensors are attached or integrated into your computer and can follow your eye gaze to detect your commands for input. Another interesting device for controlling your computer mouse is the *Glassouse*, which allows you to control computer input without the use of your hands or voice, and it appears to be a very promising and affordable approach for hands free, voice free computer control. There are also for support devices for basic communication but they do not permit computer control and all of its advantages.

Progress in assistive technology is rapidly advancing and it would be wise to have a knowledgeable assistive technology specialist evaluate your needs and make recommendations that would be best for you once you begin to anticipate that you will have problems with communication. It often takes lots of time for insurance approval before you can get you think you need.

For additional information, check out the following websites for more insight into assistive technology options:

http://static1.squarespace.com/static/54e2529ae4b0409 b06622d23/t/556f5de4e4b02b07d084e04e/1433361892429/ Computer+Access+Options+for+Individuals+with+ALS.pdf (Firefox)

http://www.abilities.com/community/assistive_eye-control.html

http://www.als-ny.org/index.php?page=for_patients&sub=assistive

http://www.alsphiladelphia.org/assistive-technology

http://glassouse.com

www.youtube.com/watch?v=eLsJXtUrLsI

www.youtube.com/watch?v=BCrHbEo_8G0

www.youtube.com/watch?v=U279Jv7C0j4

www.youtube.com/watch?v=nFp632QcQ_w&ebc=ANyPxKpptV0 H2k8ZhJszj4vhP9JTe6xZi3VWn-uQGjwTqXjXxdUN2WsHfPcfm hYyAMaDUL9tgzFzvhRpq2nieOjtzecmbDnqNA

http://www.eyegaze.com/eye-tracking-assistive-technology-device/

https://mndresearch.wordpress.com/2014/12/05/assistive-technology-and-the-power-of-voice/

http://www.eastersealstech.com/2015/12/23/steve-gleason-act-cuts-red-tape-als/

https://lifeboat.com/blog/2016/01/how-assistive-technology-is-opening-new-doors-for-als-patients

http://amyandpals.com/communication-solutions-gallery/ (Firefox)

http://www.etriloquist.com/alslinks.html

http://www.mobilityworks.com/blog/message-banking-technology-for-als-patients/

http://www.tobiidynavox.com

https://www.statnews.com/2016/07/06/als-design-residence/

http://alsn.mda.org/article/als-voice-low-tech-communication-offers-advantages

Seventy-One

Choices

When dealing with a progressive and debilitating disorder such as ALS, making wise and timely choices regarding the management of symptoms and disability could delay or prevent dysfunction, discomfort, complications, prolong your survival time, and improved your quality-of-life.

Making good choices begins with finding an excellent neurologist who specializes in neuromuscular disease and has access to or works at an ALS center. You are going to need a great deal of guidance and support, and an ALS center is where you are most likely to find it.

Making good choices begins with accepting the reality of your diagnosis, understanding your disease and its implications, acknowledging your situation and partnering with your doctor. Learn everything you can about ALS and do your due diligence before making significant decisions. In these matters, knowledge is power—the power to understand what is happening to you, the power to identify and apply your options, the power to make good decisions, the power to acquire what you need, the power to exercise self-determination, the power to be an effective self-advocate, and the power to knowledgeably audit the quality of your healthcare and caregiver management.

As you collect information about ALS, symptoms, disability, and your management options, you can to begin to critically evaluate each piece of information you collect to be sure that it is accurate, up to date, complete, and optimal for your specific needs.

Once you have carefully evaluated all of your information, you should be ready to make good decisions.

Making good choices will be the result of choosing the best alternative based on an objective evaluation of each of your options. Unfortunately, good decision making can be compromised by conflicting information, inaccurate information, incomplete information and/or by allowing emotion or bias to unduly influence your decision.

Making decisions regarding an end-of-life plan well in advance of its need could avoid a crisis and give you enough time to consider your decision thoroughly and choose what is truly best for you. Forethought about this matter can prevent unnecessary suffering or having decisions made for you because you are no longer competent to make them on your own. For example, should you suddenly enter a state of respiratory failure and lose consciousness, you could wake up on a ventilator and possibly end up in a locked-in syndrome because you had failed to write down your advanced directives or lack a health-care power of attorney (HCPOA).

http://www.ncbi.nlm.nih.gov/pmc/articles/PMC3182548/ (Firefox)

Seventy-Two

Specific Treatment for ALS

Rilutek (Riluzole)

Rilutek is the first and only medication approved by the FDA for the treatment of ALS. In one clinical trial, this medication appeared to extend an ALS patient's survival time by an average of only three months when compared to placebo. This benefit may be statistically significant, but in real life terms, it seems to be quite a modest benefit. Although these results are somewhat underwhelming, a few extra months of survival time are certainly better than zero months. Furthermore, it is possible that some individuals will have a greater benefit than the average. In my opinion, treatment with Rilutek (riluzole) can hardly be considered a major advance in the treatment of ALS, and its very high costs are difficult to justify considering its modest benefit. Nevertheless, it seems that this medication even with its modest benefits are the best we have available at this time and its limited benefits would clearly appear to out weight its modest risks when facing ALS. I have been taking Riluzole since I was diagnosed because I had the better choice and little risk. I can't say that it helped me nor can I say that I perceived any downside other than its high cost.

Stem-Cell Treatment for ALS

Stem cells can be harvested from human embryos, bone marrow, adipose (fat) tissue, and even from skin cells. Collected stem cells are placed in culture and can then be induced to form almost any kind of specialized cell, including motor neurons. Stem cells can be cultivated to grow into millions of neurotrophic cells that can produce peptides and proteins that support the growth and survival of motor neurons, which can then be used in the treatment of ALS.

Although stem cells can be induced to form motor neurons, it is difficult to imagine that cultured motor neurons will be able to actually replace dead motor neurons in ALS and somehow be able to re-innervate previously controlled muscles. Nor does it seem probable that completely atrophied muscles that were previously controlled by LMNs could be revived using this technique. However, it is entirely possible that effectively programmed stem cells might be induced to produce neural cells, including motor neurons, that could provide nutritive factors, protective factors, corrective factors, or neural growth factors that might repair damaged motor neurons, have immunosuppressive actions, and/or could be able to differentiate into healthy supportive brain glial cells. Such newly produced motor neurons might also be able to protect healthy motor neurons from damage as well as repair damaged motor neurons that have not yet died. Such a process could theoretically slow down or stop the progression of ALS symptoms in a treated individual, especially if it is administered early in the disease process.

Brainstorm cell therapeutics contends that its proprietary techniques induce stem cells to become "biological factories" secreting neurotropic factors that support the survival of neurons in neurodegenerative.

Clinical trials run by Brainstorm use an ALS patient's own bone-marrow cells to produce specially treated stem cells, transforming them into motor neurons that are then injected back into the patient's spinal cord via lumbar puncture and/or some-times into affected muscles.

Preliminary results from recent FDA-approved phase 2 clinical trials indicate that Brainstorm's stem-cell treatment in ALS is safe, and that it appears that the majority of patients treated have had an observable slowdown in the progression of their symptoms according to those conducting the clini-cal trial. Should these results be reproduced in phase 3 con-trolled trials (to begin in 2017) then this type of treatment would be the first major advance in the treatment of ALS since the disease was discovered. However, until there is definitive evidence of significant benefit for most ALS patients, the ver-dict regarding the efficacy of stem cell treatment for ALS will remain unconfirmed. Other companies (e.g., Neuralstem, Inc.) are also experimenting with neurotropic stem cells as a treatment for ALS; however, Neuralstem's treatment requires neurosurgery to inject stem cells directly into the gray mat-ter of the spinal cord. Their preliminary results also appear promising.

If phase 3 trials for stem cell treatment demonstrate signifi-cant efficacy, then I believe that such treatment could become a reality within the next five years or so. However it is most likely that it will take some combination of drugs, gene therapy, stem cells treatment, and/or other immunoregulatory treatment to defeat ALS.

It is probable that ALS has a number of factors that play a role in its causation which probably varies from individual to individ-ual; therefore, different treatments used separately or together may be needed to successfully treat this complex disease and that treatment will likely need to be customized for individual patients based on the underlying pathologic mechanism found in each patient. The rapid acceleration of scientific advances currently underway will undoubtedly bring forth effective treat-ment regimens in the coming years. A very large study on the role of genes in the causation of ALS will involve more than a thousand patients from multiple clinics and centers around the U.S. Its goal is to define genetic causes and pathology in each patient, which help in individualizing treatment.

However, for ALS treatment to be effective it would likely require that treatment be administered early in the disease's course before too many motor neurons have died.

Although certain stem cell treatment may be able to slow down the progression of symptoms in some ALS patients it is unlikely to cure the disease and so the search for a more definitive treatment(s) will continue.

Websites for ALS-treatment and additional information can be found on the following websites:

http://web.alsa.org/site/PageServer?pagename=ALSA_Ask_ Dec2011

http://www.cochrane.org/CD001447/NEUROMUSC_riluzole-for-amyotrophic-lateral-sclerosis-alsmotor-neuron-disease-mnd

www.alsa.org/research/about-als-research/stem-cells.html

www.als.net/als-clinical-trials/#

www.alsa.org/news/media/press-releases/update-on-als-brainstorm.html

www.biosciencetechnology.com/articles/2013/05/fda-approved-stem-cell-trial-dramatically-slows-als

www.neuralstem.com/cell-therapy-for-als

www.als.net/news/masitinib-als-clinical-trial-interim-report-positive/

https://clinicaltrials.gov/ct2/show/NCT02795897

http://www.alsconsortium.org/trial.php?id=179

www.genervon.com/genervon/PR20160429.php

www.quackwatch.com/06ResearchProjects/stemcell.html

Experimental Treatment for ALS
For information about clinical trials review the following websites:

http://www.massgeneral.org/als/research/participatinginatrial.aspx

www.alsa.org/research/about-als-research/clinical-trials.html

http://www.alsconsortium.org/educational_webinars.php

http://www.alstdi.org/als-research/als-clinical-trials/

https://www.mda.org/research/clinical-studies-and-trials/amyotrophic-lateral-sclerosis

http://www.genervon.com/genervon/PR20160523.php

http://alsworldwide.org/research-and-trials

https://www.youtube.com/watch?v=CaD-oF9deNY

Seventy-Three

Alternative Treatments
for ALS

I imagine that most PALS are desperate to find an effective treatment once they understand what they are facing. Unfortunately, the world is filled with charlatans that prey on desperate patients. Charlatans have one thing in common; they offer unproven and/or ineffective treatments for their own financial benefit. By unproven, I am referring to treatment that has not undergone scientific clinical trials that have been rigorously supervised approved national regulatory agencies. This includes carefully conducted double blind controlled human trials that prove whether a treatment is safe and effective based on objective scientific validation. In addition, researchers and experts in the field should have full access to the methods employed, the design of the study, and full disclosure of all of the results via publication in a refereed medical journal in order to scrutinize the research regarding its quality and significance. Further, controlled trials of proposed treatment must not only pass muster with the scientific community but also with governmental regulatory agencies such as the FDA. Legitimate clinical trials would have an institutional review board (IRB) number indicating that the protocol for the treatment study has been deemed ethical and scientific in its construct. Further, a human drug trial or treatment in the United States that has not been assigned an investigation new drug (IND) number by the FDA should not be accepted as legitimate.

On the other hand, treatment with massage therapy, physical therapy, acupuncture, and the like could offer patients better control of pain, cramping, and spasticity as well as maintain range of motion, and so on. However, none of these treatments or methods will slow down the progression of ALS, reverse symptoms, or increase survival time.

Nutritional therapy including special diets, vitamins, supplements, and minerals have been used for the treatment of ALS based on the theory that the disease is due to a nutritional deficiency. Recently, the *Deanna protocol* has been strongly promoted by its advocates based on the fact that it had a positive effect in ALS mice models and from anecdotal testimony. Nevertheless, no successful controlled clinical studies can be found in the medical literature to support that this diet is effective in treating ALS in humans. Although, it is unlikely that such a diet could cause harm, I do not imagine that a neuromuscular specialist specializing in ALS would recommend this diet to their patients until it has been scientifically validated by clinical trials. On the other hand, if an ALS patient decides to try this protocol I see no reason to object although, I would not encourage it, primarily because I would hate to raise one's hope without solid scientific evidence supporting a treatment's efficacy. For more than 40 years I have either been a principal investigator or sub investigator in more than 150 phase III clinical trials of various treatments in my specialty, so you might understand my bias toward solid scientific confirmation that a treatment has been proven to be effective and safe before recommending it to a patient.

Insurance companies will often reject claims for treatments that are deemed of unproven value.

Unproven treatments offered for ALS include: unapproved stem-cell treatment by providers working out of private clinics around the world, vitamin and supplement treatment, homeopathic therapy, herbal medicine, antioxidant or anti-inflammatory treatment, detoxification treatment, chelation therapy, antibiotic treatment, immunotherapy, and/or hormonal treatment.

Unproven and unapproved stem-cell treatment for ALS and for a variety of other disorders is currently being promoted around the world by private clinics and frequently advertised over the Internet. Treatment with unproven therapy, including stem-cell therapy, is likely to be worthless, contains no active ingredients or ineffective ingredients, or might not even contain live stem cells or ones that have been ineffectively programmed for the treatment of ALS.

Some practitioners promote the off-label use of treatment meant for diseases other than ALS to treat ALS. For example, some physicians offer treatment for ALS using antibiotics normally used to treat Lyme's disease. However, there is no accepted scientific evidence that treating ALS with antibiotics will affect the course of ALS, which would seem to make such treatment to be a waste of time and money. It is also possible that their claimed success these practitioners was the result of treating patients with the neurological manifestations Lyme's disease, which had been misdiagnosed as ALS.

It's interesting to note that the best neuromuscular specialists and neuroscientists at the National Institute of Health and at the top university hospitals throughout the United States and abroad have not been able discover an effective treatment for ALS that is ready for clinical use. If this is the case, then how is it possible that a few practitioners with no serious scientific, multicenter clinical trials to support their claims have discovered an effective treatment for ALS, which is now ready for clinical use? How is it possible that these supposedly effective treatments for ALS have eluded thousands of the best physicians and scientists in the world? The answer is simple—they have not!

The best way to determine the legitimacy and merit of a treatment for ALS is to discuss it with your ALS-center neurologist, contact the ALS or MDA Association to confirm the legitimacy of the treatment, and to directly review the scientific literature regarding the proposed treatment. If you or told that your symptoms are due to Lyme's disease or another disease then get a second and/

or third opinion from an ALS specialist at the University Hospital. If somebody wants to treat your symptoms because they claim you have Lyme's disease for they contend to have an effective treatment for ALS then get a second opinion from an infectious disease specialist or another expert in a University Hospital that will have no vested interest potential from one monetary gain in any proposed treatment. Taking such an approach should help you to quickly differentiate between what is erroneous or fake treatment and what is the right approach. Finally, I would not accept an experimental treatment for ALS outside of a major university hospital in the United States, Europe, or Israel because I believe that the odds of finding an unapproved effective ALS treatment outside of a rigorously regulated scientific environment is probably close to zero. The following websites will offer you additional information on the subject:

http://www.mndassociation.org/research/mnd-research-and-you/unproven-treatments/

http://www.alsa.org/als-care/resources/als-insight/articles/nov2014-alsuntangled.html

http://alsuntangled.com/

http://www.ncbi.nlm.nih.gov/pmc/articles/PMC3865630/ (Firefox)

scienceblogs.com/insolence/2014/05/29/weve-heard-this-story-before-raising-loads-of-cash-for-unproven-treatments/

www.quackwatch.com

www.sciencebasedmedicine.org/quack-clinics/ (Firefox)

www.sciencebasedmedicine.org/ph-miracle-living-dr-robert-o-young-finally-arrested-but-will-it-stop-him/ (Firefox)

http://www.alsmndalliance.org/about-us/policies/alternative-treatments/

http://www.todaysdietitian.com/newarchives/tdoct2007pg84.shtml

http://www.tandfonline.com/doi/full/10.3109/21678421.2013.788405

Seventy-Four

End-of-Life Plan

O nce a PALS accepts his or her diagnosis and fully understands their disease they will recognize that they have a terminal illness; however, none can accurately predict how long one will survive, nor can anyone precisely predict the clinical course. Since you can't accurately predict how things will go for you, it would be wise to prepare for both the probable and the possible. Although it might be difficult and frightening to thoroughly explore this issue, it would be wise to create a well-thought-out end-of-life plan so as to avoid unnecessary suffering and/or errors.

Although a few PALS will live for decades, almost all affected individuals with ALS should expect to grow progressively weaker over time and that paralysis will sooner or later affect all or almost all of their voluntary muscles during the course of their illness, unless one first passes away from a complication of ALS or from another disease. Difficulty in breathing will eventually develop once respiratory muscles weaken enough to cause hypoventilation. As hypoventilation advances, there is a good chance that an affected ALS patient will eventually enter into a state of respiratory failure at some point. Without intervention, worsening hypoventilation will ultimately lead to respiratory failure followed by death. In addition, patients with ALS could develop pneumonia, malnutrition, a serious infection, suffer atelectasis and/or develop airway obstruction; any of which could lead to death.

As symptoms advance, most of us will have the option of choosing various methods to prolong life. For example, one can begin noninvasive ventilation or invasive ventilation when breathing becomes compromised. You might choose to accept a feeding tube should eating or drinking become difficult or if you begin to suffer from recurrent aspiration, severe weight loss or malnutrition. If your ability to breath begins to fail, you can choose to accept life-sustaining respiratory support (e.g., tracheostomy ventilation) or refuse treatment and allow nature to take its course. Carefully consider and reconsider your options throughout the course of your illness so that you can make well-thought-out decisions long before you enter into a medical crisis and are forced to make a critical decision when you are stressed and/or compromised.

Should you choose to refuse to receive or continue with further treatment at any point in the course of your illness, be aware that your decision is both legal and ethical—and that it is your decision alone to make. It is important to understand that not accepting artificial life-sustaining treatment is entirely different from doing something to actively end one's life.

As ALS advances, with rare exception, it will be relentless in its progression. Over time, the advancing symptoms of muscle weakness will evolve into paralysis, which will increase your level of disability and at a certain point it is likely to have a negative impact on your quality of life when compensatory mechanisms have been exhausted.

During the middle stage of ALS, while limitations may be few, would be a good time to begin to consider end-of-life decisions, gain insight into this issue, and consider making the necessary preparations. This would include taking care of related legal and financial matters, some of which have been outlined in previous sections. Making such preparations well in advance makes great sense since it may require a long lead-time or you might not be up to the challenge when the disease advances.

Organize all of your important documents, and make sure your family, POA, and/or the executor of your Will all know where your documents are kept. Create a manual for your spouse or another responsible party, detailing all the necessary information and directions needed to manage your affairs (financial, legal matters, wishes, etc.). If you have information regarding matters related to managing your home, business, investments, or other important matters, then you should detail them in your manual for a time when you may no longer be available to help.

The names, addresses, telephone numbers, and e-mail addresses of your accountant, doctors, lawyer, executor of your Will, and others whose services you rely upon should be included. Include your budget, accounts, leases, automatic and regular payments, mortgage documents, passwords, bank account and other financial statements, deeds, car title, and insurance policies. It would be a good idea to train your spouse or other trusted individuals to gradually take on your day-to-day responsibilities well in advance so that they can become familiar with all your responsibilities while you are still in good enough shape to assist them. If possible, it would also be a good idea to complete all funeral arrangements well in advance so that they will be carried out according to your wishes and not be a burden to your loved ones during a time of emotional stress.

Once your ability to maintain adequate ventilation begins to fail and you can no longer be effectively supported by non-invasive ventilation, you will be faced with the decision of whether or not to begin tracheostomy ventilation or to allow hypoventilation to advance to respiratory failure and its natural consequence—death.

Most PALS in the United States choose not to begin tracheostomy ventilation when they reach the crossroad where a decision is required.

I have thought a lot about this issue, and when the time comes, I imagine that my decision will be based on the quality of life that I am experiencing at the time and the quality of life that I can realistically expect in the near future.

I will also consider how life support (e.g., TV) would affect the quality of my life and whether that would or would not be acceptable. It seems to me that if your symptoms are progressing slowly and you are enjoying your life up until the point you enter respiratory failure, it would not be unreasonable to expect that your quality of life might continue to be acceptable for a time if you are willing to live with the demands of tracheostomy ventilation.

On the other hand, if your quality of life has deteriorated to the point that you are suffering and you foresee a near future of worsening symptoms with no hope of improvement, then you might conclude that to continue to live with TV or other life support might be worse than dying. Under this circumstance, some might reject accepting or continuing to use artificial life support

Of course, many other factors could influence one's decision in this matter, including one's fear of death, religious beliefs, family consideration, and/or one's strong will to live.

Should you choose not to undergo tracheostomy ventilation and your state of ventilation deteriorates, you should expect to enter respiratory failure sooner or later. If you have provided your family and physician with advanced directives, including a *do not resuscitate order* (DNR), then as respiratory failure worsens, your physicians and medical staff will not intervene with respiratory support as long as you have provided them with clear legal health care directives.

It would be wise to plan ahead for such an eventuality with your family, your physician, and/or your hospice team. Put your instructions in written form so that your decisions will be carried out according to your wishes. Establishing a healthcare power of attorney to assure that your wishes will be followed.

If you have planned for this situation, then as symptoms of respiratory failure worsen, your physician and/or hospice team will comply with your decision and will administer sedatives, anti-anxiety medication, and/or morphine to diminish suffering from the consequences of respiratory failure, which can include "air hunger", a sense of suffocation or drowning, marked agitation, etc. In this scenario, your blood CO_2 level will rise and your blood oxygen level will fall. At a certain point, you will enter a coma and pass away. With the correct palliative treatment, your passing should be a peaceful one, devoid of unnecessary suffering.

In addition, a PALS who is being maintained on respiratory support and/or a feeding tube and finds that his or her quality of life has deteriorated to a point that it is no longer bearable and without any hope of improvement, one will have the option to change one's mind about sustaining life by artificial means and request that his or her physician or hospice team remove all artificial support and let nature take its course.

To live or not to live with ALS is a question that I imagine most ALS patients will confront sometime during their illness. Some years ago, my wife overheard someone say that if he had been diagnosed with ALS, he would have shot himself. When you consider preciousness of life, the thought of giving it up prematurely seems to be either folly or a choice driven by ignorance, fear, weakness of character or some combination of these. However, if you have really done your best to deal with this disease and in spite of your best efforts life becomes unbearable and your future is completely without hope of relief, then I can certainly understand why someone might not want to continue to accept artificial life support under such a circumstance.

When I spoke to a psychologist who had suffered many a life crisis as a quadriplegic, he told me that he found life to be meaningful and desirable even if he could at least look out his window and see any sign of life, and I clearly understood his point.

Some individuals in the late stage of ALS will suffer nearly complete paralysis and yet continue to find life meaningful and worth pursuing. I suspect that Stephen Hawking continues to have a strong will to live and has a meaningful life in spite of just about being totally paralyzed and suffering complete loss of direct speech. Perhaps his attitude is a result of his satisfying work, ambition, family and the quality of life that he has been able to enjoy in spite of his condition. For others, I suspect that the similar circumstances might be insufferable.

I find increasing disability to be frustrating at times. However, the benefits I currently derive from my relationships and what is still possible continues to bring me happiness and I find that this makes life worthwhile. These are the things that continue to spur me on, since a lot of what I enjoy continues to be possible. However, when the balance of my quality of life dips in the direction that living with advancing symptoms and disability becomes intolerable because acceptable options have been exhausted, meaning has been lost, and suffering has become great and without hope of improvement is lost, I will not be worried because I am prepared for that time.

Careful end-of-life planning will offer you the opportunity to carry out your wishes in a way that you believe to be in your best interests. In this matter, you should reach a clear agreement with your physician and/or your hospice team as to exactly how things should be handled so that your wishes are honored and that you will not suffer because of delays or errors in managing things in the end. Review the following websites for additional information and points of view:

www.alsa.org/als-care/resources/publications-videos/factsheets/reasons-for-living-with-als.html)

www.youtube.com/watch?v=_BdHm2XRlB0

www.slate.com/articles/health_and_science/medical_examiner/2015/02/end_of_life_decisions_achieving_a_good_death_with_the_help_of_a_doctor_and.html

http://o.canada.com/health-2/end-of-life-care-creating-an-exit-strategy

http://alsn.mda.org/article/peaceful-passing

www.ncbi.nlm.nih.gov/pmc/articles/PMC3182548/ (Firefox)

http://palliative.info/resource_material/pneumonia_eol.pdf (Firefox)

https://books.google.com/books?id=F8FhKb1rghcC&pg=PA 316&lpg=PA316&dq=als+and+financial+liabilities&source=b l&ots=VY6rwswX9F&sig=HAXLyCCLJ3SL95RTo8LIz_NCy2w &hl=en&sa=X&ved=0ahUKEwiegv6nwJnNAhWCFR4KHVuz AFUQ6AEIVjAJ#v=onepage&q=als%20and%20financial%20 liabilities&f=false

https://www.youtube.com/watch?v=hbk6O4QjK9A

http://www.mndcare.net.au/End-of-life/Symptom-management-at-end-of-life.aspx

http://www.rcjournal.com/contents/08.07/08.07.0996.pdf (Firefox)

http://www.thelancet.com/journals/laneur/article/ PIIS1474-4422(14)70221-2/fulltext?rss=yes

http://www.takingcharge.csh.umn.edu/conditions/end-life-and-hospice-care (firefox)

http://journalofethics.ama-assn.org/2015/06/nlit2-1506.html

http://www.comfortcarechoices.com/index.php?option=com_ content&view=article&id=81:choosing-to-stop-eating-a-drinking-at-the-end-of-life-vsed-&catid=36:articles

http://www.bioethics.jp/licht_advals.html

Part III

A Personal Experience

Seventy-Five

ALS and Me

Sometimes when it is real quiet, and I am sitting comfortably doing whatever it is that I am doing, I tend to forget that I have ALS. That is, until I try to move. At that moment, I immediately realize that I can't just stand up, walk across the room, grab a glass of water, or even turn a page without the risk of dropping the book I'm reading. When that happens, I am suddenly brought back to the reality of the limitations of my physical ability, an ability that I had previously taken for granted. My response is simply to focus on my current situation and find a way to deal with the problem at hand. Fortunately, quite a bit is possible if you know your options, apply a little ingenuity, make the necessary effort, and acquire the mobility and adaptive devices you need. As a result, I am almost always able to find a way to fulfill my needs and pursue my interests by pushing back against advancing physical constraints or by finding a way around them. By applying knowledge, effort, resources, imagination, or by getting help, I have been able to adapt to my limitations in a way that has worked for me.

Pushing back is both easy and hard depending on how you look at it. I choose to exercise those options that are still available because this allows me to continue to enjoy a good quality of life while living with ALS.

Occasionally, I consider a future of increasing paralysis and dependency, and so I concentrate on planning practical solutions for what I know surely lies ahead. In other words, I try to anticipate the trajectory of my symptoms and disability and prepare methods to deal with the disease's progression. Fortunately, I don't dwell on these issues for long. Instead, I mostly focus on the present, since I am living in the present and mostly enjoying it.

The ability to shift one's thoughts away from the negative and find a way to work around obstacles and solve problems must be a protective mechanism that we humans developed long ago. We are particularly talented in adapting to change. I continue to be encouraged by my ability to adjust and adapt to all of the ALS symptoms I have thus far encountered. Resilience also appears to be one of man's strengths. I suspect that those that take this approach have a certain mind-set and are willing to dig deep down into their potential and use all their strength to find a way.

On one hand, I have accepted that I've the bad luck to have developed an illness that is uncommon, progressive, and with rare exceptions fatal. On the other hand, I realize that I've had the good luck to develop ALS later in life, after I have had the opportunity to do much of what I've wanted to do, and that I am still am able to continue to enjoy life.

I am happy that I have been able to provide for my family's needs in spite of my disability. I appreciate that I have the good luck to have a loving supportive family, live in an environment where the support, resources, and the options I need are available and accessible. I also appreciate that my symptoms are progressing at a far slower pace than I expected, leaving me time to adjust, complete unfinished business, pursue my interests, and most of all, to spend lots time with the people I love.

Although my situation is slowly worsening, as a physician I know that my symptoms could have been far worse. Therefore, in the grand scheme of things, as strange as it may seem, I feel fortunate for what is still possible, for the time I have had, and for the time that I still have.

I have found that life continues to surprise me in that it often takes unexpected turns. When I was younger, for no apparent reason, I had a premonition that I would die young. I had actually not given much thought to my own death in decades, and when I had finally accepted the notion that I would probably live a normal life span—bam! I am hit with ALS. I think I have always known that life can be terribly unpredictable, because some events are just random in occurrence. I realize that being struck with ALS was neither directed at me personally nor related to anything over which I have or had control. It is just a matter of happenstance. I don't feel sorry for myself or even angry, because I know that life comes with no promises or guarantees. I also know that I am lucky to just be here, and I recognize that I have had quite a good run. Even now, I still find life to be quite enjoyable in spite of my symptoms, limitations and advancing disability.

I am 74 years old, and I understand and accept the fact that at some point in the not-too-distant future, I will die as a result of ALS. This doesn't particularly scare me, since I don't fear death, and I am prepared for it. I am not sure why I feel this way. Perhaps I have always been aware that death is a natural and expected part of life. I also feel that when I pass away, I will remain in a state of peace, so no worries there. However, what does upset me is the thought that I will not be around to be part of the lives of those I love and this pains me the most. I also recognize that those that remain are the ones who will suffer, because they have lost someone they love and they will have to live with that loss. Perhaps the thing that does frighten me the most about ALS is the thought of running out of acceptable options or, worse yet, losing so much function that life becomes impossibly difficult and that joy and hope are lost. Since I expect my ability to breathe will likely give out before anything like that happens, I imagine I will never be stuck in such a situation, or at least not for long.

Until I run out of acceptable options, I hope to find and enjoy meaning, happiness, love, and fulfillment most days, and so I will hold tightly onto life and fight with all my power to continue to enjoy what is still possible and worthwhile.

I have always believed that we create or play the primary role in shaping our own lives within the realm of what is possible in spite of the presence of adversity. This outlook has always worked well for me, and it now helps me deal with the impact ALS is having on me. I find that even now, I have been able to maintain a good quality of life in spite of a steady progression of worsening symptoms. As symptoms advance, I meet new challenges by modifying my environment, employing adaptive devices, compensating, adjusting, and finding ways to deal with each new obstacle. It is not so much mind over matter; rather, it's more like mind meets challenges and finds a way to overcome or get around them. I understand what is happening to me, and I know how to navigate the medical system, which makes it easier for me to get what I need. I live in an environment where information, options, help, and needed equipment are available to me. I have a loving and supportive wife and family who are here for me. Much of the burden of what is happening falls on my wife's shoulders; fortunately, Talia is smart, strong, and capable. In addition, I have Veronica, a competent and caring home caregiver aide.

Symptoms of ALS began affecting me about eight years ago, and probably even before then. One day, while lying on a lounge chair, I noticed a muscular twitching of my thigh. At first the twitching was intermittent, and I assumed that it would pass. The following summer, I noticed fasciculation (twitching) beginning to occur in other locations. I began to suffer from more frequent muscle cramps as well as increasing fatigue. I discussed these symptoms with my physician and was referred to a neurologist for evaluation. A year earlier, I had also noticed that my core body strength was weakening. This was most apparent when I tried to lift anything heavy or when I tried to get up following floor exercises at the gym.

I knew that a number of diseases, including ALS, could cause fasciculation, and I became concerned. As time passed, I underwent a series of neurological tests. When my studies initially revealed mild abnormalities, I began searching for a more palatable diagnosis than ALS. I consulted with three neurosurgeons, hoping that I might have cervical stenosis (a treatable narrowing of the spinal canal) rather than ALS. Two neurosurgeons at top-notch university hospitals wanted to operate, but I sought other opinions because I wasn't confident of their assessment and fearful of unnecessary surgery.

My neurologist, Dr. Heiman-Patterson in Philadelphia, diagnosed me with ALS in 2009. The diagnosis was later confirmed at the Mayo Clinic as well as at another ALS center outside of the United States. Although I had evidence of cervical and spinal stenosis, it became clear that it was ALS that was causing my symptoms and that surgery would have been an error.

At first, I was overwhelmed, scared, and depressed. I had been reading about ALS all along, so I knew its manifestations and outcome. I wasn't much afraid of dying but rather of living in a fully incapacitated state.

I looked for alternative answers. I went to physical therapy for a while and continued to work out in the gym, but at a less intense level. In time, I came to understand that I had to accept that my diagnosis of ALS was correct and that I would have to find a way to make the best out of the situation and figure out how to enjoy the time I had left.

In spite of the fact that I had ongoing symptoms, I decided to continue to work for as long as possible because I love my work. However, as time passed, I experienced increasing physical difficulty with fatigue and increasing muscular weakness. At a certain point, I stopped practicing medicine but continued to work on educational projects and administration. One of the really negative aspects of ALS was that it forced me to give up practicing medicine. If I'd had a choice, I would never have retired and would have continued to practice medicine until I felt that I was losing my edge.

As the disease progressed, I slowly became weaker and began to have trouble walking. My fatigue grew in intensity. After a while, I gave up going to the office and began to work on projects at home. All the while, my symptoms continued to advance, and in time I began to experience increasing symptoms of shortness of breath and marked weight loss. At that point, I felt that the end might be approaching quickly. So I rewrote my will, developed a financial plan for my family, and bought burial sites.

Soon thereafter, I found a way to receive an experimental ALS stem-cell treatment outside of the United States at an outstanding university hospital. Fortunately, following the treatment, the exhaustion and extreme fatigue I had been experiencing dramatically resolved. I also felt that the progression of my symptoms seemed to have slowed down. Was this a result of the treatment? I can't say for sure, but it does seem to me that they were related. Stem-cell treatment for ALS has been undergoing clinical trials in the United States and Israel—if found effective, it should be available to the public within the foreseeable future.

Around the time I received the stem-cell treatment, I began using a rollator so that I could walk without the risk of falling. I also began using a device to help me button my shirts. A transporter wheelchair became indispensable for longer distances. A thick ROHO air cushion raised my seat's height, which made it easier to rise and also allowed me to sit for long periods without discomfort. Following the stem-cell treatment, my appetite suddenly returned, and I was able to add an additional thousand plus calories a day to my diet with protein-rich drinks. Eventually, I regained the thirty-five pounds of weight I had lost—and then some. I bought thick-handled utensils for better control while eating. I purchased an electronically controlled bidet toilet seat to wash my behind, placed a ramp in the bathroom for easier access, and enlarged the shower and bathroom entrances. We exchanged our bed for an adjustable one that could sit me up in the morning, making it much easier to be helped out of bed. I bought an easy chair with a seat that could elevate me into a standing position. I also acquired a Hoyer lift, which when needed could lift me off the floor (in the event of a fall), help me out of bed, or be used to transfer me from chair to chair. I was advised to use paraffin baths and stretching exercises for my hands in order to prolong my ability to type and to prevent contractures. I also began using voice recognition software to type on my computer.

I continue to study ALS as well as to get advice from my ALS clinic and from other specialists about the management concerns and my options. I know that I am doing everything possible to maintain my ability to function, prevent accidents, and enjoy a good quality of life.

At this time, Talia assists me with anything I can't do for myself. When Talia is not around, Veronica, my home caregiver aide, is there to help, and it is a pleasure to have her with me. Veronica is experienced, capable, and fun. She helps me do whatever I want to do, which has had a very positive effect on all of our lives.

When I first became short of breath, I began using a BiPAP machine and mask. This instantly relieved my respiratory symptoms. A mask fit over my face and allowed me to continue to breathe comfortably throughout the night. At first, using a mask became intolerably uncomfortable. Initially I tried on more than a dozen types of masks without finding one that was comfortable. Finally, my friend Solly, a periodontist, was able to grind out part of frame of the mask that was pressing on the bridge of my nose to create a more comfortable fit. Once I started this treatment, I was no longer short of breath, and I could once again sleep through the night. I also bought rechargeable lithium ion batteries for the BiPAP machine so that I could take it with me, which extended my mobility. When my breathing further deteriorated, I began using a Trilogy ventilator throughout the day and night. It automatically adjusts the volume and pressure of the air needed to breathe comfortably and it also adjusts for leaks, which is really amazing. I now find it more convenient to use mouthpiece ventilation on the Trilogy rather than use a mask with BiPAP for respiratory support during the day.

Finally, I received a power wheelchair that was customized to fit me, it is easy to adjust and provides comfortable sitting positions. This offers me mobility and comfort throughout the day and well into the evening. Even though I can no longer walk, I still can go pretty much go anywhere I want to go, so I rarely feel stuck.

Of all the issues surrounding the management of ALS, I found that home healthcare support (a caregiver) became the most important one once I began to require physical assistance for daily tasks. One of my first initiatives was to hire Veronica so that I had someone in addition to Talia to help me each day. This has allowed me to function to the maximum of my ability while giving Talia peace of mind and the freedom to continue to work and carry out her own activities.

Having a great physician to guide and support me throughout the progressive stages of ALS has been a godsend. Dr. Terry Heiman-Patterson has set up a competent and warm multidisciplinary ALS center in Philadelphia that has offered me the services and guidance I needed. But more than that—she has shown me a level of kindness, insight, and dedication that I have found to be extraordinary as well as rare. Knowing that she is in my corner and there for me has relieved me of a great deal of anxiety and this has helped allow me to make the most out of my life while dealing with this relentless disease.

When I stopped working, I organized a personal work schedule so that I would continue to be engaged in projects that interested me each day. I began printing and archiving my photographs, worked on my digital files with Photoshop, and started to sell off photography equipment that I no longer used. I also found Lisa, a young woman who is organized and smart and in possession of good knowledge of photography to help me with my projects. With her help, I began printing again. She also helped me create a series of DVD videos for my Grandson Jake, which will allow me to speak directly to him when he is older about those things that I feel are important.

In fact, those DVDs were the genesis of a book (*Common Sense Is Not All That Common*). I knew that when Jake grew up, I would not be around to share my love, thoughts, and experiences with him, so I decided I would organize them into a book so that they could be shared with him at some point in the future.

After completing the videos and the book for my grandson, I began to work on the ALS book you are reading. The purpose of this book is to raise an affected individual's level of awareness about those things I believe one ought to know about the management of this illness and about those things that could significantly improve one's quality of life while living with ALS. This book has grown in scope and depth because I have had lots of time to consider many ALS related issues, perform research into the management of ALS's symptoms and disability. It turned out that writing this book was a lot more difficult than I had expected. I set up a schedule and began writing most days until I finished this last chapter, and then I began the long process of editing. It was both challenging and stimulating at the same time. I found that while I was writing, I would completely forget about my disability, which was a good thing. I also realized that I had a lot to share and only a limited amount of time remaining, so I had to stay focused. Writing allowed me to think deeply about issues that confront all of us who are challenged with ALS. It also gave me the opportunity to share my own experiences in a way that I thought might be helpful to others who find themselves in similar circumstances.

In spite of my limitations, I never find life boring. Family, neighbors, friends, and former colleagues visit often. I now have time to read a lot, do research, write, and work on projects that interest me. I also get to watch movies most evenings, which is something I really do love.

Each Saturday, my daughter and five-year-old grandson arrive from New York to spend the weekend with us, and we have a great time.

ALS may have slowed me down and imposed its limitations, but at the same time, I have gained a greater appreciation of everyday life and the beauty that surrounds me. Some days during the spring and summer when the weather is good, I go around the neighborhood in my power wheelchair, enjoying my neighbor's gardens and the magnificence of a clear day's blue sky. I now seem to have more time than I ever had to enjoy my friends and family along with plenty of undisturbed time to think and pursue interests.

In general, since I developed ALS, everything in my life seems to have slowed down, and my focus has changed. I now have time to see and enjoy everything around me in a new light. The other day, while shaving, I looked into the magnifying mirror and noticed, perhaps for the first time, that the color of my eyes is a shade of steel blue. I thought, "How interesting!" I had never really noticed them before with such clarity—I guess I was always too preoccupied with rushing off to work to notice what was right in front of my nose. This is kind of a metaphor for what I am now experiencing. It is amazing to grasp how adversity can offer you a new and positive perspective about your life that might have otherwise gone unnoticed. The same is true for my relationships, which I have also learned to appreciate on a new level. I realize more than ever that relationships are the most meaningful and beautiful part of my life. A few relationships have drifted out of my life; perhaps they were less than what they appeared to be. I also realize that some people are uncomfortable with illness and disability or find it difficult to maintain our relationship under these new circumstances.

On the other hand, good friends and family have always been here for me, and this continues to be the case. Sometimes friends demonstrate how much they care through their actions, and this makes me very happy. I recognize that I am lucky to have such high-quality relationships in my life. And these are the relationships that I appreciate more than ever, because they carry with them so much happiness.

ALS was quite a crushing diagnosis. I think that had I allowed the feelings of fear, anxiety, and frustration, to grow, they would have prevented me from enjoying the time that remains. Although I have suffered bouts of anxiety and negativity on occasion, I have learned to deal with them; so these negative feelings don't persist for long.

I realize that life goes on, with or without us. In this situation, I have two options: I can stay connected and engaged in life and enjoy what is still possible, for my sake and for those close to me. Alternatively, I can passively allow ALS to envelop me to the point that I become psychologically paralyzed by fear, anxiety, or depression and prematurely give up my power of self-determination and the ability to enjoy what is possible.

It appears somewhat paradoxical that this fatal disease has totally freed me from fear. I joke around with my friends that I don't have to worry about dying of cancer or a heart attack since I know that I have a short "expiration date," and it doesn't look like I will have time to develop other disease. I find that applying a little humor to my situation tends to keep things in balance.

Over the past few years, I have been working with Talia to prepare her to take over all of my responsibilities: managing our finances, dealing with the mechanics of our home, legal matters, and so on. She now manages everything competently and this has relieved me of a big burden.

I love family holidays. We now celebrate Rosh Hashanah, Thanksgiving, Hanukkah, and Passover in our home with friends and family. My brother, Irwin, visits with me for lunch once a week and shares his latest poems. Friends drop by often, and we share conversations, ideas, and jokes.

I suspect that some friends may find it difficult to see me deteriorate; others seem surprised to see how well I am doing. I try to make it easier on them by not pushing them away, and so I don't focus on my symptoms or limitations. Most accept the situation as part of life, just as I do, and we continue to enjoy our relationship since nothing has really changed between us. For those that live at a distance, there is always the phone, FaceTime, or Skype.

Some years ago, I met the mother of the author of *Tuesdays with Morrie*, a book about a man with ALS. At the time, I had asked her about the book that she was holding and then decided to read it after I heard the story. It is a book about her son's university professor who had developed ALS and his approach in dealing with his symptoms and prognosis. I was struck with Morrie's amazing and uplifting response to his situation and how well he was managing in the face of his great life challenge. In spite of his progressing symptoms, he seemed to be at peace. Of course, I never imagined that I would find myself in the same situation. Recalling this memory, I sense there are a lot of similarities regarding how each of us has dealt with ALS, and yet significant differences remain between our approaches. I realize there is no single right way to respond to ALS since each individual's course of symptoms can vary greatly, and we each have our own perspective and circumstances. Therefore, each of us must find his or her own way to deal with ALS based on our values, character, knowledge, ability, resources, and outlook.

As I researched ALS, I came to understand that I could expect to live several years on average once diagnosed. During these past years I have been able to enjoy a good quality of life; however, I know that it will end at some point in the near future. When all avenues to enjoy an acceptable quality of life have been exhausted, then I imagine that such a life would be devoid of happiness and meaning for me. Fortunately, that has not yet occurred.

I have learned to accept help from others and not be ashamed of my condition. I remember how uncomfortable I felt the first time I was pushed in a wheelchair into a doctor's office. Since then, I've learned to leave feelings of embarrassment behind, because there is really nothing embarrassing about reality. Some individuals have little understanding about these matters because they lack knowledge and/or experience. As a result, some may feel uncomfortable in dealing with the unfamiliar. Perhaps some would just like to avoid being reminded of their own vulnerability or mortality.

I tend to think about my circumstance in the larger context of my life, and as a result, I have come to appreciate the many blessings I have had over the years and the ones I continue to enjoy. I have always been able to pursue the life I wanted and have been truly fortunate to enjoy a challenging and fulfilling life's work. I appreciate that I was raised in a loving family and that today I have a loving family. I recognize that I am lucky to have no unmet needs. I wake up each morning surrounded by beauty in an environment filled with light and life. Even though my mobility is limited, I don't feel limited.

You may find it surprising that I am not anxious, depressed, or angry. I decided early on that I would not start down the road of self-pity or fear. I will not allow myself to slip into depression and waste the precious time I have left by being unhappy.

At the beginning, I cried some, but not anymore. I focus on living in the present. I have found that with each new challenge, there is almost always an alternative that I can take. I believe that each of us has the potential to adapt and adjust, and in so doing, we have the possibility of self-determination within a world of possibilities. I know that when I have truly done my best, I cannot expect any more of myself, and that is OK. Best of all, I feel strongly connected to and supported by my family and friends, and this sustains me when things get difficult.

At some point in life, each of us can expect to come up against a really tough challenge. Living with ALS is now my challenge. I have learned that one's ability to overcome difficulty is often far greater than one thinks. Even when faced with what seems to be an impossible obstacle, you are still free to choose how to respond. Once you commit to a choice or a course of action, you will be surprised what is actually possible if you use your imagination, remain determined, ask for help when needed, and learn to rise above your own fear. This approach may be difficult and perhaps uncomfortable at times. However, I prefer to struggle in the pursuit of my own agenda rather than not take on a challenge I believe it to be in my best interest. This disease does make life difficult for me, but I refuse to allow anything, including ALS, to dominate my will, thinking, or happiness while I still have options. Taking the path of least resistance or throwing in the towel when things get tough is a path that is mostly associated with a poor outcome. It is also one that often leads to failure or unnecessary difficulty, and that is just not my way.

As this illness progresses, the window of opportunity to do what I want to do will continue to close, which will make the time remaining ever more valuable, so I will have to use it wisely. I don't complain much, because it is not helpful. The weight of this disease is on all of our shoulders, and that is especially true for Talia.

Somehow it seems paradoxical that I feel quite strong now even though I continue to grow physically weaker. In spite of my continuing physical deterioration, I appreciate that my mind remains clear, my will is intact, and I am not burdened by negative feelings or loss of focus. I am looking adversity in the eye, and mostly I am not frightened. I believe in my approach, and I am confident that I am making wise choices. As my mother used to say, "If there is a will, there is a way," and I find this concept to still ring true. It seems to me that if you are willing to reach deep within yourself, you can find the strength to push on. As a result, you will be able to achieve whatever is possible, and that is often quite a lot, perhaps more than you might expect. I know that this challenge will be over one day and that the outcome is predictable. However, for the time being, I still have a few innings left, and I plan to find a way to enjoy the game while it lasts.

Surprisingly, good things can sometimes come out of adversity. For example, writing a book for my grandson that allows me to share my thoughts with him might never have happened had I not developed ALS. Nor would I have written the book you are now reading in the hope that it would offer individuals with ALS and their caregivers insight into managing this complex disease.

When given the opportunity, I have enjoyed helping others with ALS by sharing what I have learned and experienced.

Although ALS has presented me with a great challenge at this point in my life, I also know that I have had and still have the opportunity to do some good in this world, and for that, I am grateful.

I never expected life to be easy, and I realize that developing ALS is just one of many possible unexpected life events that one could experience. As a physician, I recognize how vulnerable we all are and how easily the flame of life can be snuffed out. In the J. R. R. Tolkien translation of the old English poem *Beowulf*, the poet puts forth the following thought: "Life is transitory, and light and life hasten away quickly."

The realization that life can be short is certainly not new; however, it directs me to focus on and appreciate the preciousness of life and not take it for granted. Throughout my life, dealing with challenges has helped heighten my awareness to what is possible and what is of value, as well as recognize the benefits of determination in dealing with challenges. I have found that we have the ability to find meaning and happiness in life even under very difficult circumstances—if we remain committed and make the necessary effort. As my mom would often say, "You can make yourself happy or miserable. It's your choice." I know that she was right, because even while living with ALS, I choose to make myself happy.

Acknowledgment

I would like to acknowledge and thank my wife Talia for her great help and advice in editing this manuscript.

I would also like to express my thanks and appreciation to Dr. Terry Heiman-Patterson M.D. and Sarah Feldman PT, DPT, ATP, both from the ALS Hope Foundation in Philadelphia, for reviewing my manuscript and for offering me excellent advice.

CPSIA information can be obtained
at www.ICGtesting.com
Printed in the USA
LVOW10s1126210517
535324LV00014B/638/P